'74 VICTORY LEADERS

FERGIE JENKINS
Rangers

JIM HUNTER
A's

MARK FIDRYCH

SS

Red Sox

SD

LAWRENCEBURG PUBLIC LIBRARY

A.L.
BIL

FINGERS
PADRES

Cardboard Gods

AN ALL-AMERICAN TALE TOLD THROUGH BASEBALL CARDS

Cardboard Gods

AN ALL-AMERICAN TALE TOLD THROUGH BASEBALL CARDS

JOSH WILKER

Seven Footer Press

Published by Seven Footer Press
247 West 30th Street, 11th Floor
New York, NY. 10001

First Printing, March 2010
10 9 8 7 6 5 4 3 2

Design by Junko Miyakoshi

ISBN-13 978-1-934734-16-2

www.sevenfooterpress.com

AN ALL-AMERICAN TALE TOLD THROUGH BASEBALL CARDS

I don't remember what I wished for before our wishes were the same. It didn't matter who was blowing out the birthday candles or throwing a coin into a fountain or scattering the seeds of a dandelion. When we were given a wishbone, I wanted to win, and so did my big brother, but for a long time it didn't matter which way the wishbone broke. I don't remember what I wished for before baseball.

At the end of the summer of 1975, when I was seven, we went to our first game. It was only a couple weeks after our recently reshaped family had moved into a damaged house in what seemed to be the middle of nowhere. Mom and her boyfriend, Tom, had their hands full trying to make the place livable, and they didn't have much money either, but they knew what my brother and I had begun to wish for. So they took a break from ripping up rotted carpeting and tearing down warped wooden siding and painting over swear words and crude pornographic drawings, and we drove three hours in our VW Camper to Boston. The length of the trip seemed almost unbearable to me. I couldn't wait to finally get a glimpse of my gods.

When we walked up the concrete tunnel and I saw the field for the first time, the deep green color of the grass hit me like the heartbeat of something benevolent and immense. I followed my family to our seats in a daze. You only sense that pulse a few times your whole life.

A little while later, after the game had begun, my brother elbowed me in the side.

"Hey, here's Yaz," he said. It was true. Walking to the plate was the real version of the figure from my favorite baseball card. He had big numbers on his card stretching far back in time, to way before I was even alive. He had been an All-Star year after year. He had won the Triple Crown. Everyone everywhere seemed to understand.

"Come on, Yaz!" my brother yelled.

"Come on, Yaz!" I yelled.

Everyone everywhere was yelling for Yaz.

As the game went on, the desire on the part of the crowd for Yaz to come through grew into something deeper and more desperate. A hunger. Each time he came to the plate the sound of 30,000 people pleading his name got louder. We pleaded along with the crowd again and again, our throats getting hoarse. He kept failing. His last chance came in the eighth inning with a man on second. We tossed the last shreds of our voices into the roar.

CARDBOARD GODS

1st PACK

2 + 2 = 5

Topps 1975 #533: Rudy Meoli

For a long time, I knew how to find happiness. All I needed was a quarter.

I lived in the country, far away from almost everything. Far away from the suburbs where I was born and had spent the first six years of my life. Far away from clear television signals. Far away from my favorite place in the world, where the baseball team I loved played its games. Far away from my father. Far away from all other kids except one.

Sometimes that kid, my older brother, Ian, would nod when I held up a baseball glove and a ball, and we'd go out into the yard. But sometimes he would be far away, too, lost in a thick book about distant worlds. I'd say his name and say his name, but when he was this far away he'd either say nothing or tell me to leave him alone.

But I was close enough to one thing. If I had a quarter, I could walk a half-mile to a general store and buy a pack of baseball cards.

Sometimes I wouldn't be able to stop myself from ripping open the pack within seconds of its purchase. But even while doing so, I was aware that it would have been better to wait. So most days I carried the pack home unopened. It was important to discover the new cards at home, as if in some way delaying the discovery until then helped define that faraway house as my home, as someplace special in the world.

I switched the pack back and forth from my hands to my pocket as I walked, liking how it felt in both places. I liked to feel the waxy surface of the pack and the thin raised rectangle of hard gum inside. I liked to feel the sharp edges of the cards through the pack, too, and to imagine that they'd somehow never once been touched by human hands.

When I got home I went up to the room I shared with my brother. In the early years I would do this in hopes that Ian would be there, so I could show him the new cards as they came to me. As the years went on he was there less and less, and sometimes even if he was there I'd be able to tell that he was far away, and I'd take the pack to my side of the room without saying his name.

As I write this, decades later, almost all the things that made that room my room are long gone. The poster of David "Skywalker" Thompson levitating his way to a tomahawk slam. The poster of Ace Frehley, his silver-painted eyes clamped shut, using his guitar as a phallic conduit for the infinite wonder of the cosmos. The magazine cutout of Cheryl Tiegs in a see-through fishnet bathing suit walking straight toward me with a dreamy smile. All the various lint-covered objects made of Nerf. All the piles of hand-scrawled solitaire Strat-O-Matic scorecards. The only thing that remains is the heart of the room, the box containing all the baseball cards I ever brought home. The box I've carried with me through my life.

When I brought a new pack home I pulled that box to the center of the floor on my side of the room, then I opened it so that all the cards I already had would be staring up at the ceiling, waiting to see who'd be joining them.

Then, kneeling, I opened the pack.

I wonder sometimes if the years have beaten all this out of me. Have I lost all trace of the direct path to happiness? Have I lost belief in the boundless possibilities in that slim moment when I levered my fingernail below the flap of an unopened pack?

And in the tiny clicking sound of the flap disconnecting.

And in the first strong whiff of gum.

And in the first glimpse of some unidentifiable piece of a card, a swatch of grass in a photo on the front, a row of numbers on the back.

And in the way I would always blur my vision as I pulled the white-dusted shard of pink gum from the pack, so that I couldn't yet see any names or other identifying information on a card until I placed the gum on my tongue.

And in the way the gum shattered into many pieces and then, after a moment, re-formed into an improved version of itself. For a few seconds, the lifespan of happiness, the gum was soft and sweet, and sugar coursed through my bloodstream, and I looked for the first time directly at a brand-new card and felt the sunshine coming up from it as if from some better world, some wider moment suddenly so close I could hold it in my hands.

Behold this card. Behold this world of drama and wonder. Behold the uniformed maestro at the center of everything, his head thrown back in awe, his arms outspread as if to proclaim: *Behold*. Behold this maestro's singular mellifluous name, Rudy Meoli, doubled within and without the borders of the moment in flamboyant cursive and sturdy black block. Behold the similar doubling of the timid lowercase word on the maestro's chest by a thunderous uppercase echo from above—ANGELS—as if somewhere just beyond the fringes of this world exists an invincible solidity, the answer to the question in our hearts. Behold this angel.

For a long time, I lived in an angelic state of stupidity and grace. I knew how to find happiness. I thought that something magnificent could occur anywhere. For a long time, years, I didn't understand that I wasn't witnessing the occurrence of something magnificent in Rudy Meoli's card from 1975, my first year of collecting. I didn't understand that all I was looking at was some little-known marginal who'd just squandered one of his rare chances to reveal any previously undiscovered magnificence by hitting a weak foul pop-up, the easiest of outs. Even to this day there's a faint residue of my inability to interpret the blatantly obvious in this picture. On some level, perhaps the only level of any importance in this life, I still think of Rudolph Bartholomew Meoli, a backup infielder with a .212 lifetime average and more career errors than extra-base hits, as one of the most thrilling performers of his era, a superstar in the reign of happiness and confusion.

1974 Topps #245: Cleon Jones

When I try to identify my earliest memory, I see my brother. I'm chasing after him, a toy machine gun in my hands. I wanted to be part of the war game he was playing with his friend Jimmy, but he and Jimmy were too big for me, their legs too long. I couldn't keep up. Around that time, Ian began serving as my interpreter. I could make sounds, but no one could understand them as words except my brother, who passed along my wishes to the grown-ups. I liked this arrangement. Two boys with one voice.

When I try to identify my first baseball card, I see my brother, and I see this 1974 Topps Cleon Jones. I hold it and feel something twitching, beating, like wings. I don't remember the moment it came into my hands, and in that way it's like the person I most closely associate it with. I imagine I asked for and received the pack of baseball cards that included Cleon Jones because my brother had a pack of baseball cards. But in truth I can't place Cleon Jones's arrival in my life, and in a way he never arrived in my life because, like my brother, he was always there.

I believe the Cleon Jones card came to me while we were all still living together in one house in New Jersey, even though in the middle of that year we left Dad and moved to Vermont, where the card also could have come to me. But I like to believe the card predated the move that in many ways signaled not only the beginning of my years of collecting but the true beginning of my conscious life. There has to be a beginning, a first event in any cosmology, and I have subconsciously and consciously come to believe that Cleon Jones is mine, the central figure of the creation myth in my flimsy personal religion.

And who's to say for sure that this wasn't the first moment of the universe? A loud crack had just occurred, setting everything in motion. In the very next second, Cleon Jones is going to start running as fast as he can, and from the looks of it he is going to run for a while before having to stop. It's that moment when everything has just begun, and you don't know how it'll turn out, and you can't help assuming that it'll be great.

When the gods stopped coming to me, years began rushing by in a blur, faster all the time. The most recent ones crumble upon the slightest inspection, as if manufactured from a cheaper material than they used to be. Months and weeks are even flimsier, days a succession of smudged facsimiles.

On a recent vacation, I went back to the house I lived in the longest, in East Randolph, Vermont. On my way to the house I stopped at the general store where years before almost all of my baseball cards had come into my hands.

I pulled the rental car into the parking lot and mumbled a stiff, fakely folksy "Howdy" to three younger guys sitting on the bench on the porch. Cringing over this greeting—people in the town I grew up in didn't saunter around saying "howdy"—I entered the store. The cash register had been moved to the opposite side of the store from where it once was. There was a pale, gnomish lady in her fifties behind it. I lurched up and down the aisles for a few seconds. On my way out the door the cashier spoke.

"Help you find something?"

"Baseball cards?"

"No."

With those words echoing in my head I drove to the house I grew up in, following the same short route I used to walk when bringing a new pack home. During the drive I recalled how I would open the pack in my room and place the gum from the pack in my mouth and crack it to pieces, releasing the first blast of sugar into my system so that the arrival of my newest gods coincided exactly with the sweet, fleeting bliss I'd come to need.

It doesn't last long, that sweetness. In its wake: a deeper need.

Help you find something?

Baseball cards?

No.

For a long time, I sat behind the wheel of a rental car and stared across the road at a house owned by strangers. What brought me here? What do I lack? What could I possibly hope to find?

1976 Topps #582: Mike Kekich

MIKE KEKICH
PITCHER RANGERS

In late 1969, hoping to find, at least for a day, a widening of what had become for her an unhappily narrow life, my mother boarded a charter bus from my birthplace, Willingboro, New Jersey, to a peace march in Washington, D.C. I don't remember that day, but I was there, in my father's arms, as my mother waved down to us in the parking lot from her seat on the bus. I was probably crying. I imagine that my father, an absent-minded sociologist, was holding me like an absent-minded sociologist might hold an unraveling unabridged dictionary. My brother, a little older, was probably confused. *Where's Mommy going?* My father's last words to my mother that day, so I'm told, were instructions to watch out for rock-throwing thugs hired by the Power Elite to discourage political dissent.

"That's my husband," my mother announced pointedly as the bus pulled away from the two young children clinging to the man in the button-down shirt and horn-rimmed glasses. These were her first words to the stranger sitting next to her. By the time she had boarded the bus it was very full, and she'd gone up and down the aisle twice looking in vain to find an empty seat next to a woman. Finally she had given up and sat down in the only available seat, next to the young man with the scruffy fledgling beard, hair to his shoulders, and round John Lennon specs.

The bus ride took a few hours. The young man beside her, Tom, was a good talker. He told her stories of battling forest fires in Alaska, and of tripping on Owsley acid in an Oregon forest of giant ancient redwoods, and of crisscrossing the country on a BMW motorcycle.

He had blue eyes. He had delicate hands. He had a flask of brandy under his soft wool poncho.

By 1973, the number of my parents had grown from two to three. Tom shared a bedroom with Mom while Dad slept on a foam mat in a room down the hall. They all believed it was better to blaze a new trail rather than follow the old corrupt paths that led to lies and napalm and Nixon and sadness. Why not try to add or even multiply love rather than subtract or divide?

This kind of thing was not exactly common, but in those days it wasn't unheard of either. For example, that spring two major league baseball pitchers, Mike Kekich and Fritz Peterson, traded families. Everything. Wife, kids, pets. The unusual swap, if remembered at all today, is generally treated with mockery.

But I happen to know, without ever having spoken to either of them, that when they did it they meant it. They were sincere. Maybe the family swap was in large part an extension of the fun they were all having together, but they must have believed they weren't merely pulling a pleasurable stunt. Beyond the pleasure of the moment, there must have been a hope for some as yet uninvented republic of joy.

Forget that they both had career-worst seasons, or that in general they never really were the same players again, or that Kekich decided after a few weeks that the experiment wasn't working out, a decision that came too late—his wife and Fritz Peterson already having decided they wanted to make the swap permanent. Forget all that. For a slim, brilliant moment the world seemed to be clay in their hands, moldable to any shape they desired.

My mother had become an artist by 1973, a pretty young woman with long brown hair and a rainbow spattering of bright paint on her sneakers and jeans and shirt and sometimes even on the lenses of her glasses. She worked on her paintings, big hyperreal Pop Art portraits of her friends and family, all the time, every day, and her major-chord love songs eventually covered most of the walls of our house in New Jersey. My favorite was the one of me and my brother, the two of us watching TV. We're both in our pajamas, rapt looks on our faces, sitting very close together. In fact, I'm leaning into him, my shoulder touching his arm. In the painting, we're still a year or two away from discovering baseball cards, but all the elements are in place: my need to be close to my brother, our shared instinctual desire to find some kind of pop-culture escape, our fascination at what seemed to be both a simpler and more magical artificial world beyond the intimate snarl of affection and silences in our three-parent home.

"It wasn't easy in that house," Tom told me years later. "I'd feel bad even touching your mom on the arm if your dad was around."

By 1973, Tom's beard and hair had grown into something worthy of a man who had been shipwrecked on an unmarked island for a decade. He had been a professional actor in New York and in traveling companies all over the country, and he embraced with customary zeal his new role as a part of the family's unusual experiment. He also worked part-time as a sculptor's helper for a local art-minded pharmaceutical industry billionaire, plus he and my mom made candles and sold them in a little gift shop near our house. Once they took the candles into Manhattan and tried to sell them on the street, but cops fined them for not having a permit. Cops often hassled Tom at that time. I picture him after coming home from yet another brusque, invasive frisking by hippie-loathing members of the New Jersey State Police, he and mom laying in bed and whispering their wishes about going somewhere far away from the concrete jungle, the malignant suburbs, somewhere where they could really be *free*.

I'm sure there were also plenty of neighbors who gave Mom and Tom the stink eye for their looks or our abnormal family situation or both. The saddest story my mom ever told me was about the time she tried to take my brother to his classmate's birthday party a couple houses down, only to be told by the boy's mother, through a latched screen door, that it just wasn't possible to invite everyone.

"Gotta draw the line somewhere," the woman explained. From inside the house came the sounds of the party, floating through the screen to my mom and my brother.

If I'd been older when he'd begun living with us, I probably would have resented Tom's presence, but to me having a mom and a dad and a Tom was normal. It's all I knew. Plus, he was young and energetic and fun, willing and able to play with me in an unselfconscious, roughhouse way that my shy, reserved father, who was nearly twice Tom's age at that time, was not.

I have trouble picturing my father in my sketchy memories of those days. He was gone a lot, away earning the family's only steady income at his research job in the city or holed up in the guest room that had become his room when Tom moved in. I remember he had a mustache because I recall he liked to kiss me on the cheek. I didn't like it.

"Baby fat," he'd say teasingly, pinching the other cheek, the one he hadn't kissed.

"I'm *five!*" I'd yell, scowling, angry that he didn't even know I was no longer a baby. I wriggled away from him, still rubbing his bristly kiss off the other side of my face. I see this scenario occurring on the couch in our living room, my dad just home from work. He has on brown slacks and a white button-down shirt and a tie. A normal American in any other time and place, but the oddball in our world. The television is on. *George of the Jungle*. *Ultraman*. I stare at the screen, breathing through my mouth. My brother's on the couch, too. Eventually, my father sighs, rises from the couch, and trudges up the stairs to his little room, shutting the door.

One night, my brother and I are watching TV in the front room when men and women in ski masks burst through the front door. It's Tom's birthday. Much later, I'll understand that the whole thing is a gag, that Tom and Mom's hippie friends were inspired by the ongoing Patty Hearst saga to "liberate" the birthday boy.

"We've come to free you from society's shackles!" one of the kidnappers yells in Tom's face as they seize him. Tom struggles and giggles as he's dragged from our house. Mom follows, an accomplice, a tight smile on her face like someone on a roller coaster about to crest its first peak. I can't tell if what's happening is bad or good.

Who can tell me?

I look to my brother.

"Hey, Ian," I say.

He stares at the television. *Lost in Space*. The flickering light from the screen makes his face seem to change. He's sad. He's mad. He knows things I don't know.

"Hey, Ian. Ian," I say.

Topps 1975 #407: Herb Washington

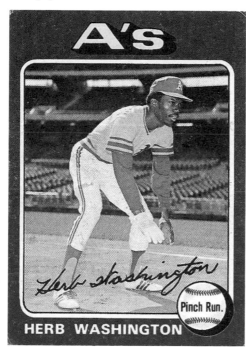

HERB WASHINGTON

Pinch Run.

Once, when I was in my twenties, I ran into an acquaintance on the F train, a guy I'll call Wendell, whom I knew from pickup games of Ultimate Frisbee in Prospect Park. We were on the train for a long time, long enough for me to decide for some reason to start filling the conversational gaps with details of my upbringing. I mentioned the three-parent experiment. I mentioned that as that experiment was crumbling, the dream of a new experiment was born, to live a completely self-sufficient life way out in the country. Mom and Tom yearned to live closer to nature, to leave the toxic concrete suburbs behind, to leave complications behind, to *get back to the land*. I mentioned that a key component of this dream was Tom going away to blacksmith school so that he could learn a trade that, in most people's minds, was as obsolete as powdered wigs and muskets. Wendell, clad in a suit, returning home from his well-paying job, had worn an expression of amused surprise throughout my dissertation, but when I got to the blacksmith thing he burst out laughing.

"My god," he said. "What were they *thinking*?"

"I know, I know," I said, because I will almost always agree with anyone about anything. But after Wendell and I parted ways—he lived in a nicer neighborhood—I began what would turn out to be a lifelong habit of imagining myself responding with fierce eloquence to his mocking rhetorical dismissal of my family's unusual choices.

"Look," I would begin, "things were different back then."

Look, it was a time to Try New Things. Not all of those things worked. But even in the mistakes, or maybe especially in the mistakes, the cockeyed grandeur of the 1970s comes through.

For example, in 1974, when Mom and Tom were making their final preparations to make what they envisioned to be a move far away from civilization and all its conventional ways, the World Champion Oakland A's added a man to their roster with no discernible familiarity with baseball and invented for him the brand-new role of designated pinch runner.

Herb Washington was and would always remain the only pure designated pinch runner in the history of baseball. Though the A's also used other players primarily as pinch runners during the mid-'70s, Washington was the only specialist to never once bat or take the field as a defender and so was the only player ever to have "Pinch Run." as his listed position on the front of a baseball card.

A's owner Charles O. Finley, a wealthy, blustering, delusional madman or visionary who in some ways epitomized the sublime and ridiculous era I have been trying my whole life to fully understand, envisioned Washington, a former college sprinter, as yet another advantage for the formidable Oakland squad. But instead of being a fortification of the already high-powered engine that had carried the A's to league supremacy throughout the early- to mid-1970s, Washington ended up being the most superfluous (hence greatest) hood ornament on the biggest, baddest, Blue Moon Odomest Cadillac in the league.

As recounted on the back of his 1975 card, Washington entered 91 games in 1974, his first season in the majors. He stole 28 bases and was caught stealing 16 times. That is not a good ratio and in fact would be identified by present-day baseball number-crunchers as counterproductive, Washington's jittery, unpolished improvisations on the basepaths killing too many possible rallies to justify the occasional extra base. He lasted only until May of the following year, adding two more stolen bases and one more caught stealing to his all-time record.

When I was a kid I did not scrutinize the stolen-base-to-caught-stealing ratio but was instead mesmerized that these statistics were included at all, for at that time and throughout the 1970s stolen bases were not among the statistics on any other card. I also completely believed the overheated back-of-the-card space-filling prose created by a nameless Topps functionary who wrote, among other things, that Washington was "personally responsible for winning 9 games for the A's in 1974."

My guess is that in a couple of these nine games, Washington merely trotted across the plate in front of a home run by one of the actual baseball players on the team, that in a few more of the nine games he scored after a series of events not of his own doing that would have led just as easily to a score by the actual baseball player he replaced, and that the game or two where his speed actually seemed to provide the winning edge were more than canceled out by his inexperienced baserunning gaffes in other games and by his taking the place on the roster of someone who could, say, field a ground ball or dump a pinch-hit single into right field once in a while. Then again, his mere presence may have inflicted psychological damage on other teams. By carrying a guy on their roster who could not hit, pitch, or field, the A's were in essence declaring to their opponents that they could kick their asses with one hand tied behind their back.

Also, and perhaps more significantly, the inclusion of Herb Washington served as a message from the A's to all the suit-wearing, sober-minded Wendells of the world that they were brave enough to try something new. Whether the useless innovation of Herb Washington signaled the apotheosis of the A's dynasty or foretold the team's impending descent at champion-sprinter speed into abject late-1970s suffering is beside the point. The point is that life is not to be methodically considered and solved like a math equation. Life, fucking Wendell, is to be sprinted toward and bungled beyond recognition.

Topps 1978 #726: Wilbur Wood

WILBUR WOOD

I won't say I haven't also wondered in the course of my life what the hell my parents were thinking. Even during my earliest years of consciousness, when I generally understood the experimentation of the adults in my family as simply the way life was, I instinctively began to reach for things that had clear rules and distinct lines between what was good and what was bad.

In fact, one of the things that would draw me into the world of the cardboard gods as much as anything else was its clean, well-defined system of statistical landmarks. You knew where you stood with the numbers on the back of a baseball player's card. If a guy hit 30 home runs and drove in 100 runs, he was a star slugger. If another guy turned in a sub-3.00 ERA, he was a top pitcher. It was as simple as that, no gray areas, no confusion.

For starting pitchers, it was all about wins. If you won 20 games, you were an ace. Conversely, if you lost 20 games, you were kind of a rag arm, a luckless mushballer (though probably not utterly incompetent; after all, your team must have seen reason to keep running you out there to take all those beatings).

These seemingly mutually exclusive starting pitcher landmarks would be well-known to me by the time I started inspecting the baffling statistics on the back of Wilbur Wood's card. In a five-year span, the aging knuckleballer with the nineteenth-century name won 20 games four times, but he also lost 20 games twice, 19 games once, and 17 games once. The most confusing year of all was one of the years when all three of my parents lived in the same house, 1973, when Wilbur Wood won 24 games and lost 20.

I could never figure out if Wilbur Wood was bad or good, but eventually I came to see him as being, in both name and deed, some kind of throwback to the rugged, spike-gashing dawn of major league baseball, when hurlers started both ends of a doubleheader and then came on in relief the next day at dusk despite massive corn liquor hangovers to strand the go-ahead and winning runs in scoring position. Wilbur Wood was beyond Old School. He was Old Testament. He was the last vestige of a time when men named Mordecai and Smokey Joe and Grover strode as giants upon the land, their won-lost records both gleaming and gory, good and bad entangled.

When Wilbur Wood hung it up, it left no one to stop the meek five-inning starters and one-out lefty bullpen specialists from inheriting the earth.

Topps 1975 #511: Texas Rangers Checklist

511	TEXAS RANGERS	TEAM CHECKLIST

Card	Player/Position	Card	Player/Position	
155	Bibby, Jim/P	106	Hargrove, M./1B	**GET ALL 24 TEAM CHECKLIST CARDS**
542	Broberg, Pete/P	131	Harrah, Toby/SS	
316	Brown, Jackie/P	60	Jenkins, Fergie/P	
470	Burroughs, J./OF	36	Lovitto, Joe/OF	Send 40¢ plus 1 Baseball wrapper to: Box 7630
518	Cardenas, Leo/SS	511	Martin, Billy/M	
12	Clyde, David/P	83	Merritt, Jim/P	Westbury, N.Y. 11590
617	Cubbage, Mike/IF	435	Nelson, Dave/2B	INCLUDE ZIP CODE.
644	Fahey, Bill/C	259	Randle, Len/2B	PRINT CLEARLY. Void where prohibited, regulated or taxed. Offer expires Dec. 31, 1975. Allow 4 weeks for delivery.
283	Foucault, Steve/P	387	Spencer, Jim/1B	
339	Fregosi, Jim/3B	493	Stanhouse, Don/P	
234	Grieve, Tom/OF	567	Sundberg, Jim/C	
412	Hands, Bill/P	178	Tovar, Cesar/OF	
362	Hargan, Steve/P			

★ © 1975 TOPPS CHEWING GUM, INC. PRTD IN U.S.A.

Though my brother and I were at the center of the adults' vision of a new life in the country—they wanted us to grow up wild and free, bounding barefoot through meadows, uncorrupted—we paid as little attention to it as possible. Instead, as it turned out, we paid attention to baseball. I'd never cared about baseball before, but in our first spring in Vermont, in 1975, my brother started playing little league and collecting baseball cards and following the regional team, the Red Sox. And what he did, I did.

This imitative way of being was something that would in many ways define my life, my imitations often going beyond mimicry to become a kind of inward orthodoxy that seized on one or another of the various pursuits of my brother as if they were the exploits of a visionary, each detail worthy of the impassioned scrutiny of a solitary monk. I understand my connection to baseball in this way. My brother liked baseball a lot. He was a better player than I would ever be, bigger and stronger, even able eventually to throw a good curveball. But I don't think he grabbed hold of its details as fiercely as I did, something I noticed early on when he tried to argue that Rogers Hornsby, and not Ty Cobb, held the record for highest lifetime batting average. It was the first time in my life that I knew more than my brother about anything, and possibly also my first experience with irony, given that I'd so passionately studied the baseball encyclopedia my uncle Conrad had recently given my brother for Christmas because I believed such study would bring me closer to my brother.

That first year in Vermont, we house-sat in a town called Randolph Center for a family spending a year as Christian missionaries in Korea. Randolph Center had many big white houses with immaculate lawns, a college with brand-new tennis courts, and a big pond called Lake Champagne with a sun-drenched wooden dock in the middle of it and a building nearby with pinball machines and air hockey tables. Very near our house, there was a small ski hill with a rope lift. In the summer, hang gliders launched themselves from the top of the hill like bright-colored ponderous birds that seemed somehow simultaneously prehistoric and futuristic.

Kids were friendly in Randolph Center, a few of them coming by to basically welcome my brother and me aboard. One of these kids was a farm boy named Buster who would go on to become the primary baseball news oracle for the nationwide sports information monopoly and who even as a preadolescent had contagious enthusiasm for baseball, baseball history, and at that time most especially baseball cards. By the time we met him, or, to put it more accurately, were swept up in his tornado of baseball mania, his baseball card collection was already the stuff of legend—the rumor was that he kept the collection in a trunk that he'd buried somewhere on the grounds of the Wiffle Ball stadium he'd built on his family's lawn to resemble a miniature Fenway Park. When asked about this he would bark laughter, then give answers as elusive as his unhittable Wiffle Ball pitches.

My brother and I had bought stray packs of cards before, but under our friend's influence we began buying packs whenever possible at the general store in town called Floyd's, which was owned by Mr. Floyd, a chipper Vermonter with a Santa Claus build and a gray-flecked flattop buzz cut. We began bringing those packs home and opening them and marking the new names received on a checklist and sorting those cards into teams and casting names already received into a reservoir for flipping and trading, the doubles pile. There were rules and unknowns, satisfactions and needs, waves of getting and undertows of wanting. The riddling pull of love. We began to collect.

We plunged into it so fiercely in that first full year away from our father that I got closer to getting every player for a single team than I ever would again. From Bibby, Jim, to Tovar, Cesar, I slowly but steadily accrued every last member of the 1975 Texas Rangers except one: Topps card number 412. Hands, Bill/P.

My brother owned Bill Hands. I can't remember clearly, but he may have even had doubles. However, it was not at all customary to simply hand over surplus cards. I understood this and was in a strange way even glad about it. The game had rules, and rules helped create a world with meaning. He proposed to trade me Bill Hands for my one and only 1975 Carl Yastrzemski. I was tempted, but even at age seven I knew that if I made such a deal I'd feel as if I'd been punched in the stomach for months afterward. By then I had fallen in love with the Boston Red Sox, and I knew that the center of the team was the ancient living legend known as Yaz. So I held tight to my Yaz card and decided to take my chances with the random gatherings within each new pack of cards.

I began to pray. I'd never prayed before. Every time I opened a pack of cards, I prefaced the opening with a silent plea for Bill Hands. His persisting failure to arrive threaded a new feeling through the revelation of each freshly opened pack, through the bright colors and sunshine, and the nobility of the names, and the exactitude of the numbers, and the sweetness of the gum, and all the other pleasures of *getting*. Below all that, faintly: an ache, an absence, an unfillable box.

Topps 1975 #634: Cy Acosta

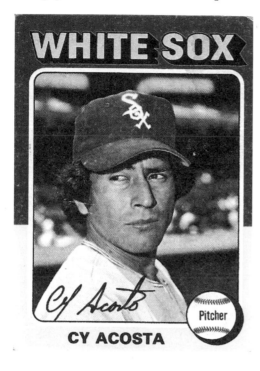

CY ACOSTA

A new practice arose alongside my pack-opening prayers: When things fail to arrive, depart. Start with a card and let the baseball encyclopedia do the rest. Start with Harmon Killebrew and go all the way back with the Lifetime Leaders in Home Runs to Babe Ruth swatting his first four-bagger in 1915. Start with Bob Gibson and go all the way back with the Lifetime Leaders in Strikeouts to Walter Johnson fanning his first batter in 1907 and Cy Young doing the same in 1890. Start with Carl Yastrzemski and go all the way back with Awards from Triple Crown to Triple Crown to the very first author of the feat, Tip O'Neill, in 1887. Start anywhere. Start in the middle of nowhere. Start with Cy Acosta and go all the way back.

In 1872, major league baseball's first Cy, Clytus George "Cy" Bentley, debuted at the age of twenty-one with the Middletown Mansfields of the National Association, a forerunner of the National League. He started 17 of their 24 games and finished the season with 2 wins, 15 losses, and a 6.14 ERA. At bat, he hit .235 with 2 triples. He died the following year, on February 26, 1873, at the age of twenty-two.

It would be eighteen years before another Cy reached the majors, but that second Cy, born Denton True Young, would retire twenty-one years later with 509 more major league wins than his predecessor, a deluge of namesakes in his wake. In chronological order depending on their first year in the majors, they are Cy Bowen, Cy Seymour, Cy Swaim, Cy Vorhees, Cy Morgan (not to be confused with Cy Morgan, below), Cy Falkenberg, Cy Ferry, Irv "Cy the Second" Young (career record: 63 wins, 95 losses), Cy Barger, Cy Neighbors, Harley

"Cy the Third" Young (career record: 0 wins, 3 losses), Cy Alberts, Cy Slapnicka, Cy Williams, Rube "Cy" Marshall (and with Roy De Verne Marshall [career record: 8 wins, 10 losses] the land of Cy merges with the land of Rube, which is almost as populous as the land of Cy, 33 major league Rubes to 35 major league Cys [the latter number not including nineteenth-century journeyman Sy Sutcliffe], Rube Foster and Rube Waddell foremost among the Rubes, who have not walked among us since the retirement of Rube Walker in 1958), Cy Pieh, Al "Cy" Cypert, Cy Rheam, Charlie "Cy" Young (career record: 2 wins, 3 losses), Orie Milton "Cy" Kerlin, Cy Perkins, Cy Warmoth, Cy Wright, Cy Fried, Cy Twombly (whose one year in the majors predated the birth of the famous painter with the same name by seven years), Cy Morgan (not to be confused with Cy Morgan, above), Cy Moore, Ed "Cy" Cihocki, Cy Blanton, Cy Malis, Cy Block, Cy Buker, and, finally, Cy Acosta.

The gap between the untimely passing of Cy Bentley and the arrival of Cy Young was eighteen years, which is the third biggest Cyless gap in baseball history. The second biggest gap is the twenty-seven years between the last pitch of Cy Buker, who played for one year for the Brooklyn Dodgers during World War II, and the first pitch of Cy Acosta.

The last pitch of Cy Acosta came three years, 186 2/3 innings, and one obscure meritless feat later (in a 1973 game, a defensive substitution involving the designated hitter brought Cy Acosta to the plate to hit, the first time a pitcher batted in an American League game after the institution of the designated hitter rule; he fanned), and with the last pitch of Cy Acosta began the longest Cyless span of all. It's now more than three decades since Cy Acosta logged his final two innings in a sparsely attended 11–3 loss otherwise featuring pitchers named Bob, Steve, Tom, Ron, Joe, and Al.

Sigh.

Topps 1975 #528: Eddie Leon

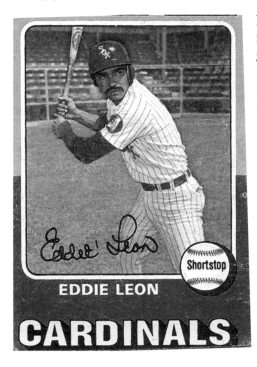

Many years after my family's move to Vermont, I got a glimpse of the expectant happiness that defined that time for Mom and Tom. I was on an aimless break from college, and I came upon a postcard Mom had written Tom while we were still living in New Jersey. At the time the postcard was written, Tom was away at blacksmith school in Kansas.

"I'm flipping out with thoughts of THERE!" my mother wrote.

She meant Vermont, the Vermont that they'd dreamed up together, the lasting answer to everything.

But our first stop in Vermont, in Randolph Center, was temporary, lasting only as long as the family who owned the house was away in Korea. Throughout our year there, I imagine Mom or Tom continued to talk to one another of THERE as being something and someplace yet to come. Near the end of our time in that house, in the summer of 1975, Mom and Tom sent in a foreclosure auction bid on a house a few miles away.

They hadn't been allowed to inspect the premises before putting in a bid, but they'd looked at the house from the road. They'd seen that it was even farther out in the country than the house in Randolph Center. They'd seen the pastures all around, the mountains cradling the green valley on all sides. They'd believed when they looked at that house that they were looking at the true beginning of the life they'd been dreaming of. They believed that the house was THERE.

Tom and I were in the kitchen of the house in Randolph Center when Mom came in with the envelope from the state. Mom looked at Tom and not at me. Then she opened the envelope with exactly the same delicious slowness that I employed to open a pack of base-ball cards. When she pried the flap open all the way she looked again to Tom. The two of them stared at one another, small, nervous smiles on their faces.

I feel as if I remember this moment intimately, even down to the detail that something about their smiles, something about the way their interlocking gazes shut out everything in the world but each other, made my stomach start to hurt. But I can't be sure about this, or about anything, because for some reason I have spent most of my adult life imagining and reimagining the past, and now I never know beyond a shadow of a doubt what actually happened and what I've invented to fill in the gaps of what's been lost. Most of the un-countable moments of life evaporate with no trace, so it's really no wonder I hold on with such desperation to what's left, my baseball cards, those actual, physical, inarguable remnants of the past. I need them now as much as I've ever needed them. I started needing them in 1975, the year I watched Tom move to Mom's side so that they could discover the contents of the letter together.

"Oh my god," Mom said.

"We won," Tom said to Mom.

"What do you mean?" I said.

"We won! We won!" Mom shouted to Tom.

We discovered the nature of this victory together, as a family: me, my brother, my mother, and Tom. We drove a few miles from the house in Randolph Center, on a winding road that went down and down. When we finally reached the bottom of the hill we took a right turn and drove past the general store where most of my baseball cards would come to me, then past the few houses of our new town. The houses started to thin out quickly, and we pulled into the rutted dirt drive of a house that seemed to be at the edge of things.

I've invented a lot of versions of the dialogue that might have occurred during the slim moment when we moved from our VW Camper to the house, that last moment before we began to under-stand what we had won, but it's just as likely that there was no dia-logue, that we all walked together in silence toward the broken door.

Inside, obscene graffiti covered the walls. *Fuck you. Suck my cock. Eat my hot an jusy cunt.* There were pictures scrawled in magic marker or carved by a knife. I learned from the images that men had gi-ant poles protruding from their midsections and women had, in the same general middle-body area, awful jagged gaping wounds, and sometimes these two things would come together, causing both parties to scream.

One room downstairs had buckling green linoleum and smashed plates and old food all over the floor. Mangy carpeting smothered the floors of the other rooms. Warped wood paneling made up some walls, while other walls had been stripped down to crumbling, gouged-away sheetrock.

There was dust everywhere, so much so that soon enough we'd all be walking around with bandanas around our mouths and noses like we were all about to rob a stagecoach. But on the first day we sniffled and sneezed, not yet figuring out that first remedy in what would become an era of tireless remedies and adjustments and innovations by Mom and Tom—and, in different, more internal ways, by my brother and me.

Upstairs there were two rooms, plus a narrow walkway along the side of the staircase that led back to a dark area that seemed to have no purpose beyond gathering trash from the family before us, including a case of Coca-Cola bottles that had all been filled with urine. After that discovery we entered the room my brother and I would share. The ceiling and walls seemed to be diseased, a pox of tiny holes everywhere, some clustered to form fist-sized lesions, plaster or pasteboard dangling from the edges.

"We'll make it better," Mom said.

"I thought we won," I said.

Ian reached and touched the border of one of the larger scars on the wall and a tiny silver ball fell out. There were these BBs all over the floor, mixed in with chunks of the ceiling and walls.

"We won an auction," Mom said.

"What's an auction?" I said.

"It's not like winning a contest," Mom said. "It's—"

She started crying a little.

"We'll make it better," she said.

On one of our first days in our new life, while Mom and Tom worked hard to get the house into a livable state, my brother and I explored the farther reaches of what was ours. We poked around the obscenity-laden garage, roamed the trash-strewn, overgrown yard, and, eventually, braved a visit to the tiny lopsided shed at the border of the property.

The shed looked as if it had been hammered together with the same inebriated rage that seemed to have caused all the destruction in the main house. The low roof was slanted, as was the doorway, which was also rife with jutting rusty nails, and the shed's one narrow window looked back on the house like an eye that had been battered to a cockeyed slit in a bar fight. Not much light got in. I wanted to leave, go back outside, but after we'd been in the shed for only a few moments, my brother discovered a loose board in the middle of the creaky floor.

He lifted it up as I came closer. There was a shallow hole in the dirt below the loose board, and as our eyes adjusted to the dim light of the shed we could see that there were objects in there. The treasures of the family before us. My brother started reaching down in.

There were some empty shotgun casings. There was a grimy teddy bear with a gaping hole in its crotch. My brother handed it to me and Styrofoam pellets leaked from its wound, clicking on the floorboards. Its fur was clammy. One of its black glass eyes was missing.

My brother kept pulling things out. There was a tube that looked like toothpaste but wasn't. There were some more Coke bottles, but these had cigarette butts in them, not piss.

Finally, my brother extracted a magazine that showed people who lived in a place with no clothing. We moved to the shed's one window and looked at it together, my brother flipping the pages. The people sipped drinks naked and laid around on the beach naked and played volleyball and badminton naked. Their limp and sagging privates seemed both sadder and scarier than the monstrous versions I had seen scrawled in magic marker or carved by knife in the main house. The color in all the photos had faded. In many of the pictures the naked people smiled broadly, as if they were very happy, as if they had finally found the paradise they'd been longing for, a place of sheer perfection.

I never, ever wanted to go there.

I began to need all the gods I could get that year, the year my budding baseball card collection moved with me into the room that had been mangled with a BB gun. The superstars with their gleaming numbers and unbroken tenures in cities that cheered for them long and loud weren't enough. I needed a teeming battalion of gods. I needed gods with warning-track power, gods with waning speed, gods who drifted from team to team, gods who got released, gods who got sent down, gods who waited and waited and never got recalled. I needed flawed gods, forgettable gods. I needed nobodies, journeymen, automatic outs. I needed gods who were neither here nor there.

I needed Eddie Leon. I needed a guy posing in a Chicago White Sox uniform while the crooked, cut-off, erroneous card he is posing on identifies him as a member of the St. Louis Cardinals and the back of the card declares he is neither a White Sox nor a Cardinal but a New York Yankee. The back-of-the-card scripture also points out that he "has been among Chisox' leaders in Sacrifices in '73 & '74."

Among the leaders. On a single team. In bunts. I don't know how you could say any less about someone without saying nothing at all. It suggests that when the White Sox really needed some bench guy of slight build and twitchy middle-infielder reflexes to go up there and lay down a beauty, they looked first to somebody other than Eddie Leon, but if their top-ranked bunter was for some reason otherwise occupied, perhaps because he'd been entrusted with the more important task of going into the clubhouse to fetch an icy drink for one of the RBI guys such as Dick Allen or Beltin' Bill Melton, well, then it was Eddie Leon's time to go up there and intentionally make an out by tapping the ball as softly as possible.

Or, to put it another way, using the capitalization style of the back-of-the-card text, then it was time for Eddie Leon to Sacrifice. To Make Sacred. And if a fallible, forgettable guy like Eddie Leon in the wrong uniform on a defective card is capable of not only *being* sacred but *making* sacred, then who in our own damaged world is beyond the reach of hope?

1975 Topps #439: Ed Brinkman

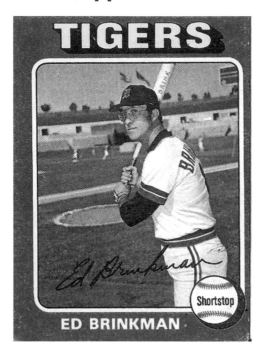

Not long after our move into the house, my father sent my brother a speedometer to fasten to the handlebars of his banana-seat bicycle. It was a thing of beauty, that speedometer, the serious black face accented by precise white numbers and hash marks and a thin silver needle. My brother rode the bike to the top of the rise in the road by our new house. I stood in the driveway and watched him disappear from sight, over the crest of the hill. Then he reappeared on the other side of the road, standing and pumping on the pedals and glancing up and down from the road to his speedometer. He yelled out intervals of increasing speed as he neared me and reached me and flew on by.

"Ten!"

"Fifteen!"

"*Twenty!*"

At that time, the tail end of the summer, sticky-pus weed-bulbs called wild cucumbers were blooming everywhere in the copious weeds of East Randolph. I had never seen these plants in either New Jersey or in Randolph Center, but they seemed to flourish in our new run-down town. The bulbs were prickly skinned sacks containing fluid as white and sticky as glue, and they had some heft to them and just happened to be a size that perfectly fit the palm of a kid. Hence, the kids of East Randolph introduced themselves to my brother and me by whipping wild cucumbers at our heads.

One day not long after the wild cucumbers had begun to fly, my brother and I rode our bikes to the town's general store to buy baseball cards. The ride passed without incident, but when we got to the cracked concrete drive of the store, a pack of kids emerged and encircled my brother and his banana-seat bicycle. They were understandably drawn to the fancy speedometer, but instead of marveling at it, as I had, they mashed wild cucumbers into its shining black face, breaking the needle and, it turned out, irrevocably fouling the interior mechanisms.

My brother, in a silent rage, tackled the main instigator and pounded on him until the kid, using some weedy East Randolph know-how, ended the barrage by yanking out a hunk of my brother's curly hair. It was the first in a series of fights between my brother and the kids of our new town. It was also the beginning of my lifelong practice of moving around in public as invisibly as possible.

I turned out to have a gift for invisibility, but even when those first solo trips to the store to get baseball cards went by without any trouble, I was unnerved by all the unknown houses, many of them dilapidated, some of them even abandoned, windows as dark as the shed window that stared unblinkingly at our house with its knowledge of violated teddy bears and awful nude valhallas.

The general store added to the feeling of foreboding. A big part of this was because the name of the store was Race's but it was owned by a family whose last name was not Race. It didn't make sense to me, compared to the store in Randolph Center that had been called Floyd's and was owned by jolly Santa-bellied Mr. Floyd. The discordance seemed to be an extension of our experience with our new house, which was really the house of the family before us, who made sure to put their suffering mark everywhere before they moved, apparently against their will, into a glum scattering of trailers a few miles away. Everything in East Randolph was provisional and nothing really belonged to anyone, and even the names of things were in question. It's no wonder that my need for the precision of baseball cards, with their definite names and numbers, increased when we moved to this new town.

The store was more dimly lit than the one in Randolph Center, and it had a cavernous back area where hulking men in hunting jackets would often be sitting, either ignoring me or staring through me as I walked toward the back to get to the open box of packs of baseball cards. A little bit later in the fall, these men would be among those authoring the procession of bloody deer corpses across the front porch of the store, which featured a large scale for weighing game. The owner of the store was the biggest of these men, and after rising and lumbering in his steel-toed shoes from the shadows and up to the register in the front, he would ring up my sale without speaking or looking at me, breath steaming in and out of his nostrils audibly. I always walked out of Race's gripping my purchase tightly, as if the cards inside the waxy wrappers were already worth far more than what I'd spent on them. As if they were worth a safe place in the world.

Most of the cards from that year, 1975, were off-center, the bordering thicker on one side than the other. In years to come I'd wonder if the process of making the cards that year was not standardized and mechanized at all but instead one that relied on the judgment and dexterity of a nineteen-year-old Coast Guard dropout named Smitty who'd just spent his break smoking a joint out by the Dumpster. But when they first came into my hands, the mistakes riddling the 1975 set made the universe captured by the cards seem to my seven-year-old self to be homely, disheveled, approachable, as if my Mount Olympus was as close at hand as a bake sale advertised by a mimeographed page tacked to an elementary school bulletin board. I needed to feel this closeness that year more than any other.

The off-balance layout was apparent in Ed Brinkman's card, which further lessened the feeling of distance between the viewer and the realm of major league baseball by presenting a figure who seemed to have called in sick to his job as an instructor of remedial math and driver's ed at the vocational high school to sneak onto the grounds of the Detroit Tigers training complex. The distance lessened further still with the discovery that this nearsighted ectomorph turned out not to be an impostor at all but a starting major league shortstop; moreover, he had been a starting major league shortstop for well over a decade. He even had his own crudely personalized bat— "BRINK"—which he presumably used in the just-concluded season to launch 14 home runs, his career high.

The total effect of Ed Brinkman's card, and of many of the cards that year, was to present for me a world that seemed flawed enough to allow even me to be a part of it, but that also was capable of the fluid dream-magic of make-believe. I could stand in the middle of my little BB-riddled room alone and hold Ed Brinkman brand new in my hands, and believe Ed Brinkman wasn't that far away from being pelted with wild cucumbers, and believe he was right beside me, and follow him from our new low valley all the way to the majors.

Topps 1976 #628: John D'Acquisto

JOHN D'ACQUISTO

PITCHER **GIANTS**

I started having nightmares, except they weren't nightmares, but we didn't know what else to call them. Years later, still trying to understand this inexplicable part of my childhood, I discovered that the accepted term for these episodes was "night terrors." I recognized the physiological and observable elements related to the term: jackhammer heartbeat, shortness of breath, the young subject running and thrashing and screaming as if unable to escape a vision of bottomless horror. But the book that described the phenomenon claimed that children who experience night terrors are not even aware of them as they happen; they are in a kind of sleepwalking trance and don't remember them the next day. Neither claim was true.

I woke in the dark, the whole house quiet, and things looked wrong, out of proportion, or as if there were no such thing as proportion, a baseball and a wall and a shoe all simultaneously gigantic and microscopically small. I got out of bed and it got worse. Jackhammer heartbeat, shortness of breath. Floor, door, staircase, stairs—everything seemed to have shed its name.

And I remembered all this the next day, my throat still hoarse from screaming. I remembered how everything had looked wrong and how this fed into a spiraling fear that there was no way back to the normal world, that the terror would be endless. I remembered the expression—fright, worry, exhaustion, helplessness—on Mom's face and Tom's face and Ian's face, no one able to stop what was happening. And beyond merely remembering, I felt it all flickering at the edges of the daylight world, the name of every object a thin, slipping rag above a kind of awful infinity.

On days like that, I went to my cards with more need than usual. I held them and read them aloud, the numbers, the names. Everything seemed a little foggy on those days, one name bleeding over its borders into the next. This was especially true if I happened to venture, as if drawn to an implacable feeling of melancholic absence and aftermath, into my dreary collection of San Francisco Giants.

I had never seen the San Francisco Giants on television. They never surfaced in *Sports Illustrated* or anywhere near the top of the most distant of all divisions, the National League West. In the All-Star Game their yearly lone representative was no more noticeable than the half-second blip in the corner of the screen made by a white-shirted extra fleeing ruin in a disaster film. They seemed to me in those years, which were just after their iconic superstar Willie Mays had departed, to be not so much a team as a state of being, or somehow a lack of a state of being. A mystery. A mist.

Gary Lucas was Gary Lavelle. Garry Maddox was Gary Matthews. When Garry Maddox was traded to the Phillies, leaving the blurring haze of San Francisco to become a distinct personality (the Minister of Defense), Gary Thomasson and Gary Alexander drifted into the ever-expanding Gary-laced void.

But it wasn't just the Gar(r)ys. I confused Ray Sadecki with Mike Sadek, Mike Ivie with Mike Lum, Jim Barr with Steve Barr and Doug Bair (and, later, Steve Farr), and for reasons that I can't explain I thought of Von Joshua as the fourth Alou. The fog of the mid- to late-'70s San Francisco Giants would also come to encompass blur-rings of identities across the years, Bob Knepper merging into Bob Kipper, Tim Foli merging into Tom Foley, Ed Halicki merging into Mike Bielecki who merged into Bob Milacki.

At the center of the fog was John D'Acquisto, who in my earliest years among night terrors and gods was one and the same with John Montefusco. As I got older I slowly came to understand the difference between John D'Acquisto and John Montefusco, but I was only able to absorb this information (which allowed me to identify several colorful individual facets of the latter figure, such as that he had won a Rookie of the Year award, had pitched a no-hitter, and was known far and wide as the Count of Montefusco) after John D'Acquisto was removed from the Giants in a trade to the Cardinals for, among others, Dave Rader, whom I then began to confuse with Doug Rader.

Trying to grab at the diaphanous handholds of names could only take me so far. When the day after a nightmare came to an end I went to bed tired and frightened, wondering if I'd make it through the night without waking up and seeing once again that everything was actually something else. It was dark and I didn't want to go to sleep. I wanted to keep saying names.

"Hey," I said. "Hey, Ian."

Topps 1976 #256: Rowland Office

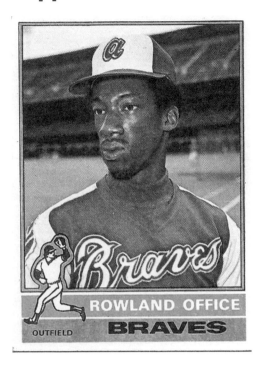

In Randolph Center, any additions to my baseball card collection had been discussed, or at least had the potential to be discussed, in a small but palpable community of Randolph Center baseball card collectors that included me, my brother, Buster, Buster's good-natured friend George (who didn't allow his good nature to keep him from swindling me, a mere toddler, practically, out of my 1974 Hank Aaron "Home Run Champion" card), and sometimes even some other kids from the town. In East Randolph, collecting baseball cards became something far more solitary, but even when I was looking at my cards by myself, I was on some level imagining that at some point I would share my thoughts and discoveries with my brother.

And though my brother would increasingly recoil from the idea that we comprised a two-boy community unto ourselves—an idea I was more than willing to embrace—in those early years in East Randolph he was often as interested in playing with me and sharing with me as I was with him. Mom and Tom worked very hard to make the bedroom my brother and I shared livable by tearing out the BB-riddled walls and putting up new ones, but my brother and I claimed the room as our own by laughing our asses off at baseball cards.

The 1976 Rowland Office card that came into our lives in our first spring in the house, after a long, cold winter, did as much as any card to achieve this goal. Something about it caused both of us to erupt, sprawling on the floor, cards scattered all around us, loose and in rubber-banded stacks. And this didn't just happen the first time we saw the card. We'd be sorting new cards into our teams, and one of us would hold up our version of this Rowland Office card for the other to see. The holder of the card would have his lips clamped shut, trying not to laugh until the other looked up to see.

Looking at the card now, I honestly don't know what caused us to roll around on our bedroom floor laughing until we cried. The name is cartoonish, the face unusually long and thin, the lips pursed as if a sour remark is about to be uttered about the stench of a team-mate's flatulence. I mean, I guess he's kind of funny looking. But now, weighed down by all my years, I also see a young guy, much younger than I am now, trying to stick in the majors, trying to hold on to what is probably the only thing he knows how to do really well. I find myself focusing on his eyes, which seem alert and un-sure, like those of a deer ready to bolt at any sign of trouble. I see a human where once I only saw a ridiculous god, a god who had and still has few peers in my imagined personal pantheon. He was the god of laughing fits, returning year after year to sacrifice himself in our brotherly rituals.

Topps 1977 #5: 1976 Victory Leaders

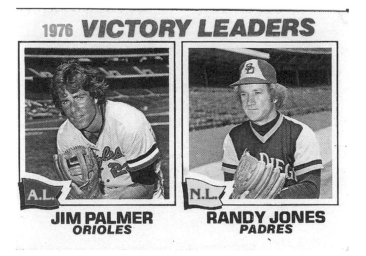

On July 28, 1976, Randy Jones went 10 innings in a 2–1 victory to push his dazzling record to 18 wins and 4 losses. After a rocky start to his career that included an 8–22 season, Jones had broken through in 1975 with 20 wins, and in 1976 he looked to be heading to superstardom. *Sports Illustrated* even featured him on their cover, wondering if he could become the first National Leaguer since Dizzy Dean to win 30 games.

By then I had finished my first year in a new class invented by the hippie parents scattered through the area. There were no grades, in both senses of the word: Kids of all ages were together in one room, and hierarchical assessment of academic achievement had been abolished. The idea was that we were free to learn what we wanted to learn, however we wanted to learn it, that every little boy and girl would find a way to burst into bloom. I learned about Indian tribes and feelings and how to say words in Russian and I wrote stories and plays and even an imitation of a television show using a cardboard box with an opening in the front that displayed a paper scroll filled with my tale in bright crayon about a bionic flea. Sometimes as I was walking to school I broke into a run.

There was a brief moment in time when it seemed the answer to everything was Yes. Anyone could burst into bloom. You didn't have to be among the few and chosen. Randy Jones—junk-ball-tossing Randy Jones, pale-skinned bozo-haired Randy Jones, thin-lipped dough-faced Randy Jones, Randy Jones in his Padres fast-food uniform, surrounded by feckless Padres teammates and empty seats and the blissfully indifferent blue of a Padres sky—was every bit as good as Jim Palmer.

Our classroom was located in the East Randolph elementary school, and kids from the regular classes made fun of us. The general gist of the taunting was that we were retarded. One day as I was leaving the general store with a pack of cards a couple kids my age from a regular class fell in behind me. One of them, Muskrat, started making marching sounds in time to my steps.

"Hu-*lef*, hu-*lef*, hu-*lef* rah lef."

"Hey, doofus," the second one, Denny, said. "How many hours in a day?"

"Hey, yeah," Muskrat said. "How many days in a week?"

"He doesn't know. They don't know shit."

"Hey, how do you spell *dog*? How do you spell *cat*?"

"Why is your hair so curly and long?" Denny said. "You must be a woman."

"Why are you a woman?" Muskrat said.

Sometimes a pack of cards couldn't do much for you. Sometimes it was full of nothing but guys you already had and checklists and highlights and league leaders. Sometimes when you got home and opened it you wished that you had picked a different pack from the box in the store. But what else was there to do? Dump the doubles onto the doubles pile, glare at the checklists, and try to learn something—you were always free to learn something—from the drab highlights and leaders.

Later in 1976, the magic dissipated for Randy Jones. He didn't get close to 30 wins and never finished another season with more wins than losses. Meanwhile, Jim Palmer, shown in the 1976 Victory Leaders card without headgear for no apparent reason other than to display that his flowing blow-dried hair is spectacularly superior to Jones's cap-crushed rusted Brillo, continued tanly vying for Cy Young awards, breezing into the playoffs, and posing for lucrative underwear ads. To this day, I find myself wishing what Randy Jones seems to be wishing—that he could somehow cross over from his photo to the golden realm of the AL Victory Leader and kick Jim Palmer in his Jockey-shorted nuts.

Topps 1976 #122 Mike Cosgrove

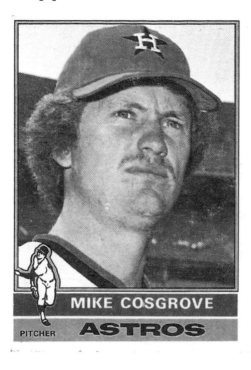

MIKE COSGROVE
PITCHER **ASTROS**

In a 1975 card that I had gotten just a few months earlier than the 1976 card shown here, a much younger looking Mike Cosgrove had oozed easy confidence, his body communicating looseness and ease, the natural balanced grace of a lefty. He stared directly at the viewer, a trace of a small, confident smile on his unblemished face, his hair straight and blond like a sun-drenched surf bum's. The back of the card contained the story of his quick rise through the minors, including the season he fanned 231 batters in 172 innings. After that he began splitting time between the minors and the majors, finally spending the majority of a season in the big leagues during the final campaign listed, 1974. Below the line for that year is a statement of praise and hope: "Mike became lefty ace of Astros' bullpen in 1974 & may be starter in 1975."

But just one year later, Mike Cosgrove no longer looks directly at the viewer. He's no longer young. The bill of his cap is misshapen, as if it has been mangled by bullies or forgotten in the rain. He wears badges of desperation indigenous to his awkward, searching decade: a perm, a dust-thin mustache. Behind him, simultaneously claustrophobic and vast, loom the unmistakable high stands of a major league stadium. He has made it; there is no joy. On the back of his card, all traces of his minor league successes have been expunged, leaving only the thin gruel of a big league mop-up man destined to vanish from the game altogether before next season's set of baseball cards hits the stores.

A friend of Mom and Tom's from New Jersey came to visit, a woman who brought her two daughters along. She'd just gotten a divorce. She and her ex-husband had been among the people who'd put ski masks on and kidnapped Tom on his birthday. Throughout the visit, she cried a lot and played side one of *The Band* over and over until I wanted to murder whoever was responsible for "Rag, Mama, Rag."

"It's so beautiful up here," she said to my mom.

"It's not like we thought," Mom said. "It's really hard."

"You're so lucky," the woman said.

"I don't paint anymore," Mom said.

The woman slept on the couch with the television on and her daughters slept in our room. They were the same ages as Ian and me but seemed older and wiser. Ian played Truth or Dare with them. I didn't want to play. It scared me. I pretended to go to sleep.

"How come he won't play?" the younger girl said.

"He's a baby," Ian said.

The days started getting shorter. I had gone through the whole summer of 1976 and hadn't gotten a Carl Yastrzemski card. I decided to write him a letter. I told him the Red Sox were my favorite team and he was my favorite player, then I asked him for his autograph.

I sealed and stamped the letter and took it out to our aluminum mailbox, flipping up the red metal flag to signal the mailman. Later in the day, when I saw that the flag was back down, evidence that the mailman had made his daily visit in the four-wheel-drive Subaru required for rural Vermont postal delivery, gravity loosened its hold just a little. My letter was on its way to Yaz!

In a certain way my real life began that day, my life in the world. Up to that point I had never wanted anything beyond what was close at hand, beyond my family, my home, my town. I began waiting for something more. The leaves started dying. Everything was going from before to after.

Instead of an encouraging personalized line of text below the numbers on the back of Mike Cosgrove's 1976 card, as there had been the year before, there is this non-sequitur: "At the turn of the century the Chicago Cubs were known as the Colts." In the photo on the front of the card, it's tempting to think the scattered figures in the distance are heckling the man in the extreme foreground, that scorn from strangers could be the cause of the complicated expression on Mike Cosgrove's face. But they are just as likely to be talking about how the Cubs used to be known as the Colts as they are to be talking about, let alone bothering to mock, Mike Cosgrove. They really have nothing to do with the likes of Mike Cosgrove. The vague repulsion or sour apprehension rippling his pasty features is his alone, the light from the dirty neon of the pawnshop within.

Topps 1978 #437: Bo McLaughlin

BO McLAUGHLIN

Everybody was going from before to after. Everybody had a look on their face like they'd just caught a whiff of a nearby landfill. Everybody was ambivalent about the length of their hair. Everybody was aging in regrettable ways. Everybody dabbled in jogging and chanting and cocaine. Everybody went back and forth from having a regular job to laying on rusty lawn furniture all afternoon unemployed. Everybody bought their children faulty mood rings and overly cheerful sex education handbooks. Everybody began wondering how to file for divorce. Everybody was a little bit country, a little bit rock and roll. Everybody wore rainbow colors and succumbed to depression. Everybody was kung fu fighting. Everybody was Bo McLaughlin.

Topps 1976 #150: Steve Garvey

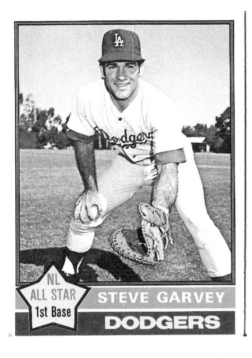

Everybody except Steve Garvey.

In 1975, *Sports Illustrated* featured a picture of Steve Garvey on the cover. In just a couple weeks, Saigon would fall, closing the book on America's disastrous military involvement in Vietnam and seeming to clinch the 1970s as a decade immune to American heroics. The year before, as the American president was being forced from office for criminally subverting democracy, the handsome, clean-cut, future *Sports Illustrated* cover subject became the first baseball player voted on to the All-Star Team as a write-in candidate. Democracy was dead? Long live democracy!

"Steve Garvey: Proud to be a hero," the cover caption read.

By the time I got this 1976 Steve Garvey card, my identity outside of baseball was as an outsider and a weirdo in my own town. The class I went to was not like other classes. My family was not like other families. There was a man in our house, Tom, who was not my father, and not only that but he had long hair and a beard and he drove around in a van with a metal chimney sticking out of the roof.

In what seems in retrospect an unbelievably dangerous move, given that the innovation introduced a blazingly hot open fire inside the rusty frame of a moving motor vehicle, Tom had rigged the van with a portable forge so that he could travel from farm to farm throughout central Vermont offering his services as a blacksmith. He soon discovered that the demand for this was next to nothing, especially since the service was being offered to wary lifelong Vermonters by a longhaired flatlander in jeans and a yellow Superman T-shirt. The few willing farmers who did have a horse or two lazing around on their dairy farms so neglected hoof care that when Tom occasionally got a job to shoe a horse, which involved clipping the animal's overgrown, infected hooves, the horse repaid the effort by kicking him in the ribs. For some time after Tom's plan to be a blacksmith had revealed itself as a hopeless case, he was still advertising the unusual nature of our family by driving all over the place with a chimney sticking out of his van.

"Why is there a chimney in your dad's van?" I was asked more than once by other kids. It wasn't really a question.

"He's not my dad," I'd say.

That denial also existed inside the walls of our house in a more intimate, more pointed way. There wasn't much discipline in my family, per my mom's "let them grow wild and free" child-rearing philosophy, and this made things even more difficult than they already would have been for the adult male interloper. Sometimes Tom tried to guide the behavior of my brother and me by speaking to us rationally. As soon as he started, however, we began drowning him out with a chant meant to convey profound boredom.

"Lecture, lecture, lecture," we droned.

Had I been put in the same situation in my mid- to late-twenties as a stepfather figure who wasn't even an official stepfather (instead forever just a *boyfriend*, both of the syllables of the word implying superficiality), I probably would have bashed the two miscreants' heads together, then hopped the nearest jet going far, far away. But except for one time when I was particularly sarcastic and Tom grabbed my arm and gave me a brief Indian burn, his frustration never boiled over into any kind of physical act. More than that, he hung in there. He stayed. Day after day, he was there.

My brother had more trouble with this enduring presence than I did, possibly because to me there had always been a Tom, whereas my brother was old enough to clearly remember a whole other family. For that matter, my brother could even remember a family that didn't include me, so my stronger attachment to Tom may also have had something to do with he and I both being intruders in the original, uncomplicated family.

I don't remember if my brother ever unleashed that trademark phrase of the boy in the broken family—*You're not my father!*—at Tom, but that was certainly the feeling underlying his side of their frequent yelling matches. These fights gave me stomachaches and sometimes worse. During one particularly vicious battle, I had to leave the house to go cry in the backyard, my hands pressed against my ears. Mom and Tom sat me down later for a talk.

"Why do you cry so much?" my mother asked.

During those years I used these baseball cards to dream myself into the True America, the one I believed existed somewhere far away. A True American was happy and painless. A True American was clean-cut and handsome. A True American looked you right in the eye, no sarcasm or fear or complicated feelings. No weird hippie food or long hair or unusual family configurations. No chimneys sticking out of vans. A True American stood tall. He didn't limp around hunched over in pain from horse kicks. He didn't skulk through his own town like an outsider and a thief when he needed to go buy more baseball cards. A True American played every game and collected 200 hits and 100 RBI every year and was elected to the All-Star Team every year and wore red, white, and blue and was proud and was a hero.

Tom eventually gave up on being a blacksmith, but it happened gradually, rather than falling in one decisive moment, like Saigon. Tom started picking up work here and there, as did Mom, and Dad kept plugging away at his sociology research job far away, sending money all the time. The idea had been to grow all our own food, but our garden always seemed to be beleaguered, weed-glutted, and stunted, no matter how hard my mom worked at it. The winters were brutal and went on forever. The nights were cold and long and sometimes punctuated by my night terrors. I ran through the house screaming past everyone calling my name and trying to tell me it was OK, but no one could ever help me, not my brother, not my mother, not Tom.

You would think that I would have come straight to Steve Garvey for help. That I would have been drawn to his first appearance in my collection, a 1976 card featuring an all-American asphyxia-blue two-plus-two-makes-four symmetry broken only by the reaching out of the 1974 NL MVP's glove hand, an aesthetic disturbance that seems to call on the viewer to complete some larger symmetrical pattern. You would think I would have jumped at the chance to imagine myself answering that call. An honorable, well-adjusted, Garveyesque boy would respond to this beckoning with a fittingly direct rock-jawed all-American reply, the baseball equivalent of a firm handshake: a straight brisk overhand strike. A logical balancing of the equation.

One day I left my free-school classroom to go to the bathroom and a couple of tough older girls cornered me in the hall.

"Hey, hippie dipshit," one said. "What's the capitol of Idaho?"

"I don't know," I said.

"See? Retards, every one of 'em," the second one said.

I tried to move past. The first one sidestepped in front of me and leaned closer, squinting. I could smell her spearmint gum.

"Hey, hippie dipshit, what's two plus two?"

Everything about Steve Garvey says that two plus two equals four. A part of me loved that kind of symmetry, loved that there was a definite answer to a question. This was the part of me that was most drawn to baseball. There were rules and numbers upon numbers, all of them adding up to a definite sum, the score of a game, or home runs in a career, or wins and losses. Though it would surprise the people who later tried to teach me geometry and trigonometry in my teenage years, one of the subjects I moved toward of my own volition in my hippie free school was math. I wanted to add two and two and get four, and then multiply those same numbers, and other numbers, and even divide them to get more complicated but no less definite answers to problems. I even wanted to do things that combined more than one operation, as on the happy day when I learned how to tabulate batting averages.

But there was more to life than two plus two equals four. I understood this from living in a house that featured plenty of things that didn't quite add up. For example, around the time I learned how to tabulate batting averages, a tree appeared in the middle of our living room.

The tree was actually a large branch with smaller branches that during a violent storm had fallen off a big tree out by the shed in the backyard. By that time, maybe a year after our move into the foreclosed property, Mom and Tom had fixed up the vandalized house by working with a resolve and passion that I have yet to be able to muster in my own adult life. They wanted the house to be more than simply livable, more than just two plus two equals four. They wanted it to be unique, singular, even a little irrational, a suitable echo of their iconoclastic back-to-the-land dream. Toward this end, they dragged the fallen branch inside and installed it in the middle of our living room so that it seemed very much as if a tree were growing up from the basement and through the ceiling. They hooked one end of a hammock to the tree and fastened the other end to the wall by the wood stove. You could lie in the hammock and look up at the tree and imagine that the line between inside and outside was blurred, that the forest off in the distance had through some impossible leap of illogic entered our home.

I was embarrassed by the indoor tree if anyone from outside my family saw it. But if no one was around I liked it. I loved it. I lay in the hammock and gazed up at as I swayed. And in the first spring that the tree lived in our living room, and for a spring or two after that, real leaves somehow bloomed from the branches.

What are you supposed to do when big and tough older girls corner you with a question like that? You're kind of damned if you do and damned if you don't. Especially if you've seen leaves bloom from a tree attached to nothing in the middle of a house.

"Four," I answered, feeling like a liar.

"Lucky guess, shit for brains."

I didn't like being an oddball outside of class, but I liked the class itself. In the big classroom that had desks and beanbag chairs scattered around randomly, we staged plays and made animated movies and built light sabers out of flashlights and colored plastic. One fall we all got a "ticket to the symphony" in the morning and in the afternoon we were led outside, to an empty meadow, where our teacher responded to our puzzlement by smiling and telling us to "just *listen*."

The following spring, we were told one morning that we were going to be taking *a trip back in time*, and that afternoon we walked down the halls past all the classes that had kids sitting at desks in straight rows. The kids in those classes all looked out at us as we paraded by. We moved out of their sight and into the day. The sun was shining, one of those moments after a long winter when your body seems to open like the petals of a flower. We took the short walk I took every day, a few hundred yards down Route 14 to our house.

When we got to our driveway, smoke was coming out of the chimney of Tom's blacksmith van. Tom stood by the van's sliding door, stoking the forge inside. We all came close, drawn to the blazing

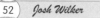

warmth and the white-hot coals. I hadn't seen him at his forge in a while. He had gotten a part-time job taking care of rats at a university lab. High weeds had grown all around the van. Tom's beard had begun its gradual retreat toward nonexistence. He was wearing his yellow Superman T-shirt, which had begun to fade.

"I thought we were going back in time," a kid said.

"Long ago, a blacksmith was important," the teacher explained.

Steve Garvey was the pinnacle of a certain centrally important facet of what my baseball cards meant to me, that sense of well-groomed normalcy and heroism and answers in a world that seemed most of the time to harbor none of those things. You would think for that reason I would have loved him, but to me he was like the superhero referenced on Tom's faded yellow T-shirt. I loved the flawed super-heroes of the Marvel universe but always disliked that clean-cut and unquestionably moral DC product, Superman. Maybe it was because nothing could ever hurt him, besides that bullshit plot gimmick, Kryp-tonite.

Tom pulled an iron rod from his van and started trying to bend it. His hands shook but the rod stayed straight across the cracking iron-on Superman *S* on his chest.

"Whew! I can't do it!" Tom announced. He acted in plays and had a deeper booming voice that he used sometimes. "Anybody else want to give it a try?"

We all knew it was impossible, like making two plus two equal five. But we all tried, the rod passing from kid to kid. The last kid to try handed the rod back to Tom, who looked a little tired. He caught my eye and flashed a quick smile, then looked down at the iron rod in his hands. He sighed.

"Oh well," he said. "Guess it can't be done."

I needed heroes. I needed gods. But Steve Garvey and Superman took it too far. In the world they ruled, two plus two could never equal five, except by mistake, and mistakes had no place in the world they ruled.

By the end of the field trip Tom had made sure that we all got a chance to make two plus two equal five. We all took a turn heating an iron rod in the forge until the rod turned white, and with Tom's help we pounded the rod on an anvil until it flattened and bent in the grasp of tongs as easily as clay, and we all used the tongs to plunge the transformed metal, which had gone from white to deep red, into an aluminum pail of water, producing a loud sizzling hiss that never ceased to amaze, and then we all got to pull the tongs out to reveal that we had not only bent an iron rod but had made it into something completely different altogether, something that made us all feel miraculous and lucky. We walked back to school gripping horseshoes.

Topps 1976 #500: Reggie Jackson

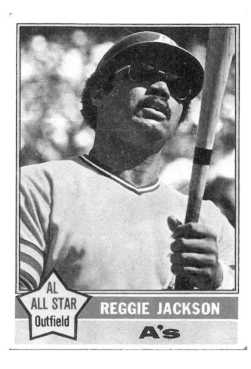

AL ALL STAR Outfield

REGGIE JACKSON

A's

Behold the All-Star. As shadows give way to sun, he pauses, reveling for a moment in his own magnificence, readying to move onto that bright stage he was born to command.

The year before I got this 1976 card, I'd caught a glimpse of the last of the A's dynasty at my first baseball game, when Ian and I had spent our voices cheering for Yaz. Our seats were in right field, close enough for the star player of the visiting team to hear us if we called his name. I don't remember if I ever did, but I do recall marveling at how he was known by everyone around me by just one name, his first name, as if the fans yelling it, or muttering it like a curse, were as intimately acquainted with him as I was with my brother.

A sense of excitement and apprehension surrounded Reggie throughout the game. Where Yaz kept failing to answer the crowd's call for greatness, Reggie kept disappointing the crowd's uneasy murmuring hope that he could be contained. Finally, late, the sky darkening and the huge, blinding banks of artificial lights flooding the field in something brighter than day, Reggie capped his methodical destruction of the home team by lashing a double to plate the go-ahead run. As he stood with one foot on second base, his hands on his hips, the crowd wove their voices together in a ragged chorus of caustic, resentful awe. Just before the bottom of the ninth the sound rose up again from everyone around me, directed at the powerful gold-clad man walking toward us, to his position, the customarily unfocused haze of unhappiness for once alighting on something specific, the strutting spectacular conquering god.

Though in the latter years of my childhood I would come to loathe Reggie Jackson as much as anyone in the crowd around me that first day at the ballpark, I now believe Reggie Jackson is worthy of my gratitude for being the loud and proud center of the baseball era I've clung to my whole life. He may even have been the best player. I would have guessed that Joe Morgan or perhaps Fred Lynn or Jim Rice outperformed Reggie during my baseball-card-collecting years of 1975 through 1980, but on closer look Morgan had a couple of subpar, injury-hampered years, as did Lynn, and both Boston sluggers benefitted significantly from playing in arguably the best hitter's park of the time; meanwhile, Reggie just kept mashing, year in and year out, wherever he earned his bulging paycheck. And on top of all that, Reggie was Mr. October, the successor to Bob Gibson as baseball's best postseason performer.

But Reggie's central position in this world, my world, was not based solely, or even predominantly, on performance. Though baseball has never been a hermetically sealed universe unto itself, it seems to have embodied the times during the 1970s with an abandon never seen before or since, seething and sparkling and belching and flailing with all the careening spasms of the epoch. And no baseball player epitomized the times more than Reggie: Reggie the iconoclast who shattered baseball's implicit ban on facial hair; Reggie the bombastic celebrity most aptly described by the *Sports Illustrated* cover caption that read "Superduperstar!"; Reggie the embodiment of the new baseball term "free agency," with all its tangled connotations of hard-won rights and individuality and base self-interest and greed; Reggie the self-proclaimed straw that stirred the drink; Reggie the biggest and loudest and most petulant and sensitive and compelling beast in the whole late 1970s Yankees dynasty known as the Bronx Zoo; Reggie the candy bar that told you how good it was when you unwrapped it; Reggie the walking 60-point tabloid headline; Reggie the one-man neverending tickertape parade. Even my father, who never cared about baseball, knew who Reggie was, and throughout his life he has mentioned the time—and not without some awe—when he stopped on his way to work in downtown Manhattan to join a crowd and watch Reggie, larger than life, pass by on a slow-moving convertible as the confetti rained down and everyone chanted his name.

But even in this card, as in all cards: transience. The faces in the crowd—faces that will watch the every move of the lordly All-Star in the foreground—have been blurred to something like Monet's lily pads, those hypnotic omens of the inevitable dusk into which we'll all dissolve. All names, even those of the greatest among us, will eventually unravel to silence. And by the time the card thrummed in my palm in 1976, the regal joy of the card's blazing gold uniform was a lie: The one and only Superduperstar had moved on, traded to Baltimore in a move prompted by Reggie's impending free agency. The magnificent early-1970s A's, the most successful baseball dynasty to never wear pinstripes, became an empty golden shell for the remainder of my childhood, gutted by the complicated, equivocal freedom of the day.

Topps 1976 #300: Johnny Bench

NL ALL STAR Catcher
JOHNNY BENCH
REDS

With my baseball cards, as with little else, I knew where I stood. I owed this feeling of solidity in part to Topps's practice of numbering their cards in such a way as to signal a four-level hierarchy of gods. If the number of a card ended in anything but a 0 or a 5, the player on that card resided on the bottom level of the hierarchy, a level so broad it included almost everyone—all the steady, colorless regulars and flawed reserves, all the has-beens and never-weres, all the green big-eyed hopefuls and graying squint-eyed hangers-on. Owchinko, Terpko, Heaverlo, Rapp, Nicosia, Barlow, Nahorodny, Knapp. One level up included players whose card numbers ended in 5; these players had made an All-Star Game or two, perhaps, or were just a couple decent if unspectacular years removed from a Rookie of the Year award, or had recently vied for, but not won, a batting crown. McRae, Wise, Hendrick, Tanana. Rising still higher, players whose card numbers ended in 0 had been to a few All-Star Games and seemed likely to be going to a few more before they were done. Madlock, Blue, Cey. And at the very top of this steep mountain were the players whose card numbers ended in 00. These were the superstars, among the best to ever play the game. There were only a handful of these players in every set.

The photo on this card, number 300 in the 1976 series, is most likely from the 1975 season, in which Johnny Bench's team, the Cincinnati Reds, won 108 regular-season games and then bested the Red Sox in a legendary World Series. Though I have since steeped myself down to the last detail of the 1975 World Series (that last detail being Yaz coming to bat with two outs in the bottom of the ninth of Game Seven with the Red Sox down a run and 30,000 voices screaming, *Come on, Yaz!* until the man they were screaming for popped out to César Gerónimo in center field), I missed the whole thing as it happened, all the action broadcast on NBC, which we couldn't get in East Randolph. In later years, I'd listen to games on the radio that I couldn't see on TV, but in 1975 I may not have even known that radio was an option, and if I did I may have not yet been able to follow a game that way. So I had to rely on my imagination and my cards to piece together what had happened to the Red Sox when they faced Johnny Bench and the Reds.

This particular card told me just about all I needed to know. With dust rising all around him, Johnny Bench is the gunslinger who has just downed one challenger and who is now eyeing the next as if to say, "You really think that's a good idea? Really?"

At times I imagined that he'd just gunned down a runner, and at other times I imagined that he'd just gunned down the whole league, including the Red Sox. At the end of the year, after the Reds again won more than 100 games during the regular season, Bench single-handedly demolished the Yankees in the Reds' four-game sweep of the 1976 World Series. That was also on NBC, so I didn't learn about it until my brother's *Sports Illustrated* showed up in the mail with Johnny Bench on the cover, launching a home run. The caption asked a question—"How good are the Reds?"—that even at age eight I understood was not really a question but a throwing up of the hands: Johnny Bench's Reds are so good, you can't even explain how good they are.

Bench's 1976 card stood out even more than the other superstar cards from that year. His gunslinger pose revealed him as a hero from an earlier, simpler time, the last of a dying breed. By then the classic Western, along with the clearly defined model of tough, decisive American maleness that fueled the genre, seemed to be limping its final gut-shot paces. John Wayne was old, and in his wake had come a new version of what it meant to be an American man. A boy growing up in the 1950s could follow the path to maleness pretty easily: Be tough, play to win, salute the flag, shoot a few savages if necessary, and let the womenfolk cook and clean and weep and such. But a boy growing up in the 1970s had to cling to the last few shreds of that simple path wherever he found them while besieged on all sides by uncertainty.

The two most popular television shows of the era, *All in the Family* and *M*A*S*H*, prominently featured characters (Archie Bunker and Frank Burns, respectively) whose histrionic embracing of the John Wayne Way was continuously lampooned as rigid, anachronistic, and just plain wrong. Meanwhile, in schoolyards all over the country, especially schoolyards that served hippie-influenced classrooms such as mine, children were encouraged to play something called "New Games," which were all, if the photos in the New Games book were any guide, invented by ambiguously gendered giggling longhairs prancing across meadows under the influence of potent hallucinogens. All the New Games valued toothless hand-holding cooperation over competition and had no real rules, only suggestive guidelines and the foundational dictate that there were never to be winners or losers. My free-school class owned the book and also a rainbow-colored parachute that served as the centerpiece for the New Games' most elaborate invention, which proved to have all the drama and enjoyment of folding and unfolding a gigantic multicolored bed sheet. I never took to New Games, but I can't say I didn't love another more powerful contributor to the decade's gamboling corrosion of What Was What and Who Was Who: *Free to Be You and Me*.

The massively popular child-targeting musical television special and accompanying massively popular album got children all over America singing along to catchy, ebullient ditties about girls doing boy things and boys doing girl things. How silly to walk in a well-worn rut! How silly to pretend to be tough or care about being first! How wonderful to be whatever you want to be! Traditional sports made a couple notable appearances, but only as a kind of foil. In one song, a gigantic real-life NFL player who had once been a member of the Los Angeles Rams' legendarily menacing "Fearsome Foursome" defensive line now comforted a boy named Dudley Pippin who had worried that he was "a sissy" because he broke into sobs. "It's all right to cry," crooned the former athlete who had once crushed guys to the turf with bone-shattering tackles. (Adding to the confusion, the hulking singer had the first name of a girl: Rosey.) In another song, "William's Doll," a boy admits to his grandmother that he considers baseball his favorite sport but says, in a line that still makes me shudder, "I'd give my bat and ball and glove / to have a doll that I could love."

Though I liked the album as much as anyone, "William's Doll" cut a little close to home, touching the same nerve that sparked my anger whenever a stranger saw my long, curly hair and thought I was a girl. This happened a few times, especially in the years before I was old enough to play little league baseball and therefore able to wear my team cap everywhere, like an ID badge proving that I was, just like my brother and all my gods, not a little girl but a boy.

Topps 1977 #634: Big League Brothers

From the back of this card: *"Paul and Rick both picked up baseballs as soon as they were old enough."*

Ian had started playing little league the year we moved to Vermont, away from our father. He wasn't very good at the beginning. After his little league games in his first year I always asked him the same question:

"Did you get a hit yet?"

The answer, no, was eventually rendered in the form of an I-Am-Going-to-Punch-You glare. By the end of the season I'd stopped asking.

That summer we played catch in the yard of the house in Randolph Center, then, when we moved to East Randolph, we played catch and hit each other grounders and fly balls in the big yard alongside the house. I can't remember him ever giving me any specific instruction, but just by playing with me hour after hour, day after day, week after week, year after year, the ball sailing back and forth between us, a shared pulse, my brother taught me baseball.

"They were teammates in little league, Pony League, High School and American Legion ball."

By the time I joined Ian on his little league team, the Mets, in 1977, he was one of the bigger and better kids in the league. Because I'd had him to practice with for two years, I was much more prepared to play than he'd been and got a hit in my first game—a single off the end of the bat, up the first base line. The following year, his last in little league, Ian was a superstar, one of the three or four best players in the league along with the hulking Stu Townsend, the mustachioed

Tony Russo, and the seeming can't-miss future major leaguer Bob Chase. I'd always idolized my brother, but that year he was one of the select few in the league to hit the ball over the fence. I actually got to pour out of the dugout with all my teammates and meet him at home plate cheering.

"In one Pony League game, Paul hit a Homer to win it for himself."

Once I got a uniform that proved I was on my brother's team, I never wanted to be without a key piece of that uniform, the grass-green cap with the white felt *M* that turned darker and darker throughout the year as I wore it everywhere, all the time. Though I also owned Red Sox caps throughout my childhood, I remember wearing my little league cap more than once on the yearly trip to Fenway. I think I was wearing that cap and screaming myself hoarse when a man in front of us turned to my mother and said I must be a kid who "ate, slept, and breathed baseball." I felt proud, and also happy to be defined. The man got it right: I was a kid who ate, slept, and breathed baseball. I was a kid who always wore the cap of the team he was on with his brother.

Without the cap, without baseball, without my brother, who was I? This question, though I never formulated it so specifically, has a lot to do with why I was drawn to this Big League Brothers card, and to all my cards in general. This card, as with other "special" cards, heightened the idea that the cards in total comprised a storybook world by using text on the back instead of centering primarily on numbers.

This text on the back of Paul and Rick Reuschel's Big League Brothers card was not the first thing that I noticed about this card, but I'm sure it gratified me when I finally got around to reading it, which would have been some time after my stomach stopped hurting from laughing by myself and then with my brother at the two stunned, doughy, beady-eyed lummoxes glowering apprehensively back at us. The story on the back of the card was of two brothers who loved baseball and who always stuck together. On other cards in the Big League Brothers series of 1977, the same basic story was told again and again—two brothers who loved baseball and stuck together, two brothers from a normal family that featured just two parents—a mother and father with the same last name as the two brothers, the father always around, tirelessly teaching both boys "the fundamentals."

I knew my life didn't match the storybook one, but as long as I had my cap on my head and baseball cards in my hand I was able to imagine myself into that world. I could see a future that always included baseball and always included my brother, the two of us side by side on the same team in the Big Leagues.

Topps 1980 #48: Rick Miller

While there has never been a salary cap in baseball, I sometimes suspect that in the mid- to late-1970s, as a reaction to the dominance of the early 1970s Oakland A's, American League owners instituted a secret Mustache Cap that restricted the amount of total facial hair each team was allowed to carry on its roster. Consider:

1. After winning three World Series titles in a row, 1972 to 1974, the roster of the overwhelmingly hirsute A's was almost completely dismantled within a couple years, as if some secret and severe penalties for over-mustaching had been levied. The skyrocketing salaries spurred by the introduction of free agency have most often been noted as the cause of this dismantling, but I'm not so sure that tells the whole story. If it does, then how do you explain the lack of a similar instantaneous dismantling of the successful National League team that had an even more star-studded roster than the A's, the Cincinnati Reds (who were all as clean-shaven as boot-camp marines)?

2. When Charlie Finley tried to hasten the dismemberment of his A's dynasty by selling two of his stars to the Boston Red Sox, Commissioner Bowie Kuhn disallowed the transaction, citing the damage it would do to competitive balance; however, I believe this justification was a screen to cover the real reason: Joe Rudi and (especially) Rollie Fingers would have put the Red Sox, already fairly well mustached, far over their facial hair allowance. Supporting this point is that Rudi later came to the Red Sox anyway, sporting his modest gun-shop-cashier 'stache, while Fingers, the facial-hair-cap-wrecking A-Rod of the Mustache Years, had to spend some years

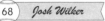

with the smooth-cheeked Padres of Enzo Hernandez and Randy Jones until the apparent lifting of the Mustache Cap in the early 1980s allowed him to join the malodorous unshaven rabble known as the Milwaukee Brewers.

3. The California Angels and Boston Red Sox constantly shuttled similarly mustached guys back and forth, as if the deals depended on the equal exchange of facial hair. The unremarkable mustaches of guys such as Jerry Remy and Joe Rudi came east, and the unremarkable mustaches of guys such as Dick Drago and Rick Burleson went west. Even when clean-cut fellows such as Denny Doyle passed between the two teams, the transaction seemed to come with hidden "facial hair to be named later" clauses that impacted (and explained the seeming imbalance of) later trades whose principals, such as clean-cut Butch Hobson and walrus-faced Carney Lansford, did not balance out on the facial hair ledger.

I'm not quite sure how Rick Miller fits into all this, but when I was a kid he seemed to drift back and forth between the Angels and Red Sox like a Mustache Years version of a Cheshire cat. Because he was obscure to me in each place for different reasons (on the Angels because they were so far away and on the Red Sox because he was always buried on the outfield depth chart), I was never completely sure which of the two teams he was on at any given moment, and so there always seemed at least a shred of him in both places, a brown medium-sized mustache hanging in the clubhouse air, waiting for the rest of him to appear and collect a pinch hit or make a diving grab in the outfield just when you thought for sure he was on the other side of the continent.

Topps 1978 #314: Paul Lindblad

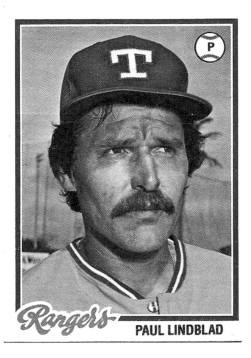

PAUL LINDBLAD

The Mustache Years weren't my father's happiest. He spent most of them living in a studio apartment in Manhattan while his family lived with another guy several hours away by bus. In that apartment, he had one window, a desk, a small table, a foam mattress that he slept on at night and rolled up and stowed in the lone closet in the morning, and some board and cinder-block bookshelves. In the hollow of one of the cinder blocks he kept a stack of curling photographs, mostly of my brother and me, the two of us changing as the years went on, our blond hair darkening, our bodies getting taller and thinner, the look in our eyes growing dimmer, warier, as if the photographer was becoming a stranger.

My card collection calmed me throughout my childhood, in part because it had elements that seemed as if they would stay the same forever. For a long time, Paul Lindblad provided one of my favorite of these comforting repetitions. As the years went on, it came to seem that Lindblad always had been and always would be

- mustache-free,
- a current or recent champion,
- a member of the Oakland A's, and
- puzzled.

But nothing and no one is immune to change. In this 1978 card, my last Paul Lindblad, the only remaining constant is his puzzled expression, which seems in the context of this card to be and perhaps to have always been a reaction to the inescapable impermanence of life.

In my first card of him, from 1975, he is shown looking clean-cut and puzzled after helping the A's win their third straight World Championship by posting the best ERA of his career, 2.06. Just below the stat line with that information is a (somehow fittingly) terse textual note further attesting to Paul Lindblad's capabilities: "Paul had 0.00 E.R.A. in 1973 series."

I'm inclined to believe the effective middle reliever plied his trade with very little ego. A man who seems to be perpetually aware that a tornado could appear at any minute on the horizon and wipe out everything in its path certainly seems unlikely to display the air of complacent self-congratulation that supposedly has a tendency to infect members of a championship squad.

I wonder now if part of the puzzlement in his face was the result of an ongoing inner debate over whether to grow a mustache. By the time he started showing up in my collection, clean-shaven and puzzled, the hoopla that the act of growing a mustache might have once created was long gone. It had been three years since the A's broke the baseball facial hair line in 1972 after Reggie Jackson showed up at spring training with a beard. A's owner Charlie O. Finley, attempting to get Reggie to shave by making him feel less special, offered money to anyone on the squad who grew facial hair; they did, Finley found that he liked it, and the A's set a trend that soon began to spread face to face around the league. Not coincidentally, Paul Lindblad, after spending several years with the A's prior to 1972, had been toiling for the Rangers that pivotal year, and by the time he returned to the A's the hippie-lip revolution had already occurred. In fact, by 1975, players on most teams were busting out beards and mustaches, muttonchops and fu manchus. To have a mustache was no longer in any way a declaration of independence. It was merely a personal choice.

And this is exactly when the world got confusing. This is exactly when the 1970s truly became the Me Decade. Everyone was on their own to make their own choices about everything. Grow a mustache, don't grow a mustache. Do your own thing, don't do your own thing. Who cares? No one. You're on your own.

For most of that decade my father was a project leader on a sociological research team charged with a massive evaluation of the effects of city services on all levels of the population. He worked hard, quietly, selflessly. A Paul Lindblad type. He showed up everyday, benefitting not only the project he was working on but also helping to feed much-needed money to the imperiled utopian dream of his distanced immediate family.

He wore a mustache for some of that decade. But this facial hair was never part of some rousing movement, large or small, like the swashbuckling 1972 A's or the "let that freak flag fly" hippies. I have sometimes thought of the mustache he wore during the 1970s as hair shrapnel, a fragment of the general hairiness of the culture of the time that seemed to have landed randomly on my dad's face. But he made a decision to grow a mustache, and he made it alone, and he wore the mustache for some years. And then, in another solitary decision, he chose to remove the mustache. I can see him shaving it off one evening in the bathroom of his apartment, then leaving the bathroom to unroll his foam sleeping mat on the floor below the one window, going to sleep, getting up the next day, and going to his job.

I don't know what he did beyond that. There were never any signs that he had a social life. During each of the yearly visits Ian and I made to see him in New York, there would always come a moment when he'd stare at us across the table of a Bun-N-Burger or Chock Full o' Nuts.

"How's your mom?" he would ask.

On some level I understood he was waiting for her, like an aging veteran who'd been demoted to the minors, hoping in spite of his ballooning ERA and diminishing innings for the call from the big club once again.

Once, not so long ago, I got him talking about those years. What got him through? We were out at a restaurant, a bottle of wine on the table, almost gone. He stared past me, a Lindbladian wince rippling momentarily across his features. He shook his head and his expression flattened.

"I absorbed myself in my work," he said.

I absorbed myself in my cards. I absorbed myself in the sameness of them, even as the sameness began to show signs that it was an illusion.

By the time I got my penultimate Paul Lindblad card, in 1977, the clean-cut pitcher was still pictured in an Oakland A's uniform, left behind in the green and gold by most of his championship-winning teammates. The expression on his face in that card suggests that he senses the end in Oakland is coming for him too. By the time the

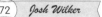

card came out, Paul Lindblad had been sold to the Texas Rangers.

And the next year, finally, Paul Lindblad was in a new uniform, far away from his normal team, far away from championships. Worst of all, he now had a mustache. The only remaining constant, his expression of melancholy confusion, was no longer the humorous center of comforting sameness but a jittery undertone revealing everything to be a temporary disguise.

Right around that time, funding was rescinded for the research project my father had absorbed himself in for several years. In such a world where the very ground can be pulled from beneath you, where your team can be taken away, where your family can be taken away, where the job that absorbs you can be lost, certain personal choices turn out to be all you really have left. They are the only things you can control. And yet, they are pointless, absurd. To grow a mustache or not to grow a mustache, that is the question. The implied answer—*What's the difference?*—lingers on the horizon like some kind of soundless cosmic tornado with the power to level your world.

Topps 1977 #418: White Sox Team Card

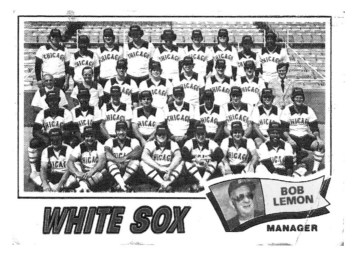

I was walking to the general store one day to buy more baseball cards, and a girl who lived in a house on the way came out onto her lawn as I was passing by. Her name was Donna and she was a couple years older than me. It was a quiet summer day—the buzz of insects, my sneakers scuffling along in the gravel. That's about it. I must have been wearing my green little league cap, which I wore all the time.

"Hey," Donna said. "Only faggots wear green on Thursday."

Embarrassment. It was like a contagious disease in the 1970s. Call it the Age of Embarrassment. Everything was unfathomable, bulging, lopsided, upside down. The first president of the decade was revealed to be a paranoid criminal and had to quit, disgraced. He was replaced by a guy known for being ineffectual and tripping over things. The replacement lost his reelection bid to a peanut farmer who revealed more than anyone wanted to know in an interview in *Playboy*, admitting he had "lust in his heart." Later, in a nationally televised speech, the embarrassingly frank president described America's "erosion of confidence"; in his estimation the whole country by the end of the 1970s was demoralized and ashamed, as if it were somehow channeling from sea to shining sea the cringe-shouldered stoop of a reedy-voiced chronic teenage masturbator.

One reason I loved being in little league as much as I've ever loved being a part of anything was that there were uniforms. At the little league game, you knew what you were supposed to wear. Outside of little league, there were all these secret rules. You wear the wrong thing and you might be a faggot.

Not that I knew what a faggot was. But I knew it wasn't good. It sounded weak and broken, something to be spit on and kicked into the woods. Because I didn't know what it was made it even worse, actually, adding to the general unease about the unknown rules of the world. I had this problem with other words, too. Whore, for example. There was one tough kid in the town, Mike, the son of the owner of the general store, who expressed his frequent loss of temper by calling whoever was pissing him off a whore, which I imagined to be a creature similar to a horse but meaner, a little stunted, scarred, vaguely carnivorous. Pussy was another of my problem words. During one walk to the store for cards, some kids surrounded me and asked me if I knew what a pussy was.

"A kitty?" I said.

"Ha! Ha! Ha! Ha! Ha!" they said.

"All right, pudlips," one of them finally said, "go run back home now."

"Yeah, go back and play with yourself," another one said.

"Ha! Ha! Ha! Ha! Ha!" they said. I didn't understand what was so funny about playing with myself. When my brother wouldn't play with me I made up little solitary games all the time. Was there something wrong with this, too?

I became a fan of *Harriet the Spy* around then. I loved the idea that the mysterious world could be rationally plumbed for clues by a kid, that an actual understandable story could be pried from its generally unfathomable depths. I went out one afternoon as if I were taking my usual walk to the general store to buy baseball cards, but in fact I had equipped myself with some of the tools used by Harriet. I had a notebook and pencil to write down clues, and I'd hung a flashlight and a magnifying glass from my belt. My plan was to walk around until I saw something happening inside one of the houses in the town, then I was going to creep up to a window and look in, and a whole mesmerizing adventure would ensue. But I walked up and down the road peeking in windows and couldn't see anything going on anywhere, just one man with gray hair sitting at a table eating cold ravioli from a can. Eventually, I started pretending I was on the trail of something instead of walking up and down the road for no reason. I switched on my flashlight and tried to shine it on the roadside gravel, but it was too bright to really see the beam.

"Hey, faggot," a kid said. It was the older brother of the kid who said *whore*. He was standing on the other side of the road from me. "Why you using a flashlight with the sun friggin' shining?"

By my calculations my brother probably started to edge into puberty in 1976, right around the time the photo on the 1977 White Sox team card was taken. Perhaps he got his first pubic hair on August 8, 1976, when White Sox players plied their trade in front of their competitors, the media, and 15,997 paying customers while dressed in wide-collared shirts and shorts. Until the time when a major league baseball team takes the field wearing flowery sleeveless summer dresses and heels, it will stand as the single most embarrassing uniform-related moment in baseball history.

This is really saying something, especially considering the other uniforms of the decade. There were the technicolor dreamsuits of the Astros, the brown and yellow McDonald's-cashier garb of the Padres, and the Indians' underrated all-red migraine producers. But none of them could match the White Sox' giant collars and knee-pants for sheer zeitgeist-embracing embarrassment.

I can see now that embarrassment permanently burrowed down deep into my blood during those years, even though I tried to avoid contracting it by trying not to break any unknown rules. The safest way to do this was to be invisible. I could be invisible by staying at home and "playing with myself," which at that time still meant making up imaginary games inside the house and out in our yard. If I had to venture into the world, I was usually able to will myself into invisibility. But I knew that complete invisibility was impossible, so I tried to avoid breaking any unknown rules by looking to my brother. How he dressed, how he walked, how he talked, how he acted: I aped his every move.

Ironically, I was mimicking a boy whose own levels of personal shame were surely higher in the 1970s than mine, since he fully entered puberty during those years. Not least among his list of

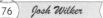
embarrassments was that he had to so often resort to passing the time with his embarrassing little brother.

In our room, I kept calling his name, holding up new baseball cards to show him. Sometimes he'd look up from his book, see the card, and smile. Sometimes he'd ignore me.

Once, I wanted him to look up and see this card. I wouldn't take no for an answer. I needed to show him the White Sox. The giant collars. The Mickey-Mouse-ears effect of the cap-crushed Afro of the incredible Oscar Gamble in the back row. The bare knees of the White Sox players near the front. The sheer hilarity of it all. I kept calling his name, aware that I was allowing an annoying whine to seep into my voice, and he finally responded, peering up from his book with a scornful, disgusted squint, as if he were looking at a faggot.

Topps 1975 #293: Dick Sharon

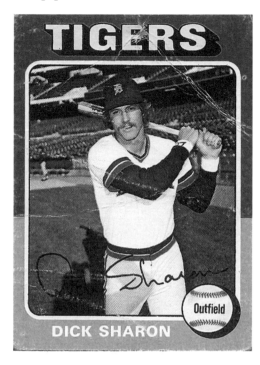

My father didn't know how to throw a baseball. Sometimes this struck me as an awful affliction, which spared him of any blame but made me fear that, since I shared his blood, I might wake up one day and be suddenly just as bad. Other times the all-important fact that he couldn't throw a baseball seemed to me to be his fault.

How could he let this happen to him? I thought. It made me angry.

My brother often checked out large library books about World War II and left them lying around open to photos of concentration camp corpse mounds. He also bought a lot of comics set in World War II: *Sgt. Rock, Sgt. Fury and His Howlin' Commandos, Weird War Tales.* Every so often the Jews would make an appearance in the panels as background for the tales of heroic American triumph, and they'd be emaciated and hollow-eyed, penned up in filthy cells or jammed like cattle into train cars or lined up meekly for the gas chamber. That's what the Jews were, as far as I knew. Thin gray prison-clothed victims.

How could they let this happen to them? I wondered. It made me angry. I thought about the Jewish blood inside me, courtesy of my dad.

He visited us every couple of months. He would arrive quietly, late on a Friday, and leave quietly on a Sunday, and be quiet all the way through, a guy you'd barely even notice. His repetitive nondescript appearances were like those of the journeyman nobodies who showed up again and again in packs of cards. Doubles, we called them, even though the worst of them showed up far more than

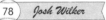

twice, eventually impressing themselves in our brains despite their apparent lack of worth, eventually gaining the power to drain the feeling of hope straight out of a pack. The king of all doubles for me was Dick Sharon, who appeared again and again and again in 1975, my first year of collecting, my first year living apart from my father, as if he were trying to tell me something, and then never returned in any later years. I held on to all those Dick Sharons as I held on to every single card that came to me, as if someday even the most useless cards might reveal a hidden value.

Like the strip of bubble gum that always accompanied another addition to the Dick Sharon collection, large boxes of M&Ms always arrived when my father arrived, peanut for my brother and plain for me. I'd never seen the boxes outside a movie theater, so they lent an air of magic to my father that he did not otherwise possess.

"Promise to brush your teeth afterward?" he asked before handing over the boxes.

"OK," we told him. We knew he didn't have any power over what we were supposed to do.

When I think of those visits, I think of him standing at the doorway of our room, looking in at us, at our sports posters, at the floor covered with baseball cards. I think of him not being able to think of anything to say. I think of him standing at the edge of the yard, watching us play catch. If my brother and I talked at all while playing catch, we talked about baseball, conversations my father could not have understood.

My father's father was a tailor from a shtetl in central Europe, where baseball didn't exist. The tailor wed an innkeeper's daughter in an arranged marriage, had three kids, the first dying in infancy, then fled to America to avoid conscription into the Austro-Hungarian army. He lived alone in the strange new country for several years, working in Manhattan sweatshops. He couldn't speak the language. At some point he sustained a serious head injury. He was hit in the head during a labor struggle, either assaulted by union goons or company goons. It was a long time ago and subsequently seldom mentioned with any detail by anyone in my father's family. The one certainty is that by the time my grandmother and Uncle Joe and Aunt Helen rejoined him in America, my grandfather was not well. He worked sporadically if at all and was profoundly withdrawn from the rest of the family, a looming, largely silent presence in the middle of a series of cramped Lower East Side tenement apartments. The living spaces became more crowded with the arrival of two more children: my uncle Dave and the baby of the family, my father.

My father remembers very few times in which his father spoke to him. One night when my father was thirteen his father came into the room where he and my uncle Joe slept and asked him in Yiddish how he was doing in school. My father was so surprised that he couldn't respond. Not long after that, my grandfather was found floating in the East River. My father remembers what my grandma kept repeating, angrily, after the police came to deliver the news.

"He did it. He did it. He finally did it."

But all I knew when I was a kid was that my dad couldn't throw a baseball, that he couldn't do anything athletic. He couldn't even run, as far as I could see. The most he would do was walk, slowly, with his hands clasped behind him like he was in one of the museums he dragged my brother and me to when we visited him. He loved to take walks and talk quietly and reverently about what he saw as the beautiful natural world all around.

"It's so peaceful here," he told me once. "Such beauty."

"East Randolph?" I said.

We were walking to the general store so I could buy more baseball cards. When we went inside, I pretended he was just some stranger who'd happened to come in the door right after me. I wasn't connected to him. I wasn't *Jewish*.

By the time my father met and married a shiksa, my mom, he had become completely irreligious. There were no traces of Jewish life in my upbringing, and even if my father had lived with us I don't think it would have been different. There were no traces of Jewish life in his tiny apartment in Manhattan, either, though I subconsciously came to think of everything in the apartment as Jewish, from the relative lack of furniture to his keeping his small black-and-white television in the closet, rarely watching it, to his crude cinder-block and board bookcases, to the yellowing Ellis Island photos in the hollow of a cinder block of his mother and father, to the persistent smell of garlic, to the giant jar of wheat germ in the refrigerator.

Occasionally my father would take my brother and me to see his mother, our grandma, and it was like venturing to the very source of the garlicky strangeness and unfamiliarity that permeated everything in my father's apartment, like going to the very heart of Jewness. I was frightened of her. She had a strange accent and was tiny and hunched and impossibly old. My father, perhaps wary of revealing to my brother and me that he was a good deal older than my mother, had always tried to evade our questions about his age by saying he was "a googol" (which he explained was a number far larger than a billion). It was one of those slippery pieces of childhood info that you neither fully believe nor disbelieve. But if he was a googol, his mother, the stooped woman who constantly forced mysterious and complicated Old World food on me, must have been as old as the stars.

"Eat! Eat!" she implored. The bowl of homemade soup in her ancient veined hands roiled with thick gray noodles and gristle. I clamped my lips tight and shook my head no. No, no, no.

When I was around her I wanted to go home. Back to my saltines and Chips Ahoys. Back to television sitcoms and baseball. Back to my painless solitary hours in my room. Back to the Nerf-soft confines of my daydreams. Back to the cardboard gods.

I had no idea that the one god who made the most visits to me, appearing again and again as a double during 1975, as if trying to tell me something, also had a Jewish father. I only learned that Dick Sharon and I were alike in that way years later. As far as I knew there were not, nor ever had been, Jewish baseball players. I knew from studying the baseball encyclopedia who Sandy Koufax and Hank Greenberg were, but I didn't know they were Jewish. From what I'd seen from my father, Jews couldn't throw a baseball and were also generally uncoordinated and pale. You'd hear them from time to time slipping and falling in the bathtub. They drove cars slowly and jerkily, their citified shoulders tensed. They listened to classical music and wore thick glasses and button-down shirts and ties. They had jobs with titles so long they were impossible to understand.

They were certainly not the dashing figure in the Tigers uniform that visited me again and again in 1975. Dick Sharon's chiseled jaw, his drooping Marlboro Man 'stache, his steely gaze and swaggering body language and smile: They all exude dashing athletic aptitude and confidence. On the back of the card, Sharon is described as a "sure-handed flyhawk." I doubt I understood what this meant, but it probably sounded to me like something that could have been used to describe one of Sgt. Rock's brave men of Easy Company or one of Sgt. Fury's colorful Howlin' Commandos. I focused my twisted attention on imagined heroes battling for victory and glory. In these imaginings the Jews were barely there at all, just figures in the background, weak and capitulatory. I tried to believe I had nothing to do with them.

How could they let this happen to them? I still wondered sometimes, unable to get them out of my mind. *Why didn't they fight back?*

I've learned some things since then. I learned that my father's oldest brother, Joe, joined the Navy soon after Pearl Harbor and saw heavy combat in the South Pacific. I learned my father's other brother, Dave, joined the Navy too, as soon as he was old enough, and when my father was old enough he also joined. There is a picture from that time of my grandma with my father and my uncle Joe, both home on leave. My uncle looks Dick Sharon–dashing in his tailored sailor uniform, while my daydreaming scholar father, barely out of his teens, looks in his baggy ill-fitting standard-issue sailor uniform like he is moments away from stumbling over a crack in the sidewalk. In between them stands my grandma, low and thick, indestructible. She had raised the family by herself, her husband unable to contribute even before he wound up floating in the East River. I can't begin to imagine what it was like to experience the hardships she had to go through, somehow soldiering on with love. Fighting back.

As for my dad, the war ended before he saw combat, but he tells a story about a camp boxing match in which he was pitted against the largest man on the base. He suspects that anti-Semitism was behind the obvious mismatch, the matchmakers hoping to enjoy a nice quick Kike beating. He never saw the first punch. One moment he was standing there and the next moment he was on the ground. He got up. Soon he was on the ground again. He got up. Then he was staring at the lights above the ring again. He got up. Down again. He got up. Someone finally stepped in and ended the match because my father would not stop fighting.

One evening not that long ago, I got my father talking some more about his father. As is often the case in these instances of me learning about my father's past, a mostly empty bottle of wine was on the table between us.

"He liked to visit different synagogues," my father said. One day my grandfather took my father to a synagogue that he had heard was beautiful. I was stunned by this. I'd never imagined that my grandfather, who had only ever existed in my mind as a distant, silent, frightening absence, could be drawn to beauty. Even more amazing was that he might want to share, and be capable of sharing, this beauty with his son.

"I remember the way the light was streaming in through the windows," my father told me softly. "The whole room was flooded with it . . ." His voice trailed off. He was thinking, remembering, carefully choosing what to pass on to me. I leaned close. I saw a little boy holding his father's hand, bathed in light.

Topps 1980 #445: Mark Fidrych

Since we got only three channels in East Randolph—ABC, CBS, and the punishingly boring PBS—the NBC network always had an air of mystery and excitement to me. Once every several months it briefly flickered into something other than a swarm of hornets in a snowstorm, the most prolonged instance of this when my brother and I, praying throughout like mediums trying to sustain contact with the dead, were able to understand most of the proceedings in an extremely fuzzy broadcast of Super Bowl XIII. But *Quark, Land of the Lost, Chico and the Man*, and the rest of NBC's lineup existed as magical but almost completely indecipherable whispers from another dimension, one that I assumed was better than my own.

Because we didn't get NBC, which televised the Game of the Week every Saturday, I saw even less baseball than I otherwise might have. Sometimes I was able to catch *This Week in Baseball* on Sunday, but I could never get a handle on when it was going to air. I believe that the first time I ever heard of Mark Fidrych was on one of those lucky Sundays when I happened upon *TWIB*. A glimpse of him was like a glimpse of everything I thought I was missing. All the shows I could never see. All the cards I'd never get. All the channels that would never come in. Here it all was, suddenly coming into focus in one magnetic figure.

Soon after the *TWIB* feature, I was lucky enough to witness Fidrych spreading his wings in real time, by virtue of a now-famous Monday Night Baseball game in Detroit between the Tigers and the New York Yankees. I can't write well enough to capture the beauty of his performance that night. I know that whenever I see it now, replayed

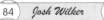

in part or in full amid a television sports landscape glutted with every televised game you could ever want, I can't help laughing. And at the end, when he waves to the adoring crowd showering down their grateful love in roaring waves, I can't help crying, either.

In 1976, the year Mark Fidrych became the all-time single-season leader in joy, my mother decided to start a business. The pure version of the back-to-the-land scenario had been that we would grow most of our food in a garden and raise sheep for meat and wool, and Tom would help get us whatever else we needed by making money or getting things in trade by being a blacksmith. But the blacksmith thing hadn't worked out, and our garden forever remained a stubborn, miserly provider, and our sheep herd was rarely able to expand beyond its usual population of one: Virginia, the fat, friendly ewe who was more like a family pet than the vital cog of a livestock operation. We needed to buy food like everyone else. So, slowly, the adults in my house entered the so-called real world.

This is what everyone has to do, right? You can't be a child forever. You have to slice that part of yourself away and put on a uniform of some sort, whether it's official or unofficial, and punch that clock. Is there a way to do this and still hang on to a wider sense of the world?

My mother believed so. She painted on a rectangular board a more colorful, warmly cartoonish version of our house and of the road, Route 14, winding past it. Above the portrait she painted "Studio 14." She and Tom hung the sign outside, announcing to the world that we were now in business. Looking at the sign, the bright colors, the cartoonish simplicity and warmth, it was difficult to tell what kind of business it was, or even that it was a business at all.

Many of the stories about Mark Fidrych focused on his antics—how he often bounded over to a teammate to slap him on the back after a good play, how he got down on his knees like a gardener to groom the mound, and, most notably, how he talked to the ball as if it were a friendly little creature capable of listening to and carrying out his gentle instructions. But he wasn't just a curiosity, a novelty. He kicked ass. He worked fast and threw everything hard, at the knees, and he couldn't ever really be touched. That Monday night game against the Yankees, he dominated the team that would eventually win the American League pennant. Afterward, Yankees captain Thurman Munson would grumble that the rookie pitcher was a showboat. But

Munson was just slow to get what everyone would eventually come to understand—even the gruff Munson, who became friendly with the Bird when they formed the starting battery in the 1976 All-Star Game: Mark Fidrych simply couldn't hide his love for the game.

Hey, you *don't* have to hide your love away! You don't have to be dour. You don't have to pretend you don't care.

In saying all this, Mark Fidrych forever became for me everything good from the decade of my childhood. He's the Pet Rock, the mood ring, the CB radio. He's the Six Million Dollar Man battling Sasquatch, Kool-Aid smashing through a wall, Fat Albert and the Gang banging on trashcans. He's SpaghettiOs and Oreos and Quik. He's a pack of smiling yahoos spilling out of a customized van in a cloud of smoke, Foghat blaring. He's Doug Henning and the Banana Splits and *Dynamite* magazine. He's Alfred E. Neuman. He's that moment when you start laughing and you don't think you'll ever be able to stop.

One day I was out in the driveway, throwing a tennis ball at the strike zone my brother had duct-taped to the garage door. A man walked by the house and asked about the Studio 14 sign in the yard.

"Is that like Studio 54?" he said.

Though I didn't understand what he was talking about, his question may have been the first contact I made with that quintessential product of the 1970s, disco.

Not long after that, my brother, my mom, and I were walking around the streets of a nearby town that actually had more than just one general store. We saw a copy of the *Saturday Night Fever* soundtrack in a store window. We went into the store and my mother asked for the record, but the only copy left was the one in the window. She convinced the store owner to sell us that one.

It was an unusual purchase. Previously, both my brother and I had begun to own our own records, a consumerist action that would eventually eclipse even that of owning baseball cards. But this time we were all in it together. When we got home, we went to the living room to hear the record for the first time, together. But the record had been damaged by sitting in sun in the store window. The needle bounded rapidly across the warped surface. There was no music, just a few truncated, pulsing yelps.

For a short while, the colors from my mother's paintbrushes began

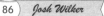

sprouting up in various places in and around our town. She made big, vibrant signs for a food co-op and a restaurant and a thrift store. She made smaller, less flashy signs for an office complex and a tiny law school.

The man who ran the law school became a repeat customer, but he would always neglect to pay for a sign until he'd badgered my mother into starting a new sign. After a while, my mother began avoiding his calls. I suppose the situation called for action on my mother's part that was squarely in that dour realm of business. No action was taken, besides the instruction to me that if I answered the phone and it was the law school guy, I had to tell him that she wasn't home.

This may not have been the beginning of the end of the sign-painting business, but it was at least concurrent to the beginning of the end. Spreading colors all over central Vermont was one thing. Collecting from deadbeats, telling deadbeats no: that was something else entirely.

In the picture on my 1980 Mark Fidrych card, the Bird attempts to simultaneously hide and caress a baseball in his hands as if cradling a terminally ill pet in a veterinary waiting room. He is four years and several trips to the disabled list removed from whispering brilliance into a baseball. The marginalia on the back of this card clings desperately to that year like a profoundly lonely middle-aged man still masturbating to the image of a beautiful woman he somehow lucked into a brief fling with the summer after college ended. Fidrych's Rookie of the Year award for 1976 is mentioned, as is his 2 innings pitched in the 1976 All-Star Game, and the space-filling cartoon along the left-hand border features a baseball player, generic except for the curly Fid-fro billowing out from under the hat, holding a giant trophy entitled "1976 MAJOR LEAGUE MAN OF THE YEAR," an award I've never heard of. The statistics alone are left to tell about the other years: in 1977 he pitched in only 11 games; the next year he pitched in only 3; and in 1979, the last season listed on the back of this card, Fidrych pitched his fewest innings yet, just 15, losing 3 games, winning none, and getting battered for 17 runs, all earned. In this 1980 card, he seems to have literally signed his name as "Mush."

What do you do when the thing you value most slips out of reach?

I remember a sign my mother made for a small recording studio, near the end, after it was clear that the sign business was going to fail. She took a long time on the sign, using many drawings to plan it out, then painstakingly transferring her design to a thick slab of wood that Tom cut into a circle. Tom also sandblasted the design Mom had created of a sun with a wise-looking, calmly joyful face in the middle of the circle so that the sun became three-dimensional. Mom painted the sun with gold-leaf paint, and when the sign was finally finished it glowed. I loved it. A photo of it appeared among a bunch of signs with an honorable mention designation in a sign-painting magazine my mother subscribed to for a while. Some years later, someone stole it, part of a larger gradual disappearance of my mother's bright signs from the world.

What do you do when the thing you value most starts slipping out of reach? There's a YouTube video of Mark Fidrych pitching in a minor league game long after his summer of joy. He was far removed from being the most famous athlete in the country, the *Rolling Stone* cover boy, far removed from having electric stuff, far removed in every way from being an elite athlete (when he records the final out he stumbles to the ground like a rec league player who's downed a six of Strohs during the game). But he knows how sweet it is to be in the game, to be on a team, and to be on a team lucky enough to win that day. He doesn't shrug off the victory as if a minor league win is somehow below him. He is happy and, since happiness only exists when shared, he immediately shares that happiness with his teammates, bounding into the scrum of minor league nobodies. He was always this way, even at the height of his fame. *We* did it, he always seemed to be saying, thanking as many people as he could, not merely slapping backs and palms but reaching out to everyone and hanging on.

Topps 1976 #199: N.L. Victory Leaders

VICTORY LEADERS
N.L.   1975

TOM SEAVER
New York Mets   22

RANDY JONES
San Diego Padres 20   **ANDY MESSERSMITH**
Los Angeles Dodgers 19

One night Mom and Tom went out, leaving my brother in charge. The phone in the kitchen rang. I got out of the hammock in the living room and went to the kitchen. I answered like I was J.J. Walker.

"Chello," I said.

"We're gonna come and get you," a low voice whispered. Click. A few seconds later the phone rang again.

"Gonna mess. You. Up." Click.

I called to my brother, who was watching *The Incredible Hulk*. When the phone rang again we got close and held the phone so both of us could hear.

"We *know* you're all alone," the voice said. "Gonna *kill* you."

"Hey, you listen—" my brother said, but the line was already dead.

"What are we gonna do?" I said. I looked out the window, into the dark. You couldn't see anything but the low branches of the front yard tree waving in the wind like a maniac.

My brother yanked a meat cleaver out of a drawer. He stalked around the house with it and checked that all the windows and doors were locked. He turned the sound on the television down. He came back to the kitchen and sat ramrod straight on a chair near the phone and stared out the window into the darkness, the handle of the meat cleaver in one of his fists, the blade sticking up straight like he was holding a flag at a parade. I sat a few feet away at the bottom of the stairs, holding my aching stomach with both arms. You could still sort of hear the Hulk throwing guys around and then the piano when it was time for David Banner to sadly move on again but mostly the only sound was wind rattling the branches of the trees.

Every once in a while a car approached, the headlights attached to a volume knob of pain in my stomach.

"I *hope* they fucking try," my brother said.

Another night I woke up halfway and could feel things starting to go bad. It always started the same way, my night terrors, with me coming half-awake and sensing that things were wrong and getting worse by the second. My brother was still up, reading, even though it was late, which meant that Mom and Tom weren't back from another evening out. I called my brother's name.

"What's wrong?" he said.

I climbed down the ladder of the loft bed Tom had built for me, past the Nerf hoop Tom had screwed to left post, past the speakers he'd mounted that played my Kiss records, past the Victory Leaders card—my only card that showed Andy Messersmith—that I'd taped to the right post. My breathing was getting more rapid and shallower. My heart was starting to race. I could feel it all about to start, and once it started it wouldn't stop.

"Hey," my brother said. He sat up in bed, pulling the covers along with him. He had a book in his lap.

"How about a little Kirk and Spock?" he said. Before waiting for an answer he started reading. It was one of his *Star Trek* novels by James Blish. I held on to the ladder to my loft bed for a while as he read. I recognized the characters. The story was unfamiliar, but after a while I started to get interested. There were two Spocks. One was real. One was just a mistake. I went and sat in the space my brother had cleared beside him on his bed. He kept reading until my eyelids grew heavy. I got up and climbed my loft bed ladder past the Victory Leaders featuring Andy Messersmith. Ian started reading to himself again. I was sleepy but still scared, the OK world a trembling curtain that could lift at any moment to show me the awful infinity.

"Hey, Ian," I said.

In the fall, on Sundays, we watched the Dallas Cowboys games they showed on CBS, which because we couldn't get NBC were the only games available to us besides the other CBS standby, the morose, colorless Joe Pisarcik–led New York Giants. After the Cowboys games we went outside and threw a football around. My brother was Roger Staubach and I was Tony "Thrill" Hill. When it was my turn to be Roger Staubach, my brother was Drew Pearson.

"I'll be Preston Pearson now," I said after a Drew Pearson score by my brother. Preston was a backup but sometimes came in and made tough, gutsy, backup-guy plays.

"Whatever," Ian said. "Who even cares? This is baby stuff."

"I'll do a buttonhook and then shake it and bake it the rest of the way," I said, pointing vaguely to where I'd be making my route.

"Whoopee," Ian droned. Just before I hiked him the ball he added, "Preston Pearson isn't Drew Pearson's brother, you know. He's not anything."

"I know that," I said, but I didn't and was disappointed. I had loved the idea that two brothers could be on the same team. My shotgun hike didn't even reach him, then I tripped a little when I started running. Ian's pass was too hard and bounced off my chest.

"Flag on the play?" I asked, rubbing where the ball hit.

"I am fucking *bored!*" my brother yelled up at the gray sky. I knew what was next.

"Go down there," Ian said, pointing. I picked up the ball and walked it to the far end zone, which was just the grass in front of the electric fence that kept the sheep in. Ian moved as far away from me as he possibly could and still be on our property. His back was to the road. I punted the ball as hard as I could but it only got about halfway to him. He ran toward it and picked it up just before it would have stopped rolling. I ran toward him, since I was supposed to try to tackle him now. When we came together I grabbed at him and he shoved me to the ground and went on to score. He spiked the ball and it bounced crazily through the electric fence and into the sheep meadow. I walked toward the road as my brother carefully stepped over the electric fence to retrieve the ball. It was getting darker. He kicked the ball all the way to me and it punched me in the ribs on the way to the grass. I picked it up and started running. Halfway down the yard, I tried to do a Tony Dorsett juke but my brother grabbed me and flung me down, ripping the ball out of my hands. I watched him run away from me for another touchdown.

Why, of all the players that ever came to me, was Andy Messersmith taped to the post of my loft bed? I'm not sure. I know Andy Messersmith was the first baseball player I remember seeing in action on television. It was right after we'd moved to Vermont, while we were still living in another family's house in Randolph Center. Andy Messersmith was on the screen, pitching. There was something else about him, something I didn't quite understand. He had a claim to being the first free agent. I didn't really understand what this meant, but it seemed significant that he was the first of something in the actual world and the first of something in my world. I guess I wanted to hold on to that feeling of those very first days collecting cards, those very first days learning the history of baseball, those very first days of being in a new place where we didn't know anyone and it was just me and my brother against the world.

Topps 1977 #89: Butch Hobson

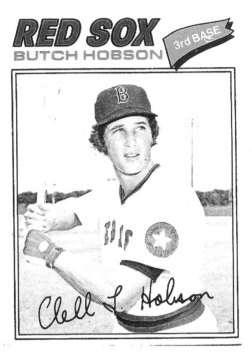

I needed to believe my brother was flawless. For a long time, this was easy. I was the one who had problems in the world. I was smaller than him, weaker than him. I had night terrors. I was scared of everything. I was colorblind. I had barely any sense of smell.

After a while, it also came out that I couldn't really see. I was riding in the VW Camper with Mom. We drove by a big field. There were a bunch of cows lying around off in the distance.

"Look at those friggin' cows," I said.

"Oh my god, what did you say?" my mother said.

"I don't know. What? Friggin'?"

"Those are hay bales."

"Oh," I said. "Really?"

"I'm terrible," my mom said, crumpling. "I'm a horrible mother! How long have you been having problems seeing?"

"I see everything," I said.

We went to an eye doctor a couple days later.

"When you're in class, do you have problems viewing the blackboard?" the doctor said.

"I don't know." I thought about my class, all the beanbag chairs scattered around, everybody wandering. "We don't really have a blackboard."

"He means are things blurry," my mom said to me.

"Things are the same as always," I said.

"Hey, four-eyes fag," an older kid said a week or so later.

My brother hit two home runs in little league that year, our last year together on our little league team. One home run meant you were flawless. Two meant O My God. The second of his home runs made it all the way to the trees beyond the chain-link outfield fence. We all poured out of the dugout and were standing by the plate yelling as he jogged around third. Everything was crystal clear because now I had glasses. I couldn't believe this was how everyone always saw things. The white chalk lines. The green blades of grass. The top of the chain-link outfield fence ringing with sunlight. The O My God trees beyond. My big brother laughing, coming home.

That summer, 1978, it looked like our favorite major league team was flawless. We went to our one Red Sox game of the year and maybe because they were way in front in first place or maybe because I had glasses, or maybe both, everything sparkled with perfection.

Also, it was helmet day. Every kid got a helmet, and my brother was just barely still young enough. Having a shiny Red Sox batting helmet made everything even shinier and even more perfect despite the weird fight that had happened on the drive down. When Yaz came to bat I shouted Yaz a million times until my throat was sore.

"Yaz! Yaz! Yaz! Come on, Yaz!"

"Can you please shut up a little," Ian said.

He was in a bad mood because he had a hangover. And mad at me because I had passed on the news to Mom out loud, on the drive down, that he had a hangover. I thought a hangover was skin hanging off your finger and didn't understand why the word made my mother look at my brother like she was going to cry.

Our team got beat up pretty badly, and some of the seats down low opened up. I couldn't believe how close we got, me and my brother. I couldn't believe no one told us we had to leave. I couldn't believe how brightly the batting helmet shined on the head of the player in the on-deck circle, Butch Hobson. I'd never been closer to a god. Ian's helmet shined the same way. I took mine off and looked at it and it shined just as bright, then I put it back on and was about to yell to Butch Hobson but it was like my throat was clogged with light. He leaned on his bat and watched the game, as if it was no big deal that they were losing the game, this one game. And it was true. They still had a huge lead in the division. They were flawless. For example: Butch Hobson, who had driven in 112 runs the year before, hit ninth in the order.

Later, as the summer wore on, the flaws would begin to show, starting with Butch Hobson's arm. Because of things you couldn't see coming apart inside him, he started to lose control of his throws to first. Some of them sailed into the seats where my brother and I had sat. You needed *real* helmets to sit there, not just the cheap plastic jobs we had gotten at the gate. The errors piled up. The division lead shrank. Both of our helmets lost their shine and I dropped mine and it cracked. Mom and Tom found some pot in the little desk by my brother's bed.

"Why do you have this?" Tom said.

"You're sneaking through my stuff now?" Ian yelled.

"That's not what we're talking about here, man!" Tom yelled.

"You smoke pot all the time, *man*!" Ian yelled. I went to the backyard and clamped my hands over my ears.

But I didn't know any of that on Helmet Day. On the way home, Ian put his new helmet over his face and went to sleep. Mom nodded off, too, her head bobbing with bumps. Only Tom and I were still awake. I discovered I could change the appearance of the headlights of the cars coming toward us by taking my new glasses off. With my glasses on, they were all just headlights, but when I went back to my true way of seeing, the headlights separated into spheres made up of many smaller lights. They reminded me of dried-out dandelion bulbs, the kind you make wishes with, but the seeds were points of light. I imagined I could make my deepest wish. What would it be? I thought about Yaz. *Come on, Yaz!* I thought about winning. I thought about me and my brother jumping around together, champions at last. I looked over at him dozing on the seat beside me. I wanted to stay awake. *Champions at last.* But as I watched the dandelion headlights floating toward us, my glasses in my hands, I started to breathe deeper and slower, and finally with one last waking wishing breath, all the seeds of light scattered.

1978 Topps #500: George Foster

GEORGE FOSTER

I remember the precise moment I found this card in a new pack. I had just bought the pack and was walking home. I was by the spot on Route 14 where an abandoned general store with an Esso sign and dust-covered windows faced, across the road, an empty metal trailer that had once been a restaurant called Chez René. Usually I was able to delay gratification for a while, carrying my standard purchase of two packs of cards all the way home before opening them, but on this day I needed that painkilling hit just a little bit quicker and slid my finger under the plastic flaps, breaking the infinitesimally thin coat of glue and releasing the scent of the gum.

I shattered the shard of gum with my teeth as I leafed through the new cards. I spotted the N.L. ALL STAR shield first, then read the name that I recognized from following its awe-inspiring march through the previous season's statistics pages in the newspapers. The broken-pieces phase of the gum gave way to the soft and cohesive sugary phase, and I heightened the moment, which would soon give way to the texture-of-a-pencil-eraser/flavor-of-spit-and-disappointment phase, by flipping the George Foster card over to affirm that the legend told by the newspaper statistics was true. After all, nothing was an inarguable fact until I saw it on a baseball card, and here it was: George Foster had hit 52 home runs during the 1977 season, the most any player had hit in my entire lifetime.

In 1978, the 50 home run plateau was mythic. Only ancient guys from the black-and-white world preceding the epoch of the cardboard gods had ever reached that Olympian height. But now George Foster had done it, and as sugar coursed through my body I held in

my hands that very same George Foster, or at least a little sliver of George Foster that had fallen like a red and brown and white leaf all the way from the forests of heaven to the rundown valley of East Randolph, Vermont. I paused for a moment, then hurried home before anyone could fuck with me.

Topps 1978 #147: Lee Mazzilli

LEE MAZZILLI

One day a year, during our visit to see our father, my brother and I would take a break from everything that really mattered and become Mets fans. They were easy to love, in part because there was nothing for us to lose by doing so, since we didn't live and die with them, and in part because everything about the team seemed to be a lovable and paradoxical mixture of spectacular and incompetent: first baseman Willie Montanez making incredible scoops of wild throws that were already several seconds too late; catcher John Stearns forming a brick wall at home plate in hopes of impeding the runner as the relay throw sailed into the dugout; Bruce Boisclair lacing a double to right and getting thrown out easily trying to stretch it into a triple. Even the lingering vestiges of the Mets' glory days seemed affected by the glittering ineptitude: Jerry Koosman dashingly windmilling and firing his way to a 3–15 record, Ed Kranepool clouting pinch-hit drives to the warning track.

By 1978 centerfielder Lee Mazzilli was becoming the star of the show. Mazzilli was good at just about everything. He could draw walks, hit for a decent average, smack 15 or so home runs and steal 15 or so bases a year, and cover a lot of ground in the outfield. You could almost say that he was faultless, a characterization that he seemed inclined to emphasize by custom-tailoring his uniforms and maintaining his archetypical feathered haircut with the level of care usually only given to invaluable cultural relics, which in a way is what it was. By 1978 my brother and I were mesmerized by feathered haircuts, and seeing such a glorious example of the new bulletproof-cool style on a baseball player was particularly enthralling. I can see him yet, king of my once-a-year-beloved Mets, his cap flying free to reveal his immaculate Scott Baio locks as he sprints across the brown Queens grass in his impeccable uniform to dive stylishly for a line drive that touches down yards away from his outstretched glove.

The morning of our Mets game in the late summer of 1978, I was eating cereal how I always ate it, without any milk and definitely without any of the cut-up bananas my father and brother had in their bowls. I was humming the home team's theme song and wondering about it.

"Are you going to be taking algebra this year?" my father asked my brother.

"We started learning some at the end of last year," my brother said, "but it was baby stuff."

"It's very im—" my father said. I started singing.

"Meet the Mets, greet the Mets, step right up and beat the Mets," I sang. I really thought these were the words.

"Why do the Mets say to everyone to come and beat them?" I said. I was reading the sports page, and I was about to tell my brother the Mets' putrid record as soon as I was done with my next bite of Cheerios when I noticed that my dad was glaring at my cereal bowl.

For whatever reason, seeing me eat cereal without any milk was the last straw for my dad. I can only guess what else was on the overloaded back of the proverbial camel whose back was about to be broken by my next unsoggy bite, but it may have been a compendium of all the ways I wasn't quite right. Here is an almost certainly incomplete list: 1) I daydreamed too much. 2) I didn't know which way to look when we crossed streets while walking around the city. 3) I didn't remember to look *any* way sometimes, lost in my own thoughts as my dad and brother talked about things I didn't understand or care about. 4) I had had a middle-of-the-night screaming bout of night terrors when we'd visited my dad's brother's family in New Jersey. 5) On another night that led to an even worse morning than the one that followed the night terrors, I'd wet the foam mattress I slept on in my dad's apartment. 6) I was, according to my dad, a "mama's boy." (Many years later, I would understand he was probably cringing at the echo in me of his own younger self.) 7) The only thing I knew about was baseball, which was silly and devoid of worth. 8) Worst of all, my picky, idiotic eating habits. Chiefly: I didn't eat fruit! 9) And now this! Milk-less cereal!

Even though I sensed that something not too great was about to happen, I went ahead and took my bite of cereal, still trying to think only about the Mets.

"Gah!" my father barked. *"You don't do anything right!"*

My brother jumped to my defense.

"No, he just likes it better when it's crunchy," he said.

"Oh my god," my father said, already mortified by his brief eruption. His head was in his hands. I wish I could say I was sitting there toughly. But yet another way in which I was not flawless was that I often burst into tears. My dad began apologizing in a devastated way that I found overbearing and confusing.

"Please forgive me," he kept saying. "Do you forgive me?"

I didn't understand what he meant. Forgive? But I wanted him to stop smothering me with the question with his big sad breathing face inches from mine, so finally I nodded, and he went back to more or less leaving me alone.

If you listed the things my father hated the most in this life, you'd come up with many of the things that made up a day at Shea Stadium. Subway rides, sports, crowds, the deafening roar of jet planes: It was all there. He spent most of the game glaring at the *New York Times* and clamping his hands over his ears for the constant procession of La Guardia arrivals and departures.

Meanwhile, as the customary beating the Mets were sustaining passed the halfway point, I started focusing on the dozens and dozens of empty seats below us, much nearer to the field. We could see Lenny Randle and Steve "Stevie Wonder" Henderson up close. We could say something to Lee Mazzilli and he'd hear us.

My father wasn't crazy about moving down, but finally he agreed, and for a second we were right there, just like we'd been at the Red Sox game earlier in the summer. But before we'd even breathed out once, a man in a blue windbreaker tapped my father on the shoulder.

"No one's even sitting here," my father whined.

"Sorry, chief," the man said. That's my clearest memory of all those games at Shea in the 1970s: staring at my father's back as we climbed farther and farther away from the action to where we belonged.

Topps 1978 #655: Lyman Bostock

LYMAN BOSTOCK

One night in September 1978, late, Ian and I were home alone and I asked him about the universe. I remember when it was because of Lyman Bostock. Ian had his light on and was reading. I was up high, in my loft bed.

"What's at the edge of it?" I said.

"The universe is expanding," he said.

"Expanding? But where? Into what?"

"It's too complicated to explain to you."

Sometimes cards had to be changed in a hurry to reflect offseason transactions. I imagine that such changes now can be effected digitally, seamlessly, leaving no trace of any previous worlds. But when I was a kid, these changes were done with an endearing crudeness that always allowed ample evidence that the past could not ever be fully erased. For example, in Lyman Bostock's 1978 card, Bostock is presented as an Angel, but the garish coloring along his neckline suggests makeup applied by a tipsy floozy more than uniform piping, and his helmet more closely resembles frosting on a personalized supermarket cake than a decal on hard plastic. He is certainly no Angel, not fully, not yet.

The universe didn't make sense. If something was expanding, then there had to be something it was expanding into. There couldn't just be nothing. I stared at the ceiling that was only a couple feet from my head. There was a little hole up there, directly above my head, and it was my theory that the hole had been made by rats who lived up above our room in a crawl space and every once in a while dug away at the ceiling with their claws when no one was looking, like prisoners chipping away at their cell wall. Maybe one day they'd claw all the way through and fall on me and bite me and I'd get the Plague. All the kids of the town would visit me, wearing surgical masks, and they'd give me presents as I shivered and coughed and said brave things. I'd have my baseball cards at my bedside. One day near the end when it was difficult to speak I'd croak to my weeping mother that she should give all my cards to my brother when the time came.

"What are you talking about?" she'd blubber. "You are gonna be just fine!"

"Hey, Ian," I said now.

He flipped the page of his book, ignoring me.

"Hey, Ian, what happens when you die?"

When I had gotten Lyman Bostock's doctored 1978 card I knew him solely as a name near the top of the list of batting averages printed in the Sunday sports section. I studied those averages religiously, as religiously as I've ever studied anything. I loved the exactness of them. I loved that there was a hierarchy, an order, Singleton and Brett near the top, Kingman and Belanger near the bottom, and I loved even more that occasionally certain previously unknown players moved into the upper echelon of that hierarchy, sometimes creeping up the list past the sturdy .280 Amos Otis types, sometimes materializing out of nowhere, as Bob Watson would do for the Red Sox in 1979 upon amassing the minimum number of at bats. I don't know which route Lyman Bostock first took, because I don't remember a time before Lyman Bostock was among the batting average leaders, and yet I also do recall thinking of him as a new guy, a youngster storming the rarefied realm lorded over benevolently by his wondrous Twins teammate Rod Carew. In general, I thought about him this way: Lyman Bostock was rising, each year a little higher. His move to the Angels in 1978 provided a temporary hiccup in his career's rising motion, but within that first year with his new team there was a microcosm of his career, a smaller rising, his batting average going up and up after a bad April.

At some point during that season I started cutting out the batting average list from the Sunday paper and taping it to the post of my loft bed, below the 1975 Victory Leaders card featuring Andy Messersmith. Each time I taped a new version of the list to the post,

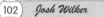

I looked for Lyman Bostock and was happy to see him rising, a little higher each week.

Ian didn't answer when I asked him what happens when you die. I stared some more at the ceiling and thought about the rats falling through and the Plague and my tragic death. Everyone weeping. Maybe they'd bury my cards with me, bawling about how much I loved them. Or maybe my cards would be covered with the Plague and they'd have to be destroyed. Or maybe they'd have to burn me *and* the cards. What would be left? A car approached that sounded sort of like our VW Camper, Mom and Tom returning, but it didn't stop. I started to really think about the whole thing, and not in a fun way.

"How can it be?" I asked out loud. "We're here and then forever we're *gone*."

"Look, just don't worry about it," my brother said.

"One minute suddenly nothing and that's it," I said, my voice rising.

"It's not going to happen for a long time."

"But it's going to happen!"

"Think about something else."

"Oh man oh man. It's going to happen," I said, starting to panic. "Omanomanoman."

I climbed down the ladder of the loft bed, past my Victory Leaders card and the latest Sunday averages, and went and sat on the stairs and gripped my stomach with both hands, rocking back and forth, overpowered by the idea that someday I would not exist.

Earlier that day, we had learned about Lyman Bostock. He'd been riding in the backseat of a car and had been shot and killed by a man aiming for someone else.

"Hey, Josh," Ian said. I didn't turn around. He was standing behind me at the top of the stairs. I heard pages riffling.

"Oh man, oh no," I muttered.

"Hey, Josh. Who is the all-time career leader in triples?"

"Oh man. I don't know. Oh god."

But then I told him. Sam Crawford.

"Ding!"

More sound of pages riffling.

"Now, all right, now who's the all-time *single season* leader in doubles? Wow, that's a lot of doubles," Ian added.

And I told him. Earl Webb. And he kept on asking questions with answers that I knew.

Eventually, I was able to get up off the stairs and go back into our room and climb my loft bed ladder past the list featuring, near the top, Lyman Bostock's name and his average. I lay down and looked at the ceiling. Four hundredths of a point shy of .300 forever.

"Hey, Ian," I said. "Can you ask me a couple more?"

Topps 1979 #500: Ron Guidry

RON GUIDRY P
YANKEES

Late in the 1978 season, my brother, whose nickname was Brillo, tried to get a feathered haircut like Lee Mazzilli. Somehow, the town's feathered haircut maestro, a young barber named Woody, was able to wrench my brother's tightly coiled curls into something that looked like what the cool kids in school had on their heads, but it lasted for only one day before puffing back out into a half-Jew-fro. My brother was angered by this, which was no surprise. My brother angrily simmered more and more. I mostly associated it with the Red Sox' ongoing collapse, which at one point caused my brother to rip his beloved copy of *Spock Must Die* into shreds.

Mom and Tom must have identified the anger as coming from a different source. One day a book showed up on my brother's bed called *The Big Book of Teenage Answers*, with a note that said "Love, Mom and Tom." I saw it first, before Ian got home. The book was written by a Bionic Woman–looking woman and a guy who looked like Steve Garvey but with cooler hair, like Lee Mazzilli's. There was a photograph of them on the back. They were both smiling with large white teeth and leaning their tan arms on curly ten-speed handlebars. I flipped through the book. A drawing of a naked woman had holes in parts of her skin to show what was inside her body. I looked at it for a while. Then I flipped around some more and stopped on a section called Ejaculation:

> You will one day begin rubbing your penis. It will grow larger and become firm. It will begin to feel so good that you will be unable to stop. It is a feeling

of uncontrollable pleasure like you have never felt before. This feeling will increase until, eventually, it climaxes with the spurting of a white milky substance from the tip of your penis. This is called ejaculation.

After this has happened, feelings of fatigue and shame will then overtake you. But there is nothing wrong with what you have done. A study has shown that 95% of all males experiment with this deed, known as masturbation. It is natural. But it is good to have a cup handy to catch the semen that issues from your penis! It can get messy!

I went downstairs and got the cup I usually used for chocolate milk and brought it back upstairs, then I climbed into my loft bed and gave it a try and found I was apparently flawed in a whole new way because nothing happened except the shame part, a little. I tried to put the book back on my brother's bed exactly the way I'd found it.

That night, my brother and I were both lying in bed. We hadn't been talking as much as we used to. What was there to talk about? The Red Sox were choking worse than any team ever had. What else was there between us anymore? But sometimes my brother needed to tell me a story as much as I needed to hear him tell it.

"Me and Dean just walked out of school yesterday," he said. I knew who Dean was. He had a flawless feathered haircut. And one other thing!

"You crushed your second home run off of Dean!" I said.

"That was a billion years ago," Ian said.

"Wait, you left school during school?" I said.

"We went to his house and he gives me this glass of water. He's like, 'Hey, here's some water, chug a lug.' But it was *vodka.*"

I knew not to say anything. But I was thinking, How could someone just walk right out of school? Weren't there any rules at all?

"We got so fucked up," my brother said.

Fucked up? I thought. I couldn't imagine what that meant. The next time I was alone, I checked *The Big Book of Teenage Answers,* but I couldn't find anything. What the hell was going on?

It was all falling apart, but there was still one last chance it could come back together. The day after the 1978 season was supposed to be over, we were let out of school early. All over New England it was the same. A half-day. A holiday. One game. A 14-game lead gone, but still one last chance to win. Amazing that I still believed: We had Mike Torrez; they had Ron Guidry.

How can I explain Ron Guidry?

At that time, I was afraid to bicycle past a Doberman pinscher who was, according to the neighbor kid who owned him, so fierce that he often chewed through his chain and went on bloodthirsty rampages. I was afraid of that dog. I was afraid of bullies. I was afraid of girls. After reading *The Big Book of Teenage Answers* I was afraid that something was horribly wrong with my penis. I was afraid of ending up in a situation where I would be forced to eat fruit, which repulsed me. I was afraid of our basement. I was afraid of the three-note Duracell ditty that ended with the sectioned battery slamming together. I was afraid of nuclear bombs. You could be sitting there on the floor of your room, sorting your newest baseball cards into their respective teams, and it could all vanish in one bright flash. I was afraid of everything ending. I was afraid of death. I was afraid most of all of my night terrors.

In light of all those fears, I can't really say that I was afraid of Ron Guidry. I mean, I wasn't afraid Ron Guidry was going to leap out from behind a snowbank and bash me with a rock. I wasn't afraid Ron Guidry was going to force me to touch my tongue to a frozen metal pole. I wasn't afraid Ron Guidry was going to burn our house down. And yet, when I hold this 1979 Ron Guidry card in my hand, more than thirty years after 1978, when he went 25-3 with a 1.74 ERA—numbers so astounding they seem inhuman, merciless, obsidian, obscene—to lead the 100-win Yankees past my team, the 99-win Red Sox, it's as if I'm holding a small box made of thin, fragile glass, a scorpion inside.

Topps 1975 # 299: Bucky Dent

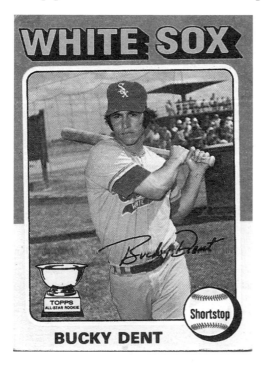

But to digress for a moment for something completely unrelated to that one-game playoff between the Yankees and the Red Sox in 1978, here's the tragic figure of Bucky Dent, the mildly promising, light-hitting young Chicago White Sox shortstop who after being named to the Topps All-Star Rookie Team in 1975 was killed in a horrific wood-chipper accident.

Some are of the opinion that this accident is a myth, and that Bucky Dent actually went on to play for several more years in the American League, and that in one notable instance he even distinguished himself as the power-hitting hero of a certain one-game playoff, that he strode to the plate in the seventh inning of that contest with two men on and his team, the Yankees, down two runs and, after fouling a pitch from Red Sox starter Mike Torrez off his foot and delaying the game for several minutes as trainers tended to the bruise, finally got back into the batter's box, now armed with a dubious new bat that teammate Mickey Rivers had, like a cardsharp producing a new deck from a hidden pocket just before going for the kill, suspiciously rushed into Bucky Dent's hands, and with this new bat Bucky Dent swung with the entirety of his scrawny might at Torrez's next offering and managed with the help of God, if you believe in God and in the idea that God has the time and inclination to micromanage wind patterns, lifted the ball just barely over the Green Monster for what stands, in this version of reality (which carries as an appendix the notion that Bucky Dent's resultant fame allowed him to be featured in a beefcake pinup poster favored by adoring brace-faced prepubescent girls from

Riverdale to Smithtown), as arguably the most famous blow ever struck in the entire storied rivalry of the Yankees and Red Sox.

All of this is preposterous, akin to the crackpot notion that the moon landings were staged on a lot in Burbank or that all Jews got a memo on September 11 to avoid downtown Manhattan. A legendary home run? Please. Beyond the contradictory indicators of Bucky Dent's slight frame and complete lack of power-hitting skills—factors which could, it is true, have been compensated for by a perfect storm of: 1) a nice fat pitch across the center of the plate; 2) an unlikely but not impossible instance of optimally solid contact; 3) the closest left-field wall in major league baseball; 4) a powerful wind gust lifting up toward heaven and out toward the Massachusetts Turnpike; and 5) possibly some cork—consider that this is the only Bucky Dent card in my entire collection, and if he had indeed played beyond this year the only way to explain his absence from my collection would be to say that I assiduously removed and destroyed any later Bucky Dent cards, as if for some reason the very sight of them caused me revulsion. But why on earth would anyone waste time doing something like that?

Clearly, the stronger Bucky Dent theory is the one in which Bucky Dent was tragically chopped into pieces, then minced into bits, then pureed into a mush of flesh and feathered hair and eye black by a ravenous, extremely efficient wood chipper before he was ever able to make any significant impact on baseball history or on the innocence of, say, a ten-year-old Red Sox fan in East Randolph, Vermont, on October 2, 1978.

3rd PACK

HALO

Topps 1978 #670: Jim Rice

JIM RICE

In the bottom of the ninth on October 2, 1978, the Red Sox had the tying run on second and the winning run on first and only one out and Jim Rice coming up. Jim Rice had already had one of the best years of all time. In fact, he'd crushed more pitches in one season than anyone in decades, as evidenced by his 406 total bases, the most in the majors since Stan Musial's 429 in 1948. All he had to do was crush one more. But he got a little under a Goose Gossage heater and flied out to right. The runner on second, Rick Burleson, moved to third. Ninety feet away. One chance left.

Yaz.

By this point my brother and I were both standing, crowding the television as if it were the faltering fire in an igloo.

"Come on, Yaz," Ian said.

"Come on, Yaz, please," I said.

It was a long winter. I continued to check the mailbox for a reply to my 1976 letter to Yaz, even when I had to trudge through waist-high snow to do it. I continued to see Yankees third baseman Graig Nettles in foul territory, the ball in his glove, both arms upraised.

In the spring I went on a school trip to Boston. We were outside the cramped Fenway Park player parking area, and I saw Jim Rice get out of a car. I pressed my face against the chain-link fence that separated us. He was no more than twenty feet away.

"Jim Ed!" I shouted.

He turned toward me. I was too shocked to say anything. After all my years of worship, I couldn't believe a god could hear me, that a god could look me straight in the eye. Moreover, I sensed that there was in Jim Rice's quick, almost flinching, squint-eyed glance toward the caller of his name a suggestion that he was haunted by a nervous, even paranoid unease with the world around him. This may have contributed to my silence as well, the possibility that Jim Rice not only was able to hear us mortals but was mortal himself. I could not think of a single thing to say. Words had been uninvented. I gulped air. Jim Rice turned away.

Life got more complicated after that. The school trip to Boston occurred during my last days of elementary school. It had been decided that even though I was only the equivalent of a fifth grader, it was time for me to leave the hippie-invented class with no grades. After several years in a classroom where everyone was free to be whatever they wanted to be, I had become a sarcastic know-it-all, undercutting most attempts by the teacher to lead the class in any constructive direction by voicing such brilliant remarks as "Great idea, teach," and "Oh boy, we've never done *that* a million times before." It was too much. I was told that in the fall I would no longer be welcome in the class and instead would have to jump into seventh grade, junior high, that different kind of school altogether, a giant building where my brother had started to change, to grow taller and tougher and quieter and further away from me.

On the ride home from Boston to Vermont, I sat with two other boys and three girls in the roofed back of a pickup truck and refused to participate in a game of Truth or Dare that mostly amounted to taking turns kissing. I could not kiss a girl. I don't know why I was so terrified, but I was. (In fact, it would be many long years before, with the help of grain alcohol, I kissed a girl, a bleary coed majoring in hotel and hospitality management.) The amazing thing was that my terror at being kissed actually drove the three girls in the back of the truck crazy. By the time we were almost home all three of them were feeding off one another on the subject of me like I was the latest disposable fad, like Shaun Cassidy or Pop Rocks or the "invisible dog" leash.

"Go with me, Josh," one of them said. I didn't understand this request. Go?

"No, go with me!" another one pleaded.

"Go with all of us," the third one squealed.

This third one was the prettiest, and she would lose interest by the next day. The second prettiest would move back to her solemn all-consuming infatuation with George Harrison within a week. The third, a burly, freckled, pug-nosed girl, kept after me the longest, cornering me periodically like she was going to steal my lunch money, but even she got tired of my stammering deer-in-the-headlights routine, finally saying, "What is *wrong* with you?" and storming away. I was relieved at first, but then I missed her; I'd never be popular again. That night in the back of the truck, returning from Boston, was, for me, like when some minor league call-up has a game, one game, when he slugs the ball all over the yard like Jim Rice. Except as it was happening all I wanted was for it to end.

"Please go with us, Josh!" all three girls said, crowding me. "Please, please, please!"

Go? I kept screaming to myself. *Go where?*

Topps 1979 #310: Thurman Munson

THURMAN MUNSON C
YANKEES

I didn't want to go anywhere. I didn't want anything to change. I didn't want time to move. But it moved. Summer came. I tried to stop time the best way I knew how, with baseball cards.

This 1979 Thurman Munson card is one of the cards that came to me that year. By that time, finding a Yankee in a pack of cards had long been like finding a mold-blackened orange in your trick-or-treat bag. I valued the never realized (nor even approached) goal of completing the year's collection too much to throw the offending cardboard in the garbage, as I would the orange, but I tried to get the Yankees cards away from the others as soon as possible and out of sight so I could engage in my time-dissolving card-aided daydreams without the sharp sliver of festering resentment in my nostrils.

Some of the cards were less offensive than others, the mushroom-cloud hair of Oscar Gamble, the innocuousness of Roy White, the hilarious storytelling ability of the author of *The Bronx Zoo*, Sparky Lyle, and the mere name of Mickey Klutts among the few effective truce-making offerings from the world of my enemies. On the other hand, some Yankees were capable of tainting the whole pack, including perennial asshole-of-the-year Reggie Jackson, simian brawl-instigator Lou Piniella, the bat-corking duo of maimer of Bill Lee's shoulder Graig Nettles and sucker puncher Mickey Rivers, and a certain weak-hitting pretty-boy shortstop who may or may not have been slowly, oh-so-painfully killed in a wood-chipper accident.

I counted Thurman Munson in that latter group. Yankees captain, leader of the bullies, picker of fights with Carlton Fisk. And here he was again, befouling my pack with his little squinting smile. This smile was probably interpreted by me as connoting that the Yankees had just won another title. Since I'd been living and dying with baseball, the Yankees had won a pennant in 1976, a World Series in 1977, and another World Series in 1978. And when I tried to escape the seemingly endless ongoing tyranny in the present by diving into the baseball encyclopedia, I saw more of the same, stretching back as far as the eye could bear to see.

Fucking Yankees, I thought.

In early August of 1979 we took our yearly bus trip to see our dad. It was unusually crowded, so I couldn't sit with my brother and had to take a seat with a short, mustachioed guy in his early twenties. We started talking and he told me he was a Yankees fan, and he reminded me a little of Thurman Munson, Yankees captain, leader of the bullies, picker of fights with Carlton Fisk. Despite that, I didn't hate him, and he was friendly, and time flew as we talked about baseball through the first few hours of the ride, before the midtrip fifteen-minute break in Springfield, MA. During that break, everybody got off the bus. I don't know where the guy sitting next to me went, but my brother and I wandered through the station and came upon a vending machine that we hadn't noticed before on any of our previous stops in Springfield.

"Check. It. Out," my brother said. In the plastic display slots were movie-theater-style boxes of candy. In one of the slots was the kind of box of plain M&Ms my father always presented to me when he arrived in Vermont for a visit, and in another slot was the box of peanut M&Ms he gave to my brother.

"I can't believe it!" I exclaimed. It seemed an amazing discovery, but we both waited a second before pumping quarters into the machine. So this was the answer to the one good mystery of our dad. We had always marveled at how he could produce these boxes that we thought were sold only in movie theaters, but he got them right here, in a bus station. This bus station. Nothing to it. You put in a couple quarters and pulled a rod. Kerplunk.

I was back in my seat shoving fistfuls of the unmagical candy in my mouth when the guy with the mustache reboarded, looking glum. I swung my knees out to let him into his window seat. He lowered himself down. He looked like he had something terrible to tell me.

"Thurman Munson died," he finally said. He went on to mention a plane crash, but I was already turning and rising to tell my brother, M&Ms clicking against the inside of smile-bared teeth. Relaying the news, my voice rang out like a recess bell. This wasn't like Lyman Bostock. I'm not proud of it now, but the moment I heard that Thurman Munson no longer existed I got happy. The Yankees would never torture us again.

When I sat back down my seatmate was staring at me. I still had a smile on my face but the man's sad, stunned glare cut all connection the smile had to anything inside me. I held the box of M&Ms out to him. He shook his head, then turned and looked out the window. The bus pulled out. I wolfed down the rest of the M&Ms before we were even back on the highway. The rest of the trip took a long time, the Munson fan staring silently out the window the whole way. I had nothing to do for hours but look at my empty box.

Topps 1980 #72: Fred Howard

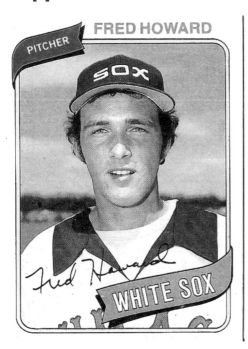

A few days later, my brother somehow convinced my father to take us to a Ted Nugent concert at Madison Square Garden. I knew almost nothing about Ted Nugent, and Ian didn't know much more than I did. I think he saw that he would be able to impress his vodka-chugging feathered-hair buddies back home if he could tell them that he had seen Nugent live.

I'd never been to a rock concert before. None of us had. It gave me a ball-shriveling inclination of how I would react if I was ever sent to war. When we got to our row, up in the highest, smokiest reaches of the arena, far from the empty stage, guys in mirrored aviator sunglasses sitting in the row behind us had their cowboy-booted feet hanging down over our seats. Though they reluctantly pulled their legs up to let us sit down, the menacing air lingered. My stomach hurt.

All around us there was a feeling like a battle was looming. This feeling crystallized with the appearance of a huge banner being paraded around by two shirtless longhaired guys to great deep roars from the crowd.

"Disco is dead but ROCK IS ROLLING!" the banner proclaimed. This seemed to spark the chant that rose up and boomed from seemingly everyone in the place but us.

"DISCO SUCKS! DISCO SUCKS!"

I looked at my brother, who was staring straight ahead, bug-eyed, seemingly as overwhelmed by everything as I was. He may also have been afraid that I'd start asking the questions that had begun to form in my head, questions that would reveal the both of us as impostors. But I kept my mouth shut, at first because I was scared of the ever-building noise, and then because I was stung by what started coming out of Ian's mouth, a repetition of words in a hesitant mumble that no one could have heard but me.

"Disco sucks, disco sucks," he mumbled in time to the thundering chant.

But hadn't we Hustled in the living room to the unwarped copy of *Saturday Night Fever* that we'd finally got our hands on? Hadn't we pooled our money for K-Tel's *Disco Dazzler*? Hadn't we had a World Series best-of-seven coin flip competition with a 2-3-2 home-and-away format and crowd noises and the thrill of victory and the agony of defeat, all to see who would win the right to buy and to be the sole proud owner of Leif Garrett's single "I Was Made for Dancin'"?

Disco sucking was all new to me, even though the most famous moment of this volatile and widespread cultural disparagement had occurred just a couple weeks earlier at, of all things, a baseball game. That night, in Chicago, the sky had rained flat black discs and lit M-80s. By the late innings, the visiting Detroit Tigers outfielders were wearing batting helmets in the outfield. A vendor reported selling forty-nine cases of beer, more than double the number he'd sold on any single night in his many years on the job. Smoldering bongs were passed from hand to hand like change for a hot dog, giant glossy paper airplanes made of promotional posters featuring a sultry blonde model known only as Lorelei swooped and dove amid the hail of explosives and Frisbeed LPs and 45s, and inebriated throngs in the parking lot jumped up and down on cars and set fire to white-suited John Travolta dolls and searched for illegal entry into the slightly more focused mayhem inside the packed stadium. As game one of the scheduled doubleheader progressed, this search gained urgency, for between games a local 24-year-old disc jockey named Steve Dahl and the aforementioned Lorelei were going to detonate a mountain of disco records.

Almost immediately after this detonation, a stream and then a gushing wave of longhaired attendees flowed onto the playing field. The desire to get onto the field was strong, as reported by an anonymous contributor to a Disco Demolition Night web page on whitesoxinteractive.com:

"One doofus tried to go over the brick wall in centerfield by using our [Disco Sucks banner]. He asked us to hold it, which we did, and he proceeded to plummet 30 feet onto the field. The sign, made of a bed sheet, ripped immediately. I remember seeing him rolling around in pain and remember reading in the paper [the next day] that there were only some minor injuries such as fractured ankles and thought he was one of them."

The revolution, the pointless, hysterical revolution, had come. Some lit bonfires in the outfield. Some wheeled the batting cage around like it was a stalled car that needed a running start. Some performed hook slides and headfirst Pete Rose plunges into where the bases would have been if they hadn't already been ripped from the ground and stuffed between giggling rib cages and the fabric of Led Zeppelin and Aerosmith T-shirts. More than one person reported seeing couples fornicating, one of these reports asserting that this occurred in at least one instance in something of an orderly fashion, the participants feverishly attending to one another in stages corresponding to the general location of the bases. Cub Scout troops and the elderly watched from the stands.

Inside the home team's clubhouse, as his teammates went through the motions of preparing for a second game that they had begun to correctly assume would never be played, Fred Howard, shown here in the only baseball card ever produced in his likeness, tried to wash off whatever residue had accrued during his stint as the losing pitcher of game one. Though he probably didn't see it this way, he had done his part. As another contributor to the web page cited above recalled: "The Sox lost the first game to Detroit, which just seemed to aggravate and energize the crowd." No one remembers Fred Howard, or even seems to have been aware of his existence, but the 1970s, that tale told by an idiot full of sound and fury signifying nothing, may not have had its decade-punctuating Woodstock without his heroic failure.

At the Garden, music ceased to exist when the band took the stage and began to play. I could no longer like the music of the Bee Gees and A Taste of Honey and Chic, and had already kissed it all goodbye, but the roar-inspiring demolisher of disco was too loud in my first encounter with it for me to respond in any way beyond a terrified cringe. After a few minutes of this terror, my cringe became a general feeling of profound embarrassment. I was embarrassed of myself for being a little bespectacled disco-loving fairy, and embarrassed of my father, who in his blue button-down dress shirt and horn-rimmed glasses looked even more out of place than I did, especially after he began stuffing conspicuously large wads of cotton into his ears the moment we sat down. Also, paradoxically, and adding to my cringe, I felt terrible that we had dragged him here, to something that a bookish noise-hating mild-mannered Bach aficionado could not possibly have hated more.

After a few prolonged explosions that I knew were songs only because they began and ended, I told my dad I needed to go to the bathroom. He came with me. I wanted a break from the noise. It was brighter than day in the empty bathroom, and, relative to the concert, extremely quiet. The quiet intimidated me. I tried to take a leak but nothing came out. Then I zipped up, washed my hands, and stood in front of my dad, the two of us alone in there. I tried to apologize. But I was mumbling, and he still had cotton in his ears. He kept saying he couldn't hear me and I kept saying I was sorry. I've always wondered if this was our defining moment. Finally he nodded, obviously faking that he had heard me. We went back to our seats.

The moment the band left the stage to the sound of gigantic human roaring, my father bolted from his seat and marched toward the exit, as strident and decisive a physical act as he'd ever performed. My brother and I had no choice but to follow, and I for one couldn't wait to get out of there. But as we were leaving, there was the distinct feeling that something was off. No one else had left their seats, and in fact a few red-eyed grinning yahoos were still stumbling in through the turnstiles as we were heading out. I imagine my brother had the greatest suspicion that we were making some sort of a terrible blunder, but since he had never been to a concert before, he didn't really know how they worked. More importantly, his skimpy knowledge about Ted Nugent left him without much clarity regarding the rock star's identity.

"Which one *was* he?" I asked my brother as we crossed Seventh Avenue. About all I knew about him, from a picture Ian had showed me, was that he played guitar *and sang*. Even though we had been very far from the stage, I had noticed that this didn't fit the description of anyone in the band we'd just seen. The two stars of the show were a guy with white pants and no shirt who sang but didn't play guitar, and a guy in shorts and a little jacket who ran and slid and sprawled and duckwalked all over the stage playing guitar but never singing.

Ian didn't answer. We rode a bus back downtown to Dad's apartment. Cotton still bulged from his ears. Nobody said anything. The following day we found an ad from the previous Sunday's news-paper and saw, listed below the much larger lurid signature of Ted Nugent, the letters "AC" and "DC" with a lightning bolt between them. We weren't sure what this meant, but we walked over word-lessly to the Crazy Eddie's on Sixth Avenue, Dad coming with us, and checked the A section of Rock. We found some albums with the lightning-bolt-split letters. My stomach twisted with my first glance of an album cover that showed a guy in shorts and a lit-tle jacket, bloodily impaled by a guitar, a shirtless man behind him mashing a microphone against his mouth. The sinking feel-ing increased when we saw a song title on another album that had words that we clearly remembered being repeatedly growled and screamed the night before, obviously not by Ted Nugent. Sin City.

"Fuck, fuck, *fuck*," my brother said. His eyes darted around like everything hurt to look at. I thought he was going to break the al-bum in half. On the cover the guy in shorts and jacket was being electrocuted. Finally Ian glared for a couple seconds at Dad, who was standing a few feet away, his glasses off, his squinting face about a millimeter from the small print on the back of a package of batteries.

Topps 1977 #317: Kurt Bevacqua

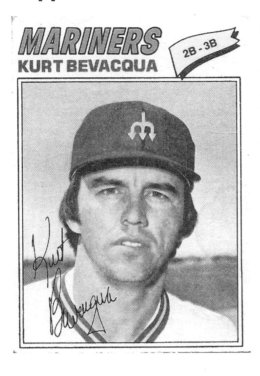

In 1979, I didn't get any Carl Yastrzemski cards. It was my first Yazless year since 1976, when I'd sent him my plea for an autograph. I kept buying packs, hoping to find Yaz. I also kept hoping to find Yaz in the mail. I checked every day for a reply, as I'd been doing for years, even though I knew such a thing was by now impossible.

What happens when reasonable hoping turns to something else? A ritual, a tic, religion, addiction. I was someone who waited until what I was waiting for began to belong to some whole other world. I was someone who was no longer satisfied with just one or two packs. I was someone who needed to keep shoving more and more gum into my mouth.

Three years earlier, my first Yazless year, Topps had included a special card in its 1976 set that showed the winner of a 1975 bubble-blowing competition among major leaguers. I never got the card myself, but my brother did and showed it to me.

"Whoa," I said.

"A bubble that big," my brother said, "is *impossible*."

The bubble was larger than the player's head. The jaws of a set of calipers strained to their breaking point, measuring the fragile, magnificent orb.

"*Kurt*," I read aloud, but then I stopped.

How did you even pronounce the last name of the one man who could do something no other human being could? The unusual collision of consonants near the end was beyond my still-growing reading abilities. I looked to my brother.

"Bevacqua," he said.

"Bevacqua," I whispered.

In 1979, I may or may not have noticed that Kurt Bevacqua seemed to have vanished. I didn't get a Kurt Bevacqua card that year or the year before. The last time I'd seen Kurt Bevacqua was in 1977, in a card that showed him to be adrift in a blurry, ethereal netherworld, wearing, or appearing to wear, the doctored cap and uniform of an expansion team that had yet to officially exist and for whom he would never play a single game. Behind him, the lifeless, bulldozed plain of a landfill, or perhaps a dormant spring training complex stripped of all its accessories. No batting cages, no pitching machines, no stands, no bases. All in all, Kurt Bevacqua seemed to be in the process of passing through some sort of veil separating the Big Leagues from the Great Beyond. He didn't seem pleased.

"What the fuck is going on?" he seemed to be saying.

The statistics on the back of Kurt Bevacqua's 1977 card supported the notion that he was vanishing. In the just-concluded 1976 season, perhaps worn out from blowing world-record bubbles, he struggled for playing time with the last-place Milwaukee Brewers, hitting .143 in an achingly paltry seven at bats. He was in his late twenties, too old to be a prospect (if he ever had been). As he rode the pine and watched his teammates rack up 95 losses, it must have at some point occurred to Bevacqua that he may not be long for the world he'd come to know. I imagine Kurt Bevacqua asking himself the inverse of the famous anthem of the big time, "New York, New York": *If I can't make it here, how can I make it anywhere?* Maybe a feeling of doom began to infiltrate the ever-wider spaces between at bats. Maybe a hazy sensation began to prevail. Maybe things that once seemed inarguably solid started to seem no sturdier than the flimsiest *maybe.* Maybe he sat on the bench trying to grip the handle of the primary tool of his trade and strange new doubts began to form.

My bat, thought Kurt Bevacqua, *is turning to fucking mist.*

One morning in early September 1979, I walked with my brother through a dense early morning fog, the whole world vanished except for us. I knew the way, because we were walking toward the elementary school near our house, the one I'd gone to for years. But I wouldn't be going inside the school anymore. It was my first day of seventh grade, and we were walking to where the bus would pick us up and take us over the mountain to the sprawling concrete structure that included the junior high and high school. I was scared. I picked up a rock and threw it into the smoky whiteness. It must have landed in the grass of the pasture I knew was out there, but I didn't hear anything.

"Hey," I said to the pasture. "Hey!"

"Shut the fuck up," Ian said. Then he said more softly, "I mean, shut up."

We were getting closer to the school but I still couldn't see it.

"Maybe the Red Sox can still come back," I began, "if they get on a r—"

"Quit dreaming," Ian said.

I knew he was right. For the first time since my Yazless year of 1976, the Red Sox weren't even in the race. Everything had been reduced to individual records. Every man for himself.

The familiar school building finally came into view, barely more substantial than the fog. We stopped at the edge of the parking lot and started waiting. I pulled a slip of paper from my pocket. It had my name on it and all my classes and the times they began and ended. My stomach began to hurt. I put the paper back in my pocket.

"Maybe Rice or Lynn can still win the Triple Crown," I said. They were both having great individual seasons.

"Quit dreaming," Ian said. He squinted into the fog in the direction the bus would be coming from. I thought about the one part of the 1979 season that still had meaning. Nobody could deny it.

"Well, at least Yaz—" I said.

"Can you please just maybe be quiet?" Ian said, and edged farther away from me.

"Here it comes," he added.

I didn't see anything, but I heard a deep grinding and groaning from the center of the fog. Then the huge flat face of the school bus appeared, its two eyes blazing.

In 1976, my brother and I had gazed together at Kurt Bevacqua's impossible feat, and together we had begun trying to approach him. For a while, his contest-winning deed could not possibly have loomed larger in our minds. It existed at the nexus of practically everything we loved most: baseball, sugary candy, the whole 1970s proliferation of crazes, most specifically the 1970s Guinness Book of World Records mania for transforming nonsensical trivialities into celebrated, numinous significance. Kurt Bevacqua and his otherworldly utterance in bubble gum anchored the glittering parade of freaks and fads and the just plain fantastic, taking the place of highest honor among such indelible figures as the man with the world's longest fingernails, the man who pulled locomotives with his teeth, the man named Robert who was so tall he seemed doomed to unbearable loneliness, the other man named Robert who was so fat—even fatter than the fattest twins in the world, that famed cowboy-hatted, motorbike-puttering twosome—that when he died he had to be lifted from his house by crane and buried in a crate big enough to transport a grand piano.

Kurt Bevacqua's bubble was at first as unapproachable as any of the impossibilities made real in the pages of the Guinness Book of World Records, but as the years went on my brother and I got better and better at blowing bubbles, learning to whisper breaths with increasing subtlety into the fragile, pendulous globe that grew like a second featureless head from our own kissing lips. If either of us had a good bubble going, and the other was in another room in the house, the bubble blower would carefully make his way to the room where the other was and alert him to the possible Bevacqua-equaling extrusion with an urgent, if necessarily soft, moaning sound in the throat. The other would look up from the comic book or TV show he was absorbed in and honor the possibly earthshaking significance of the moment with an almost prayerful silence.

We never quite got to Bevacqua, however, the bubble always popping just before immortality arrived, and my brother's interest in such things gradually waned. By 1979, it had disappeared altogether, and I was left to pursue Bevacqua in solitude, understanding even as I did so that I was childish, uncool, an understanding that made the ritual feel even more solitary than it already was.

I had to be in a certain exact place at a certain exact time. There was the schedule with my name on it and all my classes and the times they began and ended. There were bells to move everyone along. There was a locker with a combination I had to remember. There was no more wandering or lazing around making sarcastic remarks from a beanbag chair.

Meanwhile, as the 1979 season drew toward a close, Carl Yastrzemski chased the most hallowed career benchmark for hitters: 3,000 hits. If he could do it, he would be in the record books forever, an immortal beyond all doubt. I checked the box scores. I listened to the games.

"Come on, Yaz," I was thinking.

After looking earlier in the year like he was going to soar past the mark by midseason, Yaz fell into a prolonged slump that slowed his quest to an agonizing crawl.

"Come on, *Yaz*."

I started getting homework. I ignored the assignments. I started getting numbers written in red pen at the tops of quizzes and tests. This is exactly what you are, the numbers said. You are nothing special, they said.

"Come on, Yaz."

After finally scratching out his 2,999th safety, Yaz fell into a hitless trance. Planes circled overhead, trailing premature congratulatory banners. Cameras flashed all over the sold-out ballpark again and again, recording the continuing failures of an ashen-faced batter suddenly so rigid he seemed to be turning to stone.

"I just wish it were over," he told reporters.

The longer Yaz's increasingly inglorious pursuit of the record went on, the more I wanted him to achieve the immortal mark heroically, with a massive game-winning home run deep into the right-field stands, or somehow even out of the park altogether. It should shatter windows. It should stop traffic. It should make the whole world stagger and quake.

A few weeks after Yaz finally got it over with, late in a lopsided meaningless game, by pulling an ordinary grounder just past the opposing second baseman's glove, I got my first-ever report card. The grades were like the statistics of a player who is probably not going to be around much longer.

My mom was called into school, and all my seventh-grade teachers sat in a circle of chairdesks around her and took turns describing my incompetence. I can see her at this meeting, slumping in her own chairdesk, staring at the linoleum, her arms crossed tight over her stomach. Both she and Tom had gotten regular jobs by then. To hear about me from my teachers, my mom had to take half a personal day from her new position writing and editing technical manuals.

"He's so withdrawn," one of the teachers says.

"He definitely gives the impression that he doesn't want to be here," says another.

"It's almost like he wants to disappear," says another.

One afternoon when Mom and Tom were still at work and my brother was at junior varsity basketball practice, I sat on my brother's bed and opened my three last packs of 1979 cards. I shoved the gum from all three packs in my mouth and chewed for a while as I sorted through cards that included neither the latest member of the 3,000-hit club nor the 1975 Joe Garagiola/Bazooka Bubble Gum Blowing Champ. I blew a few preliminary bubbles, then stood and walked over to my side of the room and looked out the window at a driveway empty but for the rusted van at the far edge, surrounded by weeds, a chimney sticking out its roof. Then, slowly, gently, I blotted out my view with a bubble that in another time would have made my brother whisper, "Bevacqua."

Topps 1980 #573: Kent Tekulve

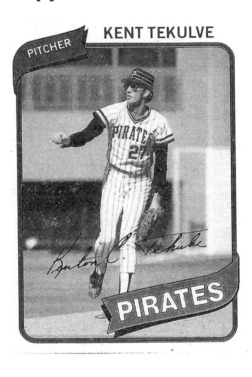

That summer, I had come upon a term in Louis L'Amour's novel *Hondo* that may have changed my life, although maybe my life was moving unstoppably in the direction of that term anyway. Hondo, this tan, unshaven, high-cheekboned guy who slept on the hard ground under the stars and engaged in knife fights with bloodthirsty Apaches and occasionally swooped down from parched mesas to rescue beautiful defenseless women from the clutches of bad guys out on the most brutal fringes of the nineteenth-century American West, was characterized at one point in the narrative as a *loner*. I clearly remember what I thought upon reading this: *When I grow up I want to be a loner.* It seemed tough, mysterious, admirable, invulnerable. You'd occasionally ride into town for your grim, manly supplies, your oats and pemmican and lye soap and bullets, and people would look at you with awe, respect, even envy.

Within a couple months of reading *Hondo*, while getting my first taste of junior high, I started to understand the realistic dimensions of the life of a loner. I sat in the back of classrooms, saying little, my homework undone, looking forward mostly to the Fudgsicle I would eat at lunch. My circle of friends dwindled to a few thin, equally myopic acquaintances that I sat with at a mostly empty corner table of the cafeteria, taking turns flicking paper footballs through one another's thumb-uprights. Outside of school, I leaned on baseball as much as I ever had, despite my brother's increasing disinterest. I was a baseball-loving loner. I could not have been more primed for the arrival in my consciousness of relief ace Kent Tekulve.

Kent Tekulve didn't seem to have anything at all in common with his fellow Pirates, that loud and vibrant collective rolling toward the last and perhaps most emblematic World Championship of the whole hairy, careening decade. The tightly knit Pittsburgh club embraced the infectious disco hit "We Are Family" as their theme song, but in that family Kent Tekulve seemed to be the odd sullen cousin who sat in the far corner at weddings, ominously fiddling below the table with the open blade of his Swiss Army knife as the rest of his extended brood clogged the dance floor laughing. He was a gray crayon in a box of multicolored Crayolas, an undernourished pigeon in the vestibule of a birds of paradise exhibit, a narrow tray of oatmeal on a buffet line otherwise bursting with towering, flamboyant culinary delectations. While Tim Foli and Phil Garner turned double plays with the polished harmony of the barbershop quartet their old-time mustaches suggested they were a part of, and strapping sluggers Dave Parker and Willie Stargell worked together to bash in runs as if swinging John Henry sledgehammers in steel-driving rhythm, and everyone in the dugout laughed and strutted and slapped five like they'd just come offstage from a sweaty, glittering ass-shaking gig with George Clinton and the P-Funk All-Stars, Kent Tekulve lurked far away in the dank, shadowy bullpen, waiting to be summoned in those rare nervous moments when all the boisterous shouts of joy shrank to troubled murmurs. This is the fantasy of all real loners: that one day the world that has shunned them, and that they have shunned, will come to them desperate for help. And that they will then stride to the very center of the predicament and, despite their thick glasses and bulging Adam's apple and mathematician wrists and ungainly, unmanly submarine delivery, earn widespread grateful weeping adoration for extinguishing the dire threat and saving the day.

Topps 1981 #29: Darryl Dawkins

CENTER
DARRYL DAWKINS
76ers

My brother no longer cared as much as I did about the likes of Kent Tekulve or Kurt Bevacqua or baseball cards or baseball in general. When he'd first entered puberty he'd found a new sport, one that better suited him in terms of all the changes he was going through, primarily his rapidly elongating limbs but also—in the new favorite game's quicker, more jagged rhythms, its intensity, its violence, its promise of flight—his mercurial moods. I liked shooting baskets with Ian on the hoop Tom had nailed to the garage, but I dreaded the moment when we would go from just fooling around to playing an actual game of one-on-one, Ian bowling me over for layups and blotting out the sky whenever I attempted to score. Nonetheless, the moment I got a chance to follow Ian into organized basketball, I did.

My seventh-grade team played its first game in November 1979. I don't remember the exact date, but it could have been November 4, the day 66 Americans were taken hostage in Iran. It could also have been a few days later, November 13, when Darryl Dawkins shattered a glass backboard with a dunk.

In retrospect, the former date was certainly more significant, punctuating not only a bad year (which had already included Three Mile Island and Skylab) but an entire decade of unprecedented American impotence and defeat. But the Dawkins backboard-shattering dunk made much more of an impact on me, especially since he repeated the feat a couple weeks later. He was a rampaging monster who could not be stopped. My brother seemed to share my awe.

"There aren't going to be any backboards left," I said. I was hovering near the edge of Ian's side of the room, close enough to see that the newspaper spread out on his bed was open to a story about Dawkins.

"The guy is nuts," Ian said. "He says he's from the planet Lovetron."

It had become a rarity that my brother and I would riff on something together. I was hesitant to say anything more about Dawkins for fear that I would blurt something stupid and childish and slam the door on the conversation before it even began. But I couldn't help myself. Darryl Dawkins was just too much.

"I hear he names all his dunks," I said.

"I know," Ian said. He got up and I thought for a second that I had said something boring that everyone knows and that Ian was getting up to leave the room. But he went to a corner of the room near the door and dug out the little orange Nerf ball from under some laundry. He walked back in my direction, passed me, and dunked the ball through the plastic orange hoop near his bed.

"The In Your Face Disgrace," he said.

The ball rolled to me. I picked it up and did my own dunk.

"The Go-rilla," I said. Ian grabbed the ball before it hit the floor.

"The Look Out Belooooow," he called, like he was yelling across a canyon. He used his right hand to slow-motion pile drive me into the cheap seats (I slow-motion fell down onto his bed) and then he slammed the ball through with his left.

I was giggling as I rose from the bed. So was he. We both reached for the ball and clonked heads.

"Gah!" I said, laughing.

"Out the way, fool!" Ian said, then he picked up the ball and bounded all the way to the far side of the room and then bounded back, all in slow motion like it was a highlight. He pretended to dribble, rocking his shoulder hilariously like a Muppet strutting with a cane.

"This one's the Greyhound Bus," he said, "because I'm going coast to *coast!*" He dunked it on the last word.

I had to sit down I was laughing so hard. I looked at the article and tried to read aloud the name of Dawkins's most famous dunk, the first one to shatter a backboard. For the record, Dawkins dubbed this cultural treasure (which referenced first his own nickname and then the last name of the big stiff guarding him) the Chocolate-Thunder Flying, Robinzine-Crying, Teeth-Shaking, Glass-Breaking, Rump Roasting, Bun Toasting, Wham-Bam-I-Am Jam. But all I could get out was the word "Chocolate" before bursting into hysterics. My brother was laughing, too, so hard that he also had to crumple down onto his bed. This went on for a while, but eventually Ian ran out of laughs and started looking at the article again as I continued to convulse with giggly aftershocks.

"Whew," I said. "Heh."

"Bam," Ian said, looking at a photo in the article of the magnificent wreckage, glass flying everywhere.

"Shit, I want to dunk it so bad," he added quietly.

"Chomentowski can dunk, can't he?" I asked. This was the budding star on the varsity team.

"It's because his hands are so big," Ian said. "His deadfinger is lethal."

I already knew that the deadfinger was a famed invention of Chomentowski and the other varsity guys, and it was when you turned your ring finger into a whip dangling down from your fist and then whacked someone in the arm or neck or head, but my brother demonstrated on me again anyway.

"Fuck!" I said.

"I can touch the net," I said, rubbing the deadfinger wound on my shoulder. This was true only because one of the nets in the junior high gym had started to unravel and a strand was hanging down.

"I can touch the rim," Ian bragged. "I can grab the rim, actually. I tomahawked a volleyball."

"Wow," I said. Many years later, I might have been able to tell that he was beginning to cycle up and away from the truth. But then I believed everything he told me, especially if it contained the element of flight.

"It was no big deal," he said.

"Did a lot of people see?" I said. "You must have been skying. Did you—"

"Fuck, don't wet your pants," Ian said. He turned the page and started reading another article. "I already told you, it was nothing."

My seventh-grade team lost its first game by a couple points, then lost its second game by a few points, its third game by several, and so on. We would lose every game that year.

Many of the pummelings were punctuated by my glasses getting raked off my face. This would generally happen during struggles for a rebound that bore a resemblance to the battle captured on the lone Darryl Dawkins card in my collection, part of my exceedingly brief and desultory foray into collecting basketball cards that occurred a couple years after my basketball career began. In the Dawkins card scenario, I was spindly Kevin Grevey, awkwardly reaching for a ball far beyond my grasp while getting gratuitously drilled in the base of my spine by Doug Collins. I would be losing my glasses in the next moment, as one or both of the opposing team's board-dominating behemoths semi-accidentally lowered their elbows into my face.

After a few of these incidents my frames finally broke, and from then on each spectacles-related calamity entailed both of my lenses dislodging from the frames and skittering across the floor. The ref eventually blew his whistle and members of both teams got down on their knees to locate the frame and lenses for me, at which point I'd then go to the bench and wrap more adhesive tape around them while my coach, a much-beloved youth league icon named Mick, rubbed his eye sockets with the heels of his hand in the manner of someone with a migraine.

My team was, as far as I could tell, Mick's first-ever losing team, which made me ashamed. Worse, I started to suspect that I was bad luck, the reason any given team might lose. I'd watched Mick coach my brother's good seventh- and eighth-grade teams, and I'd been on the losing end of several severe baseball diamond beatings by Mick's dynastic little league squad, the Yankees. I had always wished that Mick could have been my little league coach, since it seemed that everything he touched turned to gold.

Mick was revered as a great teacher of sports, especially baseball. His little league team was always getting the jump on everybody else, having preseason training camps inside gymnasiums during those never-ending weeks in Vermont when the calendar says spring but snow and freezing rain keep pounding down. Mick was dedicated, even umpiring all the games his team wasn't playing in, which probably also allowed him to probe for weaknesses among the opposition. Contrary to the clichéd image of the dominant, red-faced, win-at-all-costs little league dictator, Mick was actually quite soft-spoken and mild, though he also was able to carry an air of authority about him. I was far from the only kid who wasn't on his team who wished he was.

But the real key to his success, at least in the commonly held view, which mixed admiration with envy, was that unlike other little league managers who just picked names out of a hat when it came time to draft new nine-year-olds every year, Mick "scouted." I was never exactly sure what this scouting entailed, but I envisioned Mick pulling up to playgrounds, his car idling as he looked out from beneath his cool big league flip-down sunglasses in hopes of spotting some natural talent. I'd often wished that I'd been one of his finds.

Yes, much later, long after I'd moved away from that town, Mick was imprisoned for molesting one of his little league players. He had been victimizing children for many years, all the way back to my time. In fact, when I was in seventh grade there was a rumor that a kid on my terrible basketball team, let's call him Wayne, had claimed that while on a camping trip with Mick he'd been woken in the middle of the night by the sensation of the coach's mouth on his dick.

"No way," I said to this nauseating rumor.

"Wayne's a liar!" said another kid hearing the rumor for the first time.

"Wayne is so full of shit his eyes are brown," another kid agreed.

The whole thing was just impossible. Mick was the best!

Mick never asked me to come on one of his camping trips, a stroke of good fortune that I attribute to my ineptitude. He was drawn to good athletes. Wayne was a good athlete. And the one time Mick did do something to me that felt odd was late in that winless seventh-grade season, right after I'd stumbled into an impersonation of a good athlete and sunk two shots in a row. Mick subbed for me after my second basket and sat down next to me as play resumed. He was beaming.

"You're doing great, Josh, just *excellent*," he said, which felt good. I wasn't exactly amassing a giant stockpile of praise elsewhere in my life. As Mick spoke he let his hand fall on my bare leg. He kept it there after he'd finished talking. While watching the action on the court, he gave my thigh two long, ardent squeezes.

Not that I knew the word *ardent* at that time. In fact, I couldn't have put any words at all to that moment. Darryl Dawkins had a name for each and every one of his world-rocking dunks. I didn't have a name for anything. I didn't take any more shots that game, and when I got home the only thing I told anyone was that we lost.

1980 Topps #697 David Clyde

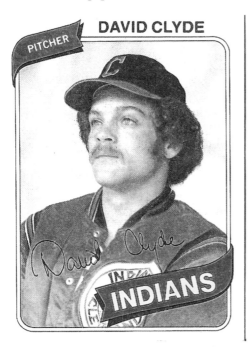

DAVID CLYDE

PITCHER

INDIANS

Earlier that season, before I knew for sure that we were never going to win, my team got off to a shaky but not utterly hopeless start in an opponent's cold, near-empty gym. It was a Saturday morning. For some reason Mick wasn't there to coach us that day. Maybe his eighth-grade team, a much more successful squad, had a game somewhere else. The young guy who filled in for him, Duncan, was in his early twenties. Like the young man pictured on this baseball card, Duncan had a sparse mustache and a dazed, faintly melancholy air. As he stared out at the action, he kept gumming his mustache with his lower lip, as if to keep making sure it hadn't evaporated. If he was anything like I would be when I got to be that age, he had taken up residence in the tenuous shadowlands of *maybe*. Maybe everything will be OK. Maybe it's not too late. Maybe what's gone can return.

Maybe in this baseball card a painted backdrop of a fake blue sky was wheeled in to cover the mildewed bricks of a windowless room deep within the Cleveland Indians' spring training barracks. Maybe this room was where the oft-disabled former number one draft pick David Clyde preferred to endure his daylight hours. Maybe the backdrop belonged to a photographer who, until his struggling business began cracking under the weight of unwholesome rumors that included the word *statutory*, made his living creating disquietingly impassioned portraits of high school seniors. Maybe the photographer had fled to Arizona with a U-Haul full of his yearbook-picture backdrops to start anew, and to avoid temptation he had steered clear altogether of wistful teenagers, instead picking up freelance work involving the negligible subjects that the pensioned, fully vested Topps photographers preferred to avoid.

When he was young, David Clyde, nationwide high school sensation, had been the opposite of a subject to avoid. He had been a sure thing, literally unbeatable, 18–0 his senior year, his left arm like something out of an old Greek myth, golden, invincible, blessed by the gods. The media swarmed. The scouts came running. But then for many years he knew little but disappointment, pain, unstoppable descent. Maybe he knew at the time this photo was taken that it was over, that he had already pitched his last major league game. Maybe on the other hand he was thinking that maybe everything would be OK. Maybe it wasn't too late. Maybe what's gone *can* return.

Maybe after the shoot he and the photographer gravitated toward one another, as those reduced to maybes sometimes do. Maybe they went for beers and shots at the topless joint out by the abandoned A&W on the frontage road. Maybe they knew enough to stay silent throughout, neither asking the other any questions about the past.

Early in the second quarter, just after the teams switched baskets, Duncan called a timeout. We huddled around him. He lower-lipped his mustache while looking over our heads and up at the scoreboard.

"Things are starting to get away from us," he said. "But look. We've still got a shot, maybe." When he lowered his gaze from the scoreboard, his eyes happened to fall on me, and they stayed on me as he said, "But we've got to make something happen right now."

I understood he would have looked at someone else if he'd known anything about our team, but it still made me feel good that he addressed his words to me. I stared back at him and nodded. The buzzer sounded. A thought occurred to me as I retook the court. It made my whole body tingle.

Maybe we can win.

The ref handed my teammate Chris the ball and Chris slapped it with his right hand, a signal to the rest of us to start milling around, pretending we had set plays. In a rare burst of on-court assertiveness, I cut hard to my left, breaking free of the listless scrum of bodies near the center jump circle. I caught the inbounds pass in stride and started dribbling toward the wide-open hoop. I had not yet scored the first basket of my career in organized ball, so as I dribbled a kind of joy bubbled up through my rib cage and into my throat.

Previous to that moment there had only been an aimless Saturday morning murmur of voices in the gym. Suddenly the murmur spiked, went weird. I'd never heard the sound before and hope to never hear it again: A generalized, ingrown gasp, like a note from a choir on a record played backward. I pressed onward, dribbling, still preposterously open, ignoring.

I stopped just inside the foul line and hoisted the side-holstered push shot that all kids use before they get the hang of a real jump shot. Improbably, the basketball grazed the inside of the rim and nestled through the net. The strange sound that had risen up all around me ceased. I turned, smiling, expecting to see my teammates smiling back. Jesus, the look on their faces. The look on Duncan's face. My own smile congealed. The players on the other team stared one more beat, still stunned, then started spasming with laughter. Eventually the scoreboard operator, also laughing, added the tally to the swelling number beneath the word HOME.

Topps 1980 #169: Luis Gomez

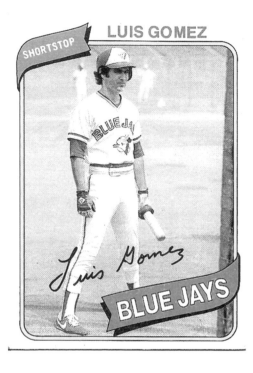

Is life a battle between good and evil or an inconsequential rest stop between oblivions? Consider Luis Gomez, the expansion team benchwarmer, waiting slack-armed for his turn in the batting cage, where he will likely have only enough time to practice bunting before a Blue Jay regular commands him to step aside. As he waits for this truncated, ignominious turn, two blurry figures hover above his narrow shoulders, each figure perfectly positioned to whisper into an ear. But what could these indistinct spirits possibly have to say to Luis Gomez? In his eight-year major league career, the utility infielder batted .210 with a .261 on-base percentage and a .239 slugging percentage. He never hit a home run. He stole 6 bases but was thrown out trying to steal 22 times. Once he was called on to pitch in a bullpen-savaging blowout. He gave up three runs in one inning. In his final game he batted eighth in the order, just above the pitcher's spot, for a lineup that was one-hit by Mario Soto. The last of Gomez's fruitless at bats was a pop-up that whimpered to extinction in the glove of the opposing shortstop. He stands here somewhere in the middle of that featureless career, waiting for a couple weak swings in the cage, and the two entities hovering near his ears seem incapable of making themselves understood. They will only mutter as they fade, the two voices indistinguishable from one another, no guidance, no angel and devil, no choice between paths, no paths at all, or maybe infinite paths, all of them leading to dissolution.

Topps 1976 #550: Hank Aaron

HANK AARON
DES. HITTER BREWERS

As I understand it, the term *mint* is used in the hobby of baseball card collecting to describe cards that have been utterly sheltered from life and its inevitable slide toward deterioration. There are other gradations below this topmost designation, but I doubt if there is a label far enough removed from mint to describe the select group of cards, my favorites, that I touched more than I touched anything else in my life. My incessant childhood pawings pushed these cards beyond the limits of the language of commerce, dulling and creasing their surfaces, corroding their edges, blunting their corners. In a monetary sense, these beloved cards have been nullified. Reduced to nothing. Handled too much, clung to too tightly. The absolute opposite of mint.

These were the cards that I kept going back to. I searched for them in their rubber-band-wrapped team, needing to touch them again and again. I needed to see, and say, the hallowed names. I needed to read and further internalize the rows upon rows of hallowed numbers in tiny type. I needed to know there is greatness in the world. There are things that won't be forgotten.

I sensed at times that I was an infinitesimally small speck, inconsequential and frail in an unfathomably large expanse of space and time. The universe went on forever and time stretched forward and backward forever and I was an almost-nothing within it. All my cards pushed back against this almost-nothing. They were *something*. The final card, from 1976, of Hank Aaron, the Home Run King, was the very pinnacle of this feeling, this *something*. Four years after I found it in a pack, I had begun to lose my grasp on the gods. That year, 1980, would be my last full year of collecting baseball cards. But I continued to cling to Hank Aaron with all my ruinous might.

I looked forward to little league that year more than ever. It was my last year of eligibility. It was the most important part of my life.

A few weeks before the season started, my father gave me a diary for my twelfth birthday. The hard cover had been made to look like denim, and there were a couple of gnomes on it. In fact, it was called a Gnome Gnotebook. I thought it was stupid and babyish. Gnomes? I wanted to ask my dad if he thought I was an infant.

"Thanks, Dad," I said.

"You must write something every day," he said. "The creative life is the most worthwhile existence available."

"OK," I said, exactly as if I were agreeing to brush my teeth after eating a box of M&Ms. I didn't touch the thing for weeks, until the evening after the first practice of my last season in little league. I had recently read Sparky Lyle's hilarious book, *The Bronx Zoo*, which had been written in the style of a diary, and I've always thought that my life as a would-be writer began with me hoping that the moment I put pencil to page I'd find myself involved in uproarious locker-room cake-sitting hijinks and riveting controversies and a white-knuckled all-important struggle for a pennant. And that was and always would be a big part of it, that desire to somehow make my thin, meandering life as meaningful as something in a book. And another big part of it was having a father, and an entire family, that believed that writing something every day was worthwhile. But I think I also started writing for the same reason that the Hudson River School of painters of the nineteenth century started creating giant romantic canvases depicting untrammeled American wilderness at the very moment that wilderness was beginning to disappear.

I don't know the exact words I used to describe that season, because several years later, in a fit of frustration, I hurled the gnomes and all my other writing notebooks into a Dumpster. But I think my first sentence went as follows: "I couldn't lay my glove let alone my bat on anything today."

Sometimes I wish I still had that Gnome Gnotebook, but it probably couldn't tell me much I don't already know. I know I didn't come close to writing daily updates throughout the season, my entries tailing off the moment I realized that writing about life didn't suddenly and automatically make it more interesting. I know the first time I ripped the Gnotebook in half was later, the following year, when for the first time I tried and failed to untangle my thoughts about a girl. I know when my junior high basketball team, bolstered by the addition of an older, bigger kid who'd been left back, finally broke through and won a game, barely, halfway through eighth grade, I cut off a small lock of my hair and taped it to a page.

My brother, who loved Hank Aaron even more than I did, had a poster above his bed of the moment when Hank Aaron became the career major league leader in home runs. The poster showed the whole field. If I remember it correctly, the pitcher, Al Downing, was still following through, as was Hank Aaron, and the other players on the field were craning their heads to follow the path of the ball. The most memorable feature of the poster was the small white circle superimposed on the photograph to highlight the location of the ball. Without it, you wouldn't notice the pale blur in the sky above the outfield. You wouldn't notice the most amazing thing of all time. Sometimes you need to see the halo.

In that last little league season of mine, the usually dominant team helmed by my seventh grade basketball coach, Mick, was suddenly awful. Mick's Yankees had won the league title the first three years I'd been in little league, while my team, the Mets, had gone 9–6, 6–9, and 6–9, two of the losses in each of those years horrific blowouts at the hands of Mick's crack squad. There was no mercy rule then, so they beat the shit out of us until it got too dark to see, final scores usually somewhere in the neighborhood of 37–2.

But in my fourth and final year, another 6–9 trudge for the Mets, Mick's team was terrible, though somehow even this got framed in professional-seeming terms, the Yankees "rebuilding" instead of just sucking. I guess Mick's scouting had temporarily failed him. Who knows, maybe he had tried to break certain habits for a while, vowing to stay away from playgrounds. All I know, or need to know, is that we finally got our chance, for once, to kick their fucking ass. There was a moment in that ass-kicking that needs a halo.

The first person I wanted to tell was my brother. When I got home from the game I went to find him. He was lying on his bed, reading one of his science fiction books, the Hank Aaron poster on the wall above him.

"I did it," I said. I was still in my uniform. I had my glove on, and I pounded it with my fist.

"Hey!" I said. My brother looked up.

"I did it! Against the *Yankees*. I smacked a fucking homer!"

Ian's eyes widened.

You?

It wasn't the reaction I was looking for.

"An inside-the-parker?" Ian asked.

"No, a real one," I said. "Gone."

"Wow," Ian said. "That's great."

He went back to reading. I walked to my side of the room and started unbuttoning my uniform. But then I stopped. I didn't want to take it off. I rebuttoned the top buttons and kneeled down and pulled out my baseball cards. There was one in particular I wanted to see, yet again, the one with more home runs on the back of it than any baseball card had ever had.

Since I was not as big or as good as my brother, and since I was so obviously flawed, and since I wore glasses (nobody who hit home runs wore glasses), I had always assumed that hitting a home run was beyond my reach. Though I was an okay hitter for average, I'd never even hit a ball off the fence. But my at bat against the Yankees provided the perfect storm—a straight medium-fast pitch right down the middle from a talented but undeveloped nine-year-old, Mike LaRocque, a good swing by me, perfect contact, and then about an inch clearance both over the chain-link left-field fence and to the right of the short metal foul pole. The more mythic little league heroes pounded their homers into the river a hundred feet beyond the center-field fence, but so what? If I knew anything from my baseball cards, it was that a home run was a home run.

I didn't really understand what had happened until I saw the infield ump circling his finger in the air. I staggered around the bases with a huge dumb grin on my face, and at home plate all my teammates mobbed me.

If I could take one moment from my life and save it from erosion and degradation, from the diminishing repetition of need, I'd choose that at bat. I'd start the memory as I was walking toward the batter's box and end it with me stomping on home plate as my teammates laughed and screamed and pummeled me. In other words, if I had a halo, I'd use it to mint those angelic seconds when I was Henry Louis Aaron.

Topps 1980 #450: George Brett

GEORGE BRETT
★A.L. ALL-STAR★
3rd BASE
ROYALS

I bought more cards in 1980 then I ever had or ever would. I read the box scores in 1980 closer than I ever had or ever would. I studied the Sunday averages more intently than I ever had or ever would, reading every name and number from the bottom of the list to the top, where George Brett was flying higher than anyone I'd ever seen.

Brett had been rising higher and higher since I'd been paying attention, but in the summer of 1980 he reached yet another, unthinkable level. Ty Cobb hit .400. Rogers Hornsby hit .400. Nap Lajoie hit .400. Dead guys hit .400. Men from the age of color photography did not hit .400. And yet, here he was, alive and kicking: George Brett!

That spring, a kid in my grade boasted to me that he'd lured two girls from our school into one of our town's many gravel pits one night. He claimed they had both insisted on ripping off their shirts, at which point he discovered that the brown-haired girl's nipples were brown while the blonde girl's nipples were white, a notion that confused and excited me.

Since my first failed try the day the book appeared on my brother's bed, I had continued periodically trying and failing to follow the directions in *The Big Book of Teenage Answers* for producing ejaculate. The day I heard the gravel pit tale I went home and gave it another shot. I closed my eyes as I got going and envisioned myself in the gravel pit with the two girls standing in front of me in button-down shirts. I unbuttoned the brown-haired girl's shirt first, because she was prettier, but it wasn't until I was imagining putting my tongue to the salty white nipple of the somewhat homely blonde girl that a hot flush shot through my body and I produced, in a dribble, a rivulet of sticky substance that was not milky, as the book had said it would be, but clear.

I had stopped bringing my chocolate milk cup up from the kitchen every time I attempted to be what the book said was an ordinary teenage boy (not that a cup would have been of much use), so I used a pillowcase to wipe up, then jammed it under my mattress, where it or one of its relatives would reside, wet or encrusted or both, for the remainder of my increasingly private life in that house.

Over the summer I periodically put aside my cards and the Sunday averages to imagine myself in the gravel pit near our house, minding my own business, when a female would appear, approaching rapidly, as if she had something of great importance to tell me. Most often this female would be Cheryl Tiegs in her see-through fishnet bathing suit. Other popular gravel pit visitors were Lynda Carter decked out as Wonder Woman and carrying her truth lasso, Bailey and Jennifer from *WKRP in Cincinnati*, a teenaged cock-gobbling nymphomaniac from a *Penthouse Forum* letter that I'd somehow gotten my hands on who was described as having "tits like melons," and a scratchy-voiced girl from my grade who had appeared at school one spring day wearing a loose-fitting T-shirt that could not conceal that she suddenly also had *tits like melons*. And once in a while I imagined myself hanging around the gravel pit, chucking rocks at the little gravel pit caves that tiny birds flew in and out of, when all of a sudden from around the corner, running, would appear the biggest-breasted woman of them all, coming for me.

The year before, during the major league All-Star Game, George Brett had been voluptuously assaulted by this woman, Morganna the Kissing Bandit, a giant-chested blonde who periodically vaulted fences and ran across the field in the middle of major league games, her increasingly famous attributes cha-chonging wildly, to plant kisses on the faces of stars such as Pete Rose, Nolan Ryan, and Fred Lynn. George Brett, as far as I can figure, was the only man to have his work interrupted twice by the affectionate interloper.

Morganna, whose measurements were 60-23-39, epitomized a key element of my entire unsavory fantasy life that went even deeper than my gnawing desire to make contact with a large naked boob or two: Somehow, someday, a woman would run right at me and smother me with an almost carnivorous affection without my having to do

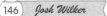

anything. The ache of puberty for me was the feeling that I existed at an impossible remove from any melon-baring deshirting, and my fantasies were as much about imagining the erasure of this infinite gap as they were about the brief guilt-laced physical euphoria they helped bring about. The image of Morganna galloping across a baseball field, of all places, to benevolently suffocate her prey with her uncontainable femininity is the Rosetta stone of all the fantasies from that summer of George Brett. In the scenarios I was the same as always, a kid whose life revolved around baseball, and then suddenly I'd be swept away by a version of sex no more complicated than a big warm wave. I wouldn't need to know anything or do anything. I could simply, passively, blissfully surrender.

After surrendering, it was back to the cards. I must have liked all the cards I got that summer, because I kept getting and getting, but I'm sure the cards in a pack that excited me the most were the ones with the word "ALL-STAR" emblazoned across the top, and of all those I can't imagine any card would have pleased me more than the one featuring the god currently soaring above the legendary .400 barrier.

Since the front of George Brett's 1980 card showed him in a moment of almost foreboding contemplation, I didn't spend much time gazing at it but instead flipped the card over immediately. The backs of the 1980 cards featured cartoons for the first time since 1977, and, even better, the cartoons referenced the player on the card instead of relating some random shred of baseball trivia. George Brett's cartoon had a caption that surely snagged my attention: "George is one of 4 baseball-playing brothers."

I would have showed it to my own brother but he no longer collected cards, so I was on my own to study the numbers. Brett's numbers for 1979 were thrilling: a .329 average and 42 doubles, 20 triples, and 23 home runs. Just looking at them was enough to get me thinking about Brett's team, the Royals, who had been a force in the American League since my love of baseball had begun, a speedy, slashing battalion of attackers that cut the Red Sox to ribbons whenever they ventured into the Royals' carpeted domain in Kansas City. As long as they weren't revealing the Red Sox as plodding, one-dimensional lunkheads, I loved envisioning the Royals in action, a dynamo of base-stealing, triple-ripping sprinters with Brett at the center, coiled low in his mystical Charlie Lau crouch and smashing anything and everything you tried to throw past him for gap-bound bases-clearing screamers.

That summer I had more time on my own than I'd ever had before, my brother off elsewhere whenever he could find a way, usually just using his thumb. Inside the house and out I made up solitaire baseball-based games involving whatever was at hand—a tennis ball, the ridges of the aluminum roof, a Nerf ball, a Wiffle Ball bat—and in those games I invented whole teams and leagues and narratives of unbearable suffering giving way to tearful limping indomitable triumph. Again and again I pitched to my knees with my arms raised like Bjorn Borg after finally fending off John McEnroe's monumental challenge at Wimbledon.

"Yes!" I cried out. Sometimes a tear or two actually streaked down my cheeks.

Before I reached that climax, I always included a Royals-like team of gazelle-thin doubles bashers somewhere in my fictional baseball world. The Red Sox were my team, and Yaz the central figure in my prayers, but when it came to fantasy I never channeled myself into the sullen lumbering carcasses of the Red Sox. To do so would be to stay within my world, within the confines of the reedy changing body I needed more and more often to escape.

Sometimes I asked my brother if I could go with him when he left the house. He said no again and again until I stopped asking. Then one day when I was kneeling on the floor of our room, looking at baseball cards, he tossed a Nerf ball at my head.

"You know how to hitchhike?" he said.

We walked through town and past the general store, not ducking in to buy any cards, and then we stopped at the corner, where a road branched off Route 14 and climbed up and out of our valley.

"Step One: always bring along a basketball," Ian said. "Then people know you're an all-American boy going to shoot some wholesome baskets instead of a maniac on angel dust who will knife them."

He didn't say this until we'd already been standing there for quite a while.

"What's angel dust?" I asked. A little later I asked, "Do cars ever come?"

"Step Two," he said. "Give up all hope of ever getting a ride ever." A minute or so later he added, "Because about two people live in this entire fucking valley."

A few minutes after that a car came down Route 14 and turned onto the road where we were standing. Ian cradled the basketball in his left arm and raised his right thumb up high. I stood behind him and kind of put my thumb up too. The car went on by.

"It's tougher with two people," Ian muttered. I thought about how close we were to the general store. I had a dollar, enough to buy four packs and go on home and shove all the gum into my mouth at once. Another truck approached. A guy in mirrored sunglasses leaned out the passenger-side window, his mouth hanging open in a smile, his tan elbow hanging down.

"Get a fucking car!" he yelled.

The driver leaned on the horn, which played "Dixie," like the General Lee.

"Fuck you!" my brother yelled as the truck disappeared over the rise. Its engine made an angry sound as it started climbing the mountain up and out of our town, away from us, a pack of hornets moving on. When the sound disappeared altogether Ian bounced the basketball once on the concrete. *Boing.* It made me think of the sharp, stunted echoes you hear in an utterly empty room.

"Step Three," my brother said. "This place is a shithole."

Topps 1980 #580: Nolan Ryan

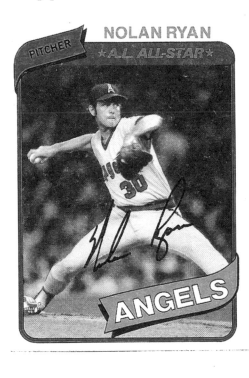

In July my teammates and I and all the other little leaguers marched in the parade down Main Street in Randolph, dressed in our uniforms, walking past cheering people with flags in their fists. The parade ended at the little league field, where every year there was a town-wide chicken barbecue picnic that coincided with an All-Star Game pitting the best twelve-year-olds from our town against a team of players from some surrounding towns. I had been selected to play in the game that year, which made me feel like a superstar even though just about any twelve-year-old boy in our town who had played all four years of little league made the All-Star Team. I didn't consider that at the time, however; instead, I focused on the dazzling word itself.

All-Star.

It emblazoned the best cards you could ever hope to find in a pack, and it called to mind the highlight of my and Ian's summer, our one chance to see all the All-Stars at once, many of them for the first time, their previously unknown skills astonishing. The power and the squat, Thing-like physique of slugger Greg "the Bull" Luzinski in 1977. The diving forkball of reliever Bruce Sutter in 1978. The cannon arm of right fielder Dave Parker in 1979. Most of all I thought about how Ian had once been a July 4 All-Star, and how I'd proudly watched him during that game, and how I would now play in the same game.

I didn't start but got one at bat halfway through the game and popped up to shallow center. I played right field the following half-inning. A batter dumped a base hit in front of me, and instead of stopping at first he tried for second. Unlike my brother, I'd not bloomed

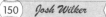

into a strong-armed pitcher in my final little league season, but after all the hours playing catch with Ian I could at least throw it fairly straight, and after I fielded the ball on a bounce I chucked it to our shortstop in time for him to apply the tag. By that time, I had already begun periodically narrating my life in my mind as it happened, combining a daydreaming loner's fuzzy disconnect with reality with an ever-growing treasury of sports terminology. *Gunned* was the not entirely accurate verb that immediately leapt to my narrating mind.

I gunned him out, I thought. *Just like Dewey Evans. Just like 1979 All-Star Game MVP Dave "Cobra" Parker.* I pounded my glove as I walked back to my position, sneaking a peek at the crowd, searching for my brother, wondering if he'd seen me unleash my *gun.*

Later, most of the people in town gathered in a field on the outskirts of Randolph and waited for night to fall. All of us went. Mom, Tom, Ian, me. I still had my uniform on, maybe because I knew when I took it off I'd never put it on again. Fireflies streaked in and around and above the clusters of people all over the darkening field, then bright explosions bloomed in the sky.

In August my brother let me come with him one day. We hitchhiked up and out of our valley to Randolph Center, where we snuck onto the grounds of Lake Champagne, avoiding the two-dollar entrance fee. We played a couple games of air hockey in the empty rec room, then moseyed on down to the lake and swam out to the empty dock in the middle. We lay there and the sun beat down on us, drying our bodies. I drifted off to a perfect golden version of sleep, then woke to the sound of a splash.

My brother was gone, but the wet ass-print of his cutoff jeans was still there on the wood of the dock, as was a trail of drops of water that must have fallen from the fringe of his cutoffs as he walked to the edge of the dock and jumped in. I got up and followed the trail of drops and didn't see him anywhere. If I didn't know the secret of the dock I would have thought it was magic or an awful tragedy. But I did know, so I jumped in and swam down under the dock to the secret air pocket underneath. My brother was there, floating in the muted light that filtered through the slats of the dock above.

"Yo," he said, his voice making a ripply echo.

His legs looked short under the surface as he pumped them to stay afloat. Little kid legs. Closer to the surface, you could see that he was becoming an adult, a few curly hairs sprouting from his chest.

I treaded water too, and the bicycling motion made me think of a dream I'd been having more and more. The dream always started with me standing in the driveway, near the basketball hoop, alone, as if everyone had gone away somewhere. Then I stepped up into the sky. It wasn't like in comic books. No unfettered soaring. Instead, I *climbed* the sky, pedaling as if on an invisible bicycle and with some effort, like going up a hill, working at it, but also ecstatic, an ache of joy in my chest for remembering how simple it was, how simple it had always been, to fly up and away from my emptied house and all through the sky above our town.

"Yo," I said to hear the little echo. My heart was starting to beat harder because of all the kid-leg pedaling.

"Yo!" Ian shouted. And I shouted "Yo!"

We got quiet again. The empty dock above us bucked in a gust, as if connected to the thumping in my chest. My heart, the seesawing dock, the spliced giggling sunlight through the slats, the deep water below, the whole wide world and beyond. A pulse runs through everything, but we hardly ever know.

As September loomed, I was back on my own, the sweet myth that summer might last forever disintegrating. I'd been buying cards for months already, the thrill of seeing the year's new card style long gone.

Any pack I could buy would be mostly doubles, guys I'd already picked up in previous packs, one monotonously recognizable personage after another, zombies in infielder crouches or with bats outstretched. Tedium, disappointment, the taste in my mouth back to what it was before I opened the pack, the stick of gum that came with the cards already a hard rubber pebble.

To this too you add prayer. You do this because without it what else is there? You do this because there's always a chance. You might just find, mixed in with all the doubles, a card like the one pictured above.

I was twelve when I found it among all the repeating Thad Bosleys and Steve Muras. There was no bigger star than Nolan Ryan. He seemed to have superpowers. Other pitchers such as Jim Palmer and Tom Seaver won more games and Cy Young awards, but only Nolan Ryan had the power to crack open the hard lid of the late summer sky and let a little of the dreamworld come leaking in. He threw the ball fast, faster than anyone ever had, faster than anyone ever

would. A twelve-year-old kid who had played his final season of little league and gone through one demoralizing year of junior high with another year about to begin could walk home from the store with this card in an unopened pack and back in his room he could open that pack and find this card and hold it in his hands and feel like he was touching a little piece of lightning from another wider world.

Topps 1981 #630: Steve Carlton

Some things are beautiful. Some things are ugly.

In September the mountains all around us rippled with a slow glowing fire, leaves turning orange and yellow and red.

In October, as Steve Carlton and the Phillies were beating an ailing George Brett and the Royals in the World Series, the leaves began to dry and fall. Brett had proved mortal after all, not only failing to hit .400 but at the most crucial moment of his career developing the ugliest malady I'd yet heard of, hemorrhoids, which as I understood it were painful bulging cysts of the asshole.

In November, baseball gone for the year and, as it would turn out, my desire to buy large quantities of baseball cards gone forever, things got uglier still, a cold wind knifing through skeletal trees and across ground hard and wan as concrete. Late that month, we went to my grandparents' house on Cape Cod for Thanksgiving. The day after the feast, since there wasn't much else to do in November, a contingent of the extended family traveled to the mall in Hyannis. My brother and I went to a record store. At first we split up, flipping through albums at different places in the alphabet, but up in the A's I found a new album by a band I thought we both liked. After we had realized we had been fools to like disco, we had switched to the unsucking Rock of this band, among others (including, prominently, AC/DC). I brought it to Ian.

"Check it out," I said. "Aerosmith's latest. *Night in the Ruts.*"

My brother half-looked, then snickered, shaking his head a little. He continued flicking through albums. I looked down at the cover.

"Night, night, night in the *ruuuts*," I sang, inventing a title track. Ian glanced at me and then moved down a couple rows. He pulled an album out and looked at the back of it. I got a glimpse of the front, which looked ugly. Down near the bottom was what looked like a shred of paper in a kidnapper's demand note. One of the words in the shred was "Sex."

"Hey, what is—" I said.

"Fuck off, huh?" Ian said. "Please?"

Some things are beautiful. Some things are ugly. As I looked to my brother to let me know which was which, my brother had begun to look to guys a year or two older than him, the members of the varsity basketball team, who had just embarked on a legendary season that would bring them all the way to the state championship game. (Ian was still on the junior varsity squad, which traveled with the varsity to all their games.) The varsity featured two brothers, the Cones, who had family in California, information that was used to explain the cutting-edge music they introduced to their teammates and that defined the clique based around the team. I assumed my flawless brother was a central figure in this clique, but since then I have come to understand differently.

"Sometimes I still wish I could, just once, dunk on fucking Chomentowski," Ian said years later, a hungry, pained look on his face as he named the varsity star.

They called my brother "Head Case," a nickname hung on him by the varsity coach, a mole-faced martinet whose voice was always hoarse from screaming. My brother was big and athletically gifted, a potential varsity star, but he had mental lapses and bursts of dubious on-court improvisation that, because they veered from the lockstep dictates of the coach's 1950s-era "Holy Cross" offense, appeared selfish (especially since they were usually ineffective), and probably the coach believed that if he harangued and browbeat my brother enough he'd eventually become the brainless pick-setting lummox in the pivot that the coach's antiquated vision of basketball required. The varsity guys ran with the Head Case nickname for different reasons, not really caring if the younger player developed, since they were already winning every game they played. They saw that there was something about my brother that didn't quite fit. Maybe they noticed his growing desperation to escape the town, their town. Maybe they noticed, as I never could, that at times he could be a bullshitter.

I think of the day he went to the Cones' house with his Tony Alva skateboard. The Cones had built a skateboarding ramp, and I suspect that my brother, a subscriber to *Skateboarder* magazine, had told them on more than one occasion that he was something of a demon on a skateboard. I don't know how I know this except maybe that my brother was unusually quiet when he came home from their house, but my feeling has always been that when he got to the Cones' place he had to reveal that he had been blowing hot air all along. Maybe up until the moment he got to the top of the ramp he had believed, had needed to believe, that he would naturally be able to perform the acrobatic feats he'd seen guys doing in the photos in *Skateboarder* magazine. But while the Cones rolled up and down the ramp with lidded-eye ease, snickering, Head Case fell flat on his big-mouth face, his expensive spotless board flying out from under him.

The Cones and the rest of the varsity had that snickering gazing-down-from-on-high attitude in general, and it and the notoriety they got for being such a successful team brought them into conflict with the nonathletes of the school, particularly those who still had shoulder-length hair and found beauty in the unironic grandeur of Arena Rock. Music defined the borderlines of this conflict, which occasionally boiled over into fistfights. If you were with the jocks, as my brother wanted to be, you better know what ruled and what rotted. You better know to snort at *Night in the Ruts*. And you better know your shit backward and forward about the new jagged sound the Cones were bringing back from the sophisticated distance.

I gave my brother space in the record store, but I kept checking on his location. Eventually I looked up and didn't see him. Had he bolted without saying anything? I was about to step out of the store to look for him out there when he emerged from a hidden corner in the back and walked past me without even a glance.

"Hey," I said. "Hey, Ian."

He left the store and started walking even faster. I followed and called his name again. I kept saying his name; he kept walking. I was a few paces behind him but I started slowing down. It was like watching a train pull away, or like my voice had been removed. Like my brother didn't know me. A man in a light-colored suit jacket passed me, moving briskly. I watched him clap my brother on the shoulder.

The two of them went back into the store and disappeared behind a door in the back. I followed them as far as I could and peered through a small window in the door. I could see my brother sitting in a metal chair, staring down at his knee, a cassette of Elvis Costello's *Get Happy* on the table in front of him. There was a rack of posters near the door on my side and I hid my face in there, pretending to look at a Ted Nugent poster. I was crying because my brother was a stranger.

My mother was paged on the mall intercom. She and Tom appeared. They let Mom in through the door in the back, and several minutes later she reemerged with Ian. The four of us walked through the mall toward the exit, Mom and Tom in front, me and Ian in back.

I started to whisper a question to Ian, but before I got any further than "Why" he knocked the wind out of me with a backhand punch to the stomach.

The varsity team won all their games until the Division II championship game at the big auditorium in Barre, when they got beat by a team—so the general thinking in my town went—that was unfairly advantaged because they "recruited," a thinly veiled reference to the presence on the opposition of a couple of black guys. The 20–1 Randolph Galloping Ghosts of 1980–81 had a celebratory party nonetheless, and my brother went to it. I've heard that if either of a pair of identical twins gets hurt, the other twin will feel the pain. Nothing like this ever happened with me and my un-identical, un-twin brother, but the night of that party as I sat at home I was overwhelmed with dread for my brother. I knew something was going wrong. And though he didn't tell me about that night for years, I eventually learned that he had drunkenly dozed off at some point only to be woken by some kind of a prank played on him by the varsity guys, I forget what, maybe something as simple as them pouring a glass of water on his head. He flew into a rage and kicked in the driver's-side window of the car that belonged to the team's star, Chomentowski. I can see their faces, a mix of shock and scorn.

"What the *fuck*, Head Case," one of them said, the tone conveying an unequivocal message. You will never belong.

We were teammates that spring, my brother and I, for one last season, together on one of the town's two Babe Ruth league teams. I was worse, relatively speaking, than I'd ever been in little league, and my brother, who had been a pitching ace, had been reduced to being an emergency starter. He had one notable moment, nearly pitching a no-hitter, but the game was against a coed team of thin, easily distractible hippie youths, and anyway he lost the no-hit bid in the last inning when one of the longhaired boys or girls stopped daydreaming long enough to loop a single just in front of the late-breaking mediocrity logging a couple pity innings in left field. I picked up the cheap hit on one bounce, already starting to replay the moment in my mind, already starting to believe I could have done more. I tossed it back in the general direction of the infield, unable to look at the tall boy on the mound.

Some things are beautiful. Some things are ugly. It's all in the eye of the beholder, I guess. I bought a few packs of cards that year, 1981. That's it. I thought then and I think now that the cards from that strike-marred season were the ugliest of any that have ever come to me.

And I count this Steve Carlton card as the worst of the bunch, the ugliest card I own. It hasn't gotten any prettier since it first came into my hands, either, especially when the beady-eyed recluse pictured in the card was quoted in a 1994 article by Pat Jordan as claiming that world events were heavily influenced by "12 Jewish bankers meeting in Switzerland" and that the AIDS virus was created "to get rid of gays and blacks."

I'm sure the moment I discovered the card its ugliness undermined any excitement at finding an All-Star in the pack. Centering the ugliness is the bright red blob mushing down one of history's more ill-advised perms while also shadowing the sharp, avian features of the subject's ashen face, his smile strangely off-putting, verging on an acidic grimace, his neck wrinkled, the top of his chest appearing clammy, clinging to the chafing polyester of the cheap candy-striped uniform, the blur of gray behind him less like sky than hardened Kaopectate, the drab block lettering along the top of the border sucking the joy out of the All-Star distinction it proclaims, the yellow block lettering of the player's name along the bottom turning what could have been a moment of gleeful recognition of a superstar into a yellow-green unease.

The bulbous, crudely rendered cap icon on the lower left, a leaden image made even less appealing by the joyless block lettering jamming the crown, helps drag the overall impression of the card into that of a senseless dumping ground. Worse, the baseball icon in the lower right—a litigious blight on the cards that season, 1981, when Topps by court order relinquished its benign monopoly—signals that everything, even baseball cards, is part of a fight, a grab for power, that the noise and clutter of the real world had invaded the realm of my gods.

"I'm finally getting out of here," my brother said. We were lying in our beds. The lights had been off for a while. My eyes had adjusted. The wind was blowing the trees around outside.

"What do you mean?"

"I'm going away to another school in September. A boarding school."

Some things are beautiful. Some things are ugly. I stared at the little rat-claw scar just above me in the ceiling.

"Adios, shithole," Ian said.

Topps 1975 #274: Vicente Romo

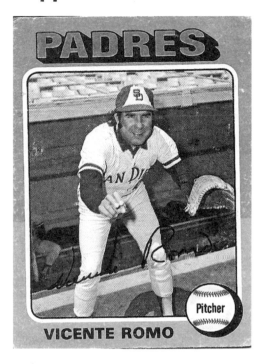

No one can ever know what's going to happen from one day to the next. Vicente Romo was an effective relief pitcher for some time—as the back of this card puts it in the customary caveman syntax of baseball card prose, Romo was "one of club's top firemen"—before being suddenly released by the Padres back in 1975. One minute you could be horsing around during one in a seemingly endless succession of yearly Topps photo shoots, playing air piano or putting a hex on the opposition or leeringly blocking a ball girl from exiting the field, and the next minute you could be packing up your locker.

When Romo was released, he had a perfectly even record: 31–31. He wasn't great. He wasn't terrible. He'd just completed a 5–5 season, proving that he had mastered this kind of reliable albeit somewhat dubious consistency. Nonetheless, after his release from the Padres he didn't latch on with another major league club in 1975. Perhaps word had gotten around that his best days were behind him. After all, he was thirty-one years old, no longer young enough to be counted among the developing guys who might suddenly blossom into something better than what they were. He didn't play in the majors in 1976, either, or in 1977, 1978, 1979, 1980, or 1981.

But in 1982, the first spring after my brother went away, Vicente Romo returned. The incredible, improbable comeback of a man who had been out of the majors for exactly as long as he'd been in the majors was only slightly overshadowed by Romo finishing the season with an underwhelming 1–2 record. He vanished from whence he came when the season ended and did not reappear on a major

league roster in the next year, or the one after that, or the one after that, and so on. But even to this day some part of me continues to believe that Vicente Romo will return once again to even his record and prove that anything that's gone might someday return.

Topps 1980 #97: Bill Lee

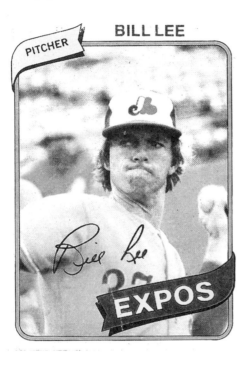

BILL LEE

PITCHER

EXPOS

Ian came back once in a while on school breaks and sometimes we lay in our beds with the lights off, talking. His going away had softened the tension, the thwarted, unfocused desire to escape that had surrounded him in the years leading up to his departure. He did most of the talking as we lay there, telling me about guys in his dorm, guys on his basketball team, guys on campus who pulled hilarious legendary stunts. I learned the names of all these strangers and built them all into larger-than-life figures, my brother's world always my world of myth. It's been two and a half decades and I could still tell you the first and last names of dozens of his classmates and make an accurate estimation of the scoring averages of the starting five players on his basketball team in both his junior and senior years, and rank in approximate order of desirability the girls he most desperately wanted to declothe, even though I never had personal contact with any of these people.

In those late-night conversations, my life didn't really come up. What could I say? My basketball team continued to suck, and that was about all I had going. When the conversation seemed to be thinning out toward nothing, I leaned on the subject that had formed the center of the language of two boys with one voice.

"This could be the year," I said one night. It was early in the 1982 season, and the Red Sox had been hanging around near the top of the division. "If Eckersley can keep it together, they might do it."

"I haven't really had time to notice," Ian said. "But who the hell's their catcher now? This sophomore dweeb in my dorm had the game on in the TV room and a guy comes up to bat about the size of a fire hydrant. He had no *chance* to get a hit."

"Muggsy Allenson," I said glumly.

"No Fisk, no Burleson, no Lynn. I don't know," he said.

"If Ojeda does what he did last year," I said, but I didn't finish the thought. "They better do something quick if they want to get Yaz a title before he hangs it up."

I started imagining it, the parade, old Yaz riding past, waving to us as we wept. I got tears in my eyes.

"No Carbo, no Tiant, no Hobson," Ian said. "And what about Bill Lee? Is he even anywhere anymore?"

The house felt empty without Ian. In truth, it had already begun to feel empty even before that, as everyone was living more and more within their own individual orbit. In the early years in that house, Mom and Tom had thrown parties, big ones and small ones, inviting all their hippie friends from the food co-op. By 1982 these parties had become a thing of the past. Mom and Tom both had regular 9-to-5 jobs and came home tired.

One warm spring day the three of us drove to a lake and rented a canoe. I sat in the middle without a paddle, Mom sat in front, and Tom sat in back. They were good at keeping the canoe straight. Nobody said much. After a while I drew in a breath and opened my mouth to speak, but I didn't want to hear my own voice wrecking the gentle sounds of the paddles in the water. The question stayed on my tongue.

Where are we going?

No hippie ever played major league baseball. Bill Lee probably came the closest, but he was really more an eccentric libertarian iconoclast than a member of any explicit or implicit movement. Still, I was drawn to him. Some of the things he said and did reminded me of the adults at the parties Mom and Tom used to have. He appeared in a magazine wearing a space suit and a Red Sox propeller beanie. He ranted about the stupidity of the establishment. He caught pop flies behind his back.

I was drawn to Bill Lee because he was the closest thing in the majors to the kind of adult that I was around, and also because,

unlike most Red Sox hurlers, he had been pretty good at beating the Yankees. Keenly aware of this, Yankees teammates Mickey Rivers and Graig Nettles had (so I choose to believe) conspired during a 1976 bench-clearing brawl to ambush Lee and rip his pitching arm out of its shoulder socket. He struggled with arm troubles the next couple of years, and in December 1978 the Red Sox, with the strong recommendation of manager Don Zimmer, a narrow-minded baseball lifer who hated and was hated by the nonconformist lefty, shipped Lee to the Expos for Stan Papi, who proceeded to hit a Stan Papiesque .188 for the Red Sox while Lee turned in a classic "fuck you, Red Sox" year, going 16–10 with a 3.04 ERA.

By 1982, I had toyed more than once with the idea of following Bill Lee to the Expos. I liked to fantasize in many ways about shucking my identity, and one of those fantasies involved leaving the Red Sox behind. After their 1978 collapse, everything about them seemed weighed down with a faint but inescapable aura of dread. Even when they clung to an early season division lead, as they did in 1979 and 1982, there was this feeling that they'd find a way to surrender it, which they did, and in such a pronounced way as to reveal that they hadn't ever really had much of a chance. They'd let most of the stars of my childhood get away, and the guys who remained just got older and slower and more prone to hit into double plays or groove fat 3–1 fastballs that opposing batters crushed into the center-field bleachers. After some of the more painful losses, I imagined announcing my defection by sending a second letter to Yaz.

Dear Yaz,

Not that you will ever write back or even read this probably but I've thought it over and I decided I have had it. I am going to become a Montreal Expos fan.

Sincerely,

Josh Wilker

P.S. Forget about sending me an autograph (unless you really feel like it).

The Expos played almost exactly as close to my house as the Red Sox did, yet I had never been to an Expos game, nor knew anyone who ever had, and no one in my entire town or anywhere in Vermont or anywhere that I had ever been appeared to be an Expos fan. Nobody cared about them, while my current team made everyone want to jump off bridges three times a week. That was the primary allure of the fantasy of abandoning my team for the Expos. It could never really hurt if I never really cared.

I still had night terrors every once in a while. One night when Ian was away at school and Mom was away somewhere, too, I went screaming through the house until I ended up near enough to Tom for him to reach out and take my hand.

"It's OK, it's OK," he said, holding on.

Ian had once headed off my encroaching night terrors by reading to me from his Star Trek book, but once they started no one had ever gotten them to stop before they'd run their entire course to hoarse-voiced exhaustion. Not until the night Tom reached out and held my hand in a house that had never felt emptier.

Bill Lee's major league career came to an end in 1982 when his one-game walkout to protest the release of teammate Rodney Scott resulted in the Expos showing him the same door they showed Scott.

Mom, Tom, and I took our only overnight trip ever as a threesome around then, a gray weekend visit to Montreal. I can only remember that there didn't seem to be much to do. I bought an Expos cap. We wandered the streets, ate in a restaurant where you ordered in French, and sat around the hotel. The highlight of the trip was when we went to see a documentary, which as far as I know was never released in the U.S., about Bill Lee. Here he was in all his glory, talking about sprinkling marijuana on his pancakes, cursing Don Zimmer for his beady-eyed, self-righteous, slow-witted devotion to traditional thinking, lauding meditation as a way to take a snapshot of your mind at any moment, and blaming the chronic back problems that besieged Americans on the fact that we, unlike the more enlightened Japanese, were slavishly devoted to the con game of chairs. With his bushy beard and his good-natured motormouth communist-inflected rantings, he seemed more than ever like one of Mom and Tom's friends from the old days.

The film made it seem as if Bill Lee might still live in Montreal, even though the team had given him the heave-ho. For the rest of the trip I wore my new Expos cap and kept my eyes peeled for him, hoping to see him so I could break the gathering silence by yelling his name.

Topps 1978 #152: Ivan DeJesus

IVAN DeJESUS

I learned from my cards that some people are special. Some people aren't. The sluggers, the All-Stars: They can swing for the fences. They are men, not sheep. They are never asked to follow. They are never asked to bunt.

Early in our time in East Randolph, Mom and Tom fixed up the shed where Ian and I had found the magazine with the naked people in it. This shed was going to be a key part of their back-to-the-land dream. The sheep would live here. The sheep would give us food and clothing and maybe even goods in trade. Our first two sheep were named Virginia and Wool, and after they mated Wool got made into little white wax paper packages for our meat freezer. Other sheep followed, either coming out of Virginia covered in blood or in a truck, imported to impregnate Virginia, but the non-Virginia sheep proved to be more trouble than they were worth, often escaping through the electric fence that was always shorting out, resulting in tiresome and embarrassing sheep hunts through the town. Also, all the sheep except for Virginia were dumb and devoid of personality. After a while, in line with all the other elements of the back-to-the-land dream eventually dropping by the wayside, we kept just Virginia, and got nothing out of her beyond her modest lawn-mowing skills. Big bags of her shorn mane filled up our mud room, never getting processed into wool. But she was a great creature, a huge, bellowing, intelligent matriarch, and we loved her, and she at least knew us, and possibly even loved us back. You could go to the electric fence and if you cupped your hand like you had grain she would walk over, and she would stay even when you showed her your empty hand, and you could scratch her on the head, which she liked.

Sometimes I think the last at bat of the back-to-the-land dream was when Virginia got so old and rickety that there was no way of justifying her continued presence in our lives, and so she was taken where all our other sheep had been taken, and she returned in white wax paper packages that stayed in the bottom of the meat freezer until the house was sold.

Other times I like to believe the last at bat of that dream was when Tom strung a tightrope across the inside of our garage. It was that spring when I learned my brother would be going away. By then Tom had been working a regular full-time job for a few years. His life had come to resemble in some ways the very thing he and Mom had so desperately wanted to escape. Previous to meeting my mom, Tom had been unsure about whether to pursue a professional acting career or to venture further into the experimental theater and experimental living he'd been increasingly attracted to. When he fell in love with my mother and they began to dream together, he saw the back-to-the-land-dream as the answer to the question of what to do with his life. *Embrace the role of a lifetime, your lifetime, the only one you'll ever get.*

So what do you do when that role ossifies into something ordinary, the role of a follower, the role of someone being told to lay down a bunt?

Tom's response was to ignore the sign and swing for the fences. Despite a relative lack of experience in musicals, he got the lead role in the Randolph theater company's production of *Barnum*. He would sing. He would dance. He would yank a tablecloth out from under dishes and cutlery. He would juggle. He would walk a tightrope.

On the first performance of the three-night run, the show climaxed with Tom walking across the tightrope strung across the stage. We weren't at that performance, however, and went the next night, when someone snapped a photo and he lost his balance halfway across. The production had prepared for this possibility and killed the lights as he faltered, keeping them off as he scurried backstage, then flicking them back on a couple seconds later when Tom reappeared on the platform at the far end of the tightrope, an arm raised in triumph.

I have to hand it to Randolph, the closest thing I've got to a hometown. Tom got a bigger cheer than he would have if he hadn't failed. I know this because I'd heard a smaller version of that cheer from the people of that town who helped make my time in little league such a beautiful oasis.

"Good *swing!*" they would yell every time I tried with all my might and missed.

My mother was always foremost among those adults cheering "Good *swing.*" If anyone in my family knew what it meant to try and keep trying, it was her. She had thrown herself into painting. She had thrown herself into inventing a new kind of family. She had thrown herself into living what had been envisioned as a joyous self-sufficient life in the country. She had thrown herself into creating and maintaining her own sign-painting business. She threw everything she had into each of the daring, ambitious tries. Swinging from her heels. Covered in paint. Covered in sawdust. Covered in dirt. On her knees working in the garden for hours. On her knees working on a sign for hours.

When all those attempts had come and gone, I see her sitting at the kitchen table and staring blankly out the window. I eventually came to associate these semicatatonic states of hers with the word "depression." I see her going to work every day to write and edit technical manuals, not what she'd envisioned when she'd written on a postcard "I'm <u>flipping</u> <u>out</u> with thoughts of THERE!" to Tom while he was in blacksmith school. I see her coming home every day from that job, the backseat covered in tear-soaked tissues. The layer of tissue wads would be particularly thick on days when she had seen her therapist.

At the time, I hated this therapist, whom I blamed for making my mother sad. Now I understand it as yet another brave try by my mom. She always kept going, kept swinging, kept trying to figure it out, one way or another.

I see her taking me, in that first year that my brother was gone, to see Allen Ginsberg play music at a hall in the state capital, Montpelier. Ginsberg the beatnik had inspired my mother in the early 1960s when she'd first moved to New York, fresh out of college, and had inspired her again later in the decade when he'd been a prominent figure in the hippie counterculture that seemed to my mother to be swinging for the fences. She wanted me to see this great man, this weird sprawling force of nature who would have rather gone insane, as he almost did early in his life, than give up this lone precious at bat called life and follow orders to bunt.

I was only fourteen, however, and though I would later come to revere Ginsberg almost as much as I would come to revere his friend Jack Kerouac, I was exactly the wrong age to stomach a bug-eyed wet-lipped strange-voiced middle-aged maniac with a sweating bald pate and wild Larry Fine tufts who sawed inexpertly on a variety of musical instruments and caterwauled atonal ditties that always, even if they were about secret CIA plots to assassinate justly elected foreign leaders, eventually circled around to how great it was to suck a teenaged cock.

"Can I have the keys?" I said at intermission.

I went out to the car and listened to a few innings of a Red Sox game on the radio. This was the 1982 team that I'd earlier expressed hope in when talking to Ian late at night on one of his visits home. But as I sat alone in the dark listening to them get thumped I understood that all the gleaming promise of the star-studded 1970s teams had vanished for real, along with the dispersal of most of the roster. What was left?

"Come on, Yaz," I said.

The next spring, I was twice ordered to bunt in what turned out to be the final game of my baseball career. I was fourteen and on a bad Babe Ruth team that got worse as the season wore on. But we eventually found a team even worse than us, probably the same ragged collection of hippie teens that my brother almost no-hit the year before. We got a good lead early, yet when I came to bat our coach gave me the sign from the third-base coach's box to lay down a bunt. I think he was trying to let me know that my opinion of myself as a baseball player, which I'd formed while doing pretty well in little league, was outdated. I was a scrub now, a bench guy. I wasn't as happy to throw away my at bat as Ivan DeJesus appears to be, but I followed orders and laid down a good bunt. The coach never acknowledged it. By my next time up we were really pounding them. Everyone was having fun but me. I looked up the third-base line to the coach and he touched his belt again, the bunt sign. I couldn't figure out if he was an idiot or if he was punishing me. Either way, I

was through with baseball. I lashed a double, probably my first solid hit since little league. As I stood on second base I didn't look at the coach. My whole body tingled from making perfect contact. My first and greatest dream life had ended.

Topps 1979 #376: Gorman Thomas

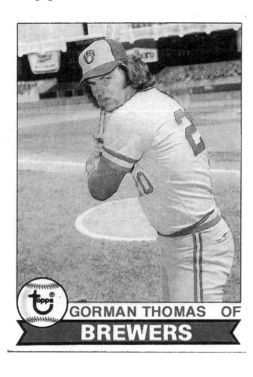

GORMAN THOMAS OF
BREWERS

Before this goes any further: What the fuck? Specifically, what the fuck are the Milwaukee Brewers doing in the National League? When I last looked, I mean really looked, back at the end of my childhood, that unbroken ladder of years seemingly aimed in the direction of the gods, there was no clearer representative of the American League than the Brewers. They never sent their keg-bellied hungover hurlers to the plate. They never hosted games below the ceiling of a retractable dome. They never allowed their simple brutish contests to be marred by the calculating timidity of sacrifice bunts. They had the beards and long greasy hair of motorcycle thugs and guzzled Miller High Life and gnawed bulging wads of tobacco and slugged long home runs or struck out swinging. They listened to Waylon Jennings and Hank Williams Jr. on their way to discharge shotguns at wildlife. They smashed into outfield fences and bought mescaline from hippies before pounding them with tire irons. Didn't they? I mean, now that the Milwaukee Brewers are in something called the Central Division of the National League I don't feel I can make confident assertions about anything. But I can at least say this: As much as any team was ever one guy, the Milwaukee Brewers in the late '70s and early '80s were Gorman Thomas. And Gorman Thomas did not ever show his grizzled, menacing face in the National League. Until October 1982, that is, and that was only because by then the Brewers had laid waste to all the American League teams in their path and the only thing left for them to conquer was the St. Louis Cardinals of the National League, which they probably would have done if the majority of the games in the

1982 World Series were played in an American League park and not upon the fake National League turf of Busch Stadium. After those four National League games, Gorman Thomas was never the same, and neither were the Brewers, and come to think of it, neither was I.

Topps 1978 #450: Tom Seaver

TOM SEAVER

And what's Tom Seaver doing in a Cincinnati Reds uniform? Tom Seaver was known as the Franchise, a nickname nodding to the fact that he *was* the New York Mets. He had always been the New York Mets. He would always be the New York Mets. And yet, here he is: Something else.

As he glares out from under his new red cap, his approach appears unaltered: *Give me the fucking ball and I'll win.* Still, no one is immune to the erosion of the unbroken ladder of years. After a few years in exile from the New York Mets, Tom Seaver seemed to be close to joining me among those who'd recently let go of playing baseball. In 1982, his final year with the Reds, he went 5 and 13 with a 5.50 ERA.

What do you do when the unbroken ladder of years disappears?

My mom came up to my room one night. It was the spring of 1983. She asked me if I thought I might want to try going away to school, as Ian had done.

"I don't know," I said.

Eventually, she drove me down to western Massachusetts to the boarding school my brother would be graduating from soon. A guy in the admissions office interviewed me. I had no extracurricular activities to tell him about, beyond my horrible basketball team. I didn't like any subjects in school. Still, words somehow came out of my mouth when it was my turn to talk.

"Good stuff, good stuff," the interviewer kept saying.

A few weeks later, my mom got word that they would be willing to get her started on another heavily loan-burdened tuition payment plan, similar to the one she was already on for my brother.

"So what do you think?" she asked me.

"I don't know."

By then, Tom Seaver had been traded back to the Mets. It wasn't exactly a triumphant return. All the Reds could get for the future Hall of Famer was Lloyd McClendon, Charlie Puleo, and a minor leaguer named Jason Felice. Reunited with the Mets, his struggles continued. One night early in Tom Seaver's second go-round in New York, I stumbled into a return of my own. A couple buddies and I had gotten an older guy to buy us some rum. We were wondering where to drink it. I'd never gotten drunk before. We ended up, probably at my suggestion, at the little league dugout where I'd spent a lot of good moments, including my first and only minutes as a kid who had just made perfect contact and hit a home run.

The brief, inexplicable triumph of that day struck me as unreachable the moment I sat down on the wooden bench, gripping, instead of a bat that had just been used to hit a home run, a liter bottle of rum-spiked Coke. As I looked out through the chicken wire at the field, I was surprised by the smallness of the diamond, by the closeness of the outfield fence, by how easy it would be to hit a home run. A sharp ache spread through my chest as I realized the impossibility of going back to that much simpler world. You can only go forward, never backward. I started drinking. The ache gradually gave way to one of the best feelings I'd ever felt. It began to really hit me when we left the dugout. We were running toward an older kid's truck that had appeared in the nearby parking lot. My strides had a slow-motion buoyancy, as if gravity were loosening its grip. We piled into the back and rode around shitfaced and laughing under the stars for the rest of the night, the bumps in the road lifting us up into the air like we were unbuckled astronauts far beyond the earth's pull.

That fall, I went away to the boarding school in western Massachusetts. I spent the first weeks in a state of barely concealed terror. All the other students seemed impossibly sophisticated, way out of my league. One day I had been the sole inhabitant of a rural, socially retarded kingdom of daydreams, solitaire Strat-O-Matic baseball, and *WKRP in Cincinnati*–based masturbation, and the next day I

was stiffly traversing a rolling green campus of solemn ivied build-
ings and sharp-witted upper-middle-class Izod-clad sophisticates in
slightly muted Spandau Ballet haircuts who had long ago lost their
virginity on the sunsplashed decks of Nantucket sailboats. Initially,
my only way of dealing with the terror of the situation was to seize
hold of my strong resemblance to my brother. *You're just like your
brother*, I was told repeatedly, often as a filler for the uncomfortable
silences that surrounded me like a force field.

I wasn't crazy about being an echo, but being an echo was better
than being nothing at all, especially if it was Ian's echo. He had done
well at the school, or so I thought, playing on the varsity basketball
team, acing English papers, serving as an official Student Leader
of his dorm. Years later, I found out he carried an ineffably deep
loathing of the memory of himself at that school. During his two
years there, he had forced his unruly collection of adolescent hurt,
yearning, and anger inside the borders of a desperate impersonation
of a well-adjusted, high-achieving paragon of old-money virtue. I
was impersonating an impersonation.

One bright and sunny Sunday a month or so after my arrival I slipped
into the TV room on the first floor of my dorm. The TV room was
for defectives, especially on a bright and sunny Sunday when you
could be out talking and laughing in your polo shirt with a gaggle of
beautiful girls in front of a leaf pile, your lacrosse stick perched on
your shoulder. My other stints in the TV room thus far had been sad,
shame-filled congregations with other dateless and misshapen fellows to watch Michael Jackson and Prince prance around on *Friday
Night Videos* while the regular kids groped one another through L.L.
Bean garments under the soft, English Literature–enhanced boarding-school stars. But on this particular Sunday I had no company at
all. It was just me and the television.

In this one instance, I didn't care what anyone thought. I had
to watch television on this particular Sunday, for it was October 2,
1983. It was Carl Yastrzemski's last game.

Come on, Yaz. I was able to say this to myself at first, but as the
game went on and he kept failing to homer, my little prayer began
to sneak out of my mouth. By Yaz's last at bat I was pleading out
loud to the television, my cracking voice slapping off the concrete
TV room walls. He settled into his familiar stance, twirling his bat
forward and leaning toward the mound slightly, as if trying to hear

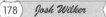

the pitcher's internal monologue. The TV thinned the crowd noise to a hollow buzz, but I could still tell that they were all shouting the same syllable as me, everyone wasting the last of their voices on that yawing, fizzling, incantatory sound.

"Come on, Yaz!" I hollered. *"Come on, Yaz!"*

The Red Sox wouldn't be going to the playoffs that year. Not even close. Yaz would be leaving without a World Series win. Yaz would be leaving. This was it.

The pitcher was a journeyman with a bland mustache. He had trouble finding the strike zone with his first three pitches. Yaz, not wanting to end it all with a walk, ultimately had to lunge at a high fastball. He popped out to the second baseman. Before the following half-inning began, he took his position in left in front of the Green Monster, and then Chico Walker ran out to replace him. As Yaz jogged toward the dugout, the crowd rose and cheered him one last time, but I just sat there trying not to look like a dweeb in the TV room crying.

I fell behind in all my classes, especially trigonometry. Numbers had once been the haven of certainty in my life. Ladders of numbers. Numbers that swelled and waned like the tide, numbers that gleamed, numbers that wheezed, clownish, laughable numbers, awe-inspiring numbers, numbers that seemed to tell stories much clearer than anything else in the world. 3,000 hits—like Yaz had gotten. 400 home runs—like Yaz had gotten. 200 strikeouts, every season—like Tom Seaver had gotten every year from the year I was born up until he showed up on a card as a Cincinnati Red. 300 wins—like Tom Seaver looked like he might fall short of as he faltered through his second stint with the Mets. These were numbers I understood.

As my first year at boarding school was ending, Tom Seaver left the New York Mets again, this time latching on with the Chicago White Sox, where he had to wear a jersey with wide horizontal stripes that made him look kind of old and kind of fat. Despite appearing (as most of the White Sox did) as if he'd be more at home lofting high-arcing softball pitches with one hand while gripping a sixteen-ounce can of Old Style with the other, he turned things around in Chicago and began stomping rather than limping toward 300 wins. He would steamroll past 300, the number no match for the relentless man.

As for me: One afternoon in the spring of my junior year at boarding school, I took one look at the impenetrable questions on my trigonometry final exam, then spent the remainder of the test period filling a blue examination booklet with an apology to my teacher. It may as well have been my suicide note to the world of numbers. Afterward, a senior drove up over the border, into Vermont, where the drinking age was still eighteen, and bought so many bottles of booze that when he got back we spread them out on a kid's bed and took a picture of them. So many bottles you couldn't even count them all. The giddiness was palpable. We were about to blast all the numbers clean out of our heads.

Topps 1980 #218: Jose Morales

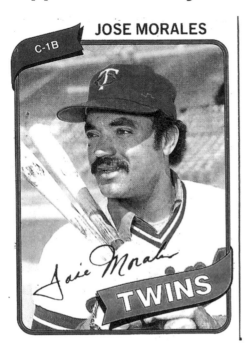

JOSE MORALES

C-1B

TWINS

I started kindergarten the same year José Morales reached the major leagues, 1973, and continued to attend school every year of his quietly competent, useful career as a right-handed bat for hire. But not long after his final at bat in 1984, I got busted at boarding school for staggering around drunk at a dance, and the following spring, while still on probation, I got caught smoking bong hits in my dorm room. A committee of faculty and students held something called a "judicial" to decide if I should be expelled.

I brought along my friend Matt as a character witness. We arrived early and were standing outside in the dark, waiting to get called into the hearing, when a hulking, pock-faced Middle Eastern student I sort of knew shambled out of the shadows. It was a strange time for a student to be walking around without a care in the world. Probably it was "study hours," when you're supposed to be quietly studying in your room or quietly studying in the library, with no movement from one to the other allowed. Movement did sometimes occur, but sneakily.

"What the fuck are you two shitheads doing here?" he bellowed. He had an accent that made "the" and "shitheads" sound like "thee" and "sheetheads." I cringed, rabbitlike, at the volume of his voice. He lit a cigarette, carelessly flaunting another rule, and I explained to him in a grave murmur that I was about to go into a hearing that would *decide my future*.

"*They* gonna decide your future?" he said.

"Well, I don't know. I guess."

He took a long drag, then exhaled, eyeing me the whole time.

"Listen to me," he finally said, his voice booming. "You must fucking do as I say. You must go in there. You must go in there and tell them. To *suck!* Your *fucking! Dick!*"

I should have taken his advice. Most of the proceeding entailed a red-faced math teacher berating me for being an embarrassment to the school.

"My friends like me," I replied at one point, lamely, as if my relationship with the small group of guys I smoked pot with was going to contribute to the greater glory of the institution. I think I also noted that I'd briefly had a radio show on the campus station.

A couple days later I was summoned to see the campus dean. She told me I was expelled. I stood up to leave.

"Where do you think you're going?" she exclaimed incredulously. "I'm not done with you. Sit down."

I sat down. I wish I hadn't. I wish I'd told her to suck my fucking dick.

I came home for what would turn out to be the last time. Mom and Tom had decided to go their separate ways. Mom wanted to go to graduate school for art history in New York City, and Tom wanted to stay in Vermont. I don't really know any more details. Soon the house would be sold and all its less essential but not completely disposable contents, such as my baseball card collection, would be packed into a storage unit.

I'd been kicked out with very little time left in my senior year, and after an unsuccessful and humiliating trip with my mom to the local high school to beg for admittance in time to graduate with the local seniors, the only thing that remained for me in Vermont was to wait for the next administration of the General Educational Development (GED) exam in the state capital.

One day while waiting around for the test I smoked the last of some hash oil I'd bought at boarding school and had a stunningly vivid hallucination of my brother and me as the longhaired hippie toddlers we'd been, laughing and running in slow motion through a meadow of sun-drenched shin-high grass. I sat there holding my hash pipe and wept. I missed my brother. I missed sharing not only the world we lived in but the world we'd created together, the other world that came to us a pack at a time, fifteen colored rectangles to a pack.

The GED test took place in the courthouse building in Montpelier. There was only one other test taker, a sixteen-year-old kid hoping to join the air force. He chewed on his lip while we waited to get under way.

"Shit, you think there's gonna be algebra on this fucker?" he asked me.

"I don't know," I said.

I don't remember if there was algebra, but the test turned out to be pretty easy. I finished while the air force kid was still laboring away. I went out and stood on the steps of the courthouse, waiting for my mom to pick me up and pretending not to notice the guy on the other side of the steps who was pretending not to notice me.

His name was Mike, and he was the son of the man who owned the general store in East Randolph where I had bought all my baseball cards. He was the kid in elementary school who had peppered his speech with the word "whore." We'd been friends, sort of, in grade school, but I hadn't spoken to him in years. The silence between us had grown out of the general silence of victimhood that gradually engulfed all the members of our terrible seventh and eighth grade basketball teams as the losses continued to mount. By ninth grade, Mike had had enough of basketball. I kept playing and losing. We took different classes. Mike probably spent his Friday nights getting wasted and fornicating in cars while I was still home watching *The Incredible Hulk*. If I hadn't gone away to boarding school for my junior and senior years, I probably would have finally had some contact with him again, either buying shitty brown pot from him or handing him the dribbling spout of a beer keg at a cold, drizzly party in the woods. By the time I took my GED test, Mike had become a fat, glowering man smoking a cigarette outside a courthouse. I'd heard that he'd been arrested for some drug charge, and probably his presence at the courthouse had something to do with that. I stared down for what seemed like hours at the boarding-school in-joke phrases I'd scrawled with a magic marker all over my Converse All-Stars. Finally my mom pulled up.

Her expression was still the weary stone face she'd worn when she'd picked me up from boarding school the day of my expulsion. On the way home on that earlier day, I'd broken the first of many long, painful silences by saying, as if we were characters in an over-wrought melodrama, "I'll make you proud someday, Mom!"

My mom, who would be saddled for years to come with the large loan she'd taken out to send me to the school, let my bombastic vow hang in the air for a while before replying in a flat monotone, "That's not the point." I'd backed off any further pronouncements in the following weeks, but the moment after the GED test seemed to demand at least a stab at ceremonial verbiage. I thought about the test itself, and then about the lip-gnawing air force kid who was probably still flailing away at "the fucker."

"Well, looks like I'm gonna be the valedictorian of my class," I said. My mom wasn't exactly in a mirthful mood, but she did later pass on the line to her friend Barbara, and Barbara filled our home for the last time with the sound of whooping, happy laughter.

I went to spend the summer at my grandfather's house on Cape Cod. I didn't bring my cards with me, but if I had I'm sure I would have eventually started leafing through them during those first long, empty days of my first borderless summer. I might have come upon José Morales's 1980 card and seen evidence of his desirable usefulness everywhere. Judging from his picture, he was confident and pleasant and relaxed, a calming, positive presence in a clubhouse. He raked like a first baseman, as shown by his .291 career batting average after seven years in the league, but he could also serve his team by manning the most specialized and difficult position on the field, catcher. And, as the back of the card text pointed out, he was that rare player who could sit on the bench all game long until needed, then come into the action cold and produce: "Established major league record with 25 pinch-Hits for Montreal Expos during the 1976 season."

I was the opposite of José Morales. I didn't know how to do anything. Eventually, my grandfather got me a job at a nearby Shell station. The night before my first day, I spent the lulls in the action of a Red Sox game on TV trying to flatten out a Shell cap with a crown that seemed unusually high. But every time I pushed down, it popped back up. I sat on it for a while, then went into the bathroom to see if it looked any different on my head, but it seemed even higher than before. Under the brim, my face looked grim and old.

I was also required to wear a collared shirt very similar to the one poking out from under José Morales's jersey in his 1980 card. I don't know what José Morales did during his first borderless summer of 1985, beyond the unbroken ladder of years, but I pumped gas, shoved dirt around windshields with a squeegee, and, upon request,

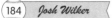

opened hoods and searched for dipsticks, sometimes actually finding them and not having to lie that I had checked the oil. I made change. I waited for the day to end.

Sometimes people saw my high Shell cap and collared José Morales shirt and assumed I was competent, that I could help them address problems with their cars. I didn't know anything about cars. Other motorists swerved into the station and asked me for directions. I didn't know how to get anywhere. To be useful, I would have needed someone screeching to a halt by the pumps and demanding to know the name of the current owner of the single-season major league record for pinch hits.

Topps 1977 #25: Dwight Evans

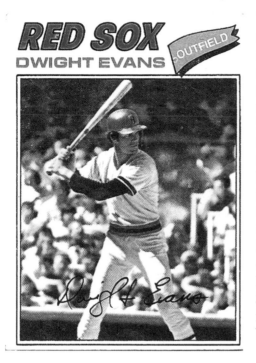

The Shell station required my services only through the busy season. In September, I had to move on. For the first time in my conscious life, my name wasn't on any roll-call sheet. I wasn't expected anywhere. I couldn't go back to East Randolph because the house had been sold. Mom had moved to New York, renting a room in a middle-aged woman's apartment on Twenty-third Street. Tom had moved into a condo in Montpelier. Dad still had his studio on Eleventh Street, and my brother lived in an NYU dorm room a few blocks away from him.

I reacted to the scattering of my family by reaching in the direction of my increasingly distant gods. My aunt and uncle lived in Boston and offered to let me stay in their guest room, so I spent the first blank autumn of my life closer to the Red Sox than I'd ever been.

I went to a couple games at Fenway by myself before the 1985 season ended with the Red Sox' record at 81–81, perfectly nowhere. They seemed impossibly far from being a team that might one day win it all. Almost everyone from my childhood was gone, and none of their replacements could match them, save for a young but strangely leaden and methodical producer of singles and Green Monster doubles, Wade Boggs. With Boggs getting on base all the time in front of him, Jim Rice still found a way to drive in more than a hundred runs that season, but he had begun to hit into an alarmingly high number of double plays. Other than Rice and reliever Bob Stanley, who had somewhat unfairly become the pear-shaped, sad-faced figurehead of the Red Sox' persistent habit of coughing up leads, the only other holdover from the old days was right fielder

Dwight Evans, who that year would win his fifth Gold Glove in a row and eighth overall. With Rice fading and Boggs's robotic excellence inspiring in the hometown crowd only admiration and respect, not love, Dwight Evans coaxed the deepest roars from me and everyone else in the half-filled stands.

In his late-blooming prime Evans did everything with a majestic calm, the absolute opposite of how I felt that fall with nowhere to go but Fenway. The way he loped out to his position in right field. The way he warmed up his famous arm by throwing laser beams out of a sleepy, feline half-windup to some bullpen lackey armed with the added protection of a catcher's mitt. The way he slowly strode to the plate, letting the pitcher stew in the rising sound of the crowd. The way he then coiled himself down into his disciple-of-Hriniak stance, different from the stance he had shown in the 1977 card I'd gotten years before, the newer stance a back-slanting crouch, weight on his right foot, left foot bent and extended with toe just touching the dirt, bat back and nearly horizontal and loose-gripped and slowly pulsing in measured counterpoint to the larger, louder thrumming chant of his nickname, *Dewey*, on all our tongues.

I worked part-time at an ice-cream parlor for a couple months, until one day the manager tried to get me to hand out fliers in the store mascot costume, a (Chocolate) Moose suit. I refused, so he just sent me out as myself. It was the middle of November, baseball as gone as the leaves, and as I held out slips of paper to passersby ignoring me I was struck by the feeling that there was barely anything even holding me to the sidewalk. I eventually dumped the fliers into a trash can and just walked around for a while, but I couldn't escape the feeling that at any moment I might start skittering down the street like an empty pack of cigarettes caught in a gust. A couple days later I quit and took a bus toward the heaviest concentration of my family, Manhattan. I stayed for a few weeks at my dad's apartment, sleeping on a spare foam mat that collided at its foot with the foot of the "master" foam mat. In the mornings I'd pretend to sleep as Dad stepped over me to get up and get ready for work. Sometimes I'd meet my mom at a diner for lunch, an oddly formal, grown-up meeting, a knapsack full of art textbooks on her side of the booth, a newspaper I'd fished from the trash on mine. At night I saw my brother, who lived in an NYU dorm just a short walk away from my father's apartment. We got stoned as he and his roommate took turns putting on bass-heavy dub records turned up so loud we wouldn't have been able to speak even if we'd wanted to. The unbroken ladder of years was gone, as was the sense that Ian was climbing a couple rungs higher than me, in a direction that he understood. Now we were both just adrift. What was there to say? Better to dissolve together into the deep, warm throb of a Robbie Shakespeare bass line as if it were the echo of the heartbeat of something benevolent and immense.

Eventually I left his dimly lit room and stumbled back to Dad's place, where he would already be asleep, all the lights off. His apartment had only one room with a door, the bathroom, and since I often came home too high to sleep, I spent most of my late nights there sitting on the shut lid of the toilet, reading *On the Road* for the first time, slowly, ecstatically, my shining face inches from my father's toenail clippers and rusty can of Barbasol. I wanted my life to be like the one in that book—exciting, adventurous, everything hallowed—but I had no idea how to make it happen.

In January, desperate to retreat from the shapelessness of life beyond school, I got into a small state college situated on top of a mountain in northern Vermont. Halfway through my first semester, my friend John and I reanointed our reggae-laced afternoon pot smoking as a round of special Season Opener bong hits and were coughing and red-eyed with the radio tuned through static to WDEV, the Red Sox radio affiliate in Vermont, as Dwight Evans got the 1986 season started with a bang by leading off the first inning with a home run.

"*Dewey . . . Dewey,*" we rasped.

That summer I returned to Cape Cod. My brother had gotten a summer job outside Boston, in Framingham, on a crew that ripped apart rooms with crowbars and sledgehammers. I made my way to Fenway more often that summer than I ever had or ever would, taking a quick bus ride in from Hyannis to meet up with Ian when he was free. He'd just completed his third year of college, but he wasn't really very close to finishing. Soon he'd drop out and get a job driving a UPS truck.

Before one game, we ducked into a souvenir store outside Fenway and Ian bought a closeout item, probably the cheapest thing in the store, a white painter's cap with the word *YAZ* on the front and various career achievements listed on the sides. He put on the cap and we walked right up to the bleacher ticket window and bought our tickets and went into the game. We were no longer able to yell for the player honored on Ian's two-dollar cap, but late in the game, with men on base, Dwight Evans strode to the plate. It was the summer of 1986 and the Red Sox had been winning. We'd been starting to wonder if there was anything beyond the usual early season mirage, but this wondering only verged on full-throated belief when Dewey crouched down into his stance amid the rising chant.

"*Dewey . . . Dewey,*" we sang.

I wanted to avoid another stint at the Shell station, so I got a job canvassing door to door for Greenpeace. I did okay my first day on the job, but later it was sorted out that part of the reason for the success was that I had inadvertently strayed from my prescribed route and horned in on the potential donors on another canvasser's turf. This got sorted out as my supervisor drove me and the other canvasser back to the office. My supervisor eyed me in the rearview mirror.

"You're like some kind of an evil genius," he said in a reedy, snickering voice. He was a thin blond guy a year or so older than me who went to Tufts, which I have ever since pictured as being populated largely by thin blond guys making cutting, ironic comments. On my second day, I made a little less money than I had on the first, and on the third day I made still less, and so on.

I watched a lot of Red Sox games with my grandfather that summer. He wasn't really that big of a sports guy, but he was willing to watch whatever made me happy, so long as it didn't interfere with his late afternoon viewing of *M*A*S*H*.

The television was in his room. I sat on his orthopedic bed and he sat on his La-Z-Boy, both of us using remote controls to lift and lower our torsos and legs until we were in suitable game-watching position. During lulls in the action my gaze sometimes drifted from the screen to the curling black-and-white snapshots under dusty glass on the wall behind the television. Sometimes I looked to my left at my grandmother's bed, where she'd died. Sometimes I found myself staring at my grandfather's purple-splotched hand as it lay flat on the La-Z-Boy armrest. His lungs were giving out, and he was connected by blue tubes to an oxygen machine that emitted a constant low-level hum from the next room.

During one game, my grandfather suddenly maneuvered the La-Z-Boy into an alert 90-degree angle and began blowing air through a disconnected French horn mouthpiece. He had been the leader of a Dixieland band in his younger years, and more recently, until his lungs started giving out, he had played the French horn in a band of similar old guys who all dressed up in maroon uniforms and performed numbers such as "The Hokey Pokey" at a bandshell in nearby Chatham every Friday night. The sound produced by the mouthpiece was a meager, rangeless brapping.

"I do this to keep my lips in shape," he explained after he had been tooting away for several minutes. An unwelcome thought formed in my mind. *In shape for what?*

The things he played on the mouthpiece were all indecipherable, with one exception. In a late inning the Red Sox got something cooking, and the old man took a deep breath and blew a monotone, spittle-thin version of the cavalry call—"Brapada brap pa braaa."

I didn't like it. It was too corny and hopeful. Even though the Red Sox had been playing well that year, and even though I was starting to believe, I still preferred to approach each game armored with the protective conviction that my team would blow it, no matter what.

"Brapada brap pa braaa," my grandfather played again. He glanced at me and smiled, his frayed gray eyebrows rising.

"Brapada brap pa braaa," he played.

"Charge," I finally said.

On days when it rained really hard Greenpeace canceled the canvassing. Those rainouts were among the greatest days this chronic life avoider has ever known. It's been more than twenty years and I still can't get over them. The job of knocking on door after door to cheerfully recite a scripted spiel about the encroaching environmental apocalypse and the need for monetary contributions made my stomach hurt, plus I was terrible at it. I came to love waking to the sound of rain. It meant the pressure was off.

On what would be my last day at that job, I left my route after a couple hours of doors slamming in my face and wandered over to a Cumberland Farms. I bought a Coke and, to cheer myself up, a pack of baseball cards. I was leafing through the cards back at my pickup spot when the smirking blond guy from Tufts pulled up. He stared at my baseball cards.

"A kid give those to you?" he asked.

The next morning I found myself praying for a giant rainstorm so I could get stoned, make Steak-umms with melted American cheese, and watch television all day with my grandfather. But the sky was blue with no hope of rain, not a cloud anywhere. I felt like I might puke. I called the office. The blond guy answered.

"I can't do this anymore," I said. "I'm really, really sorry."

"Ha. Don't be," he said.

I spent a few days as if they were rainouts, then rode my grandfather's disintegrating bike down to the Shell station to see if they were hiring.

That fucking summer. I think of the song "Sledgehammer" everywhere. Cars full of college girls in bikinis pulling into the station, that song blaring for a couple minutes, then fading as the girls disappeared. Later, back home, I cast myself in scenarios in which, instead of being profoundly oblivious to me as I washed the windshield, the girls in the front seat noticed me peeking down at the tops of their breasts and yanked me into the car to rip off my high cap and collared shirt and so on.

And I think of my bike ride home at night from Greenpeace, before I quit. Halfway through the eight-mile trek, as I passed from the ocean side of the Cape to the bay side, the road turned from a long gradual uphill to a long gradual downhill, and the traffic thinned to almost nothing. I coasted through the dark, riding atop the white line on the shoulder of the road. Most nights I stopped and swam at a pond where my grandfather had done slow old-guy laps before his lungs gave out. I floated on my back, looking up at the stars, listening to the thump of my heart as if it were the heartbeat of the whole dark lake below and all the star-studded blackness above.

My grandfather would be in bed by the time I got home, his main oxygen machine humming in the dining room, the clear plastic tube snaking under the shut door into his room. He always made sure there were beers in the fridge for me and frosted mugs in the freezer. Most nights I got home too late to catch the Red Sox game on the radio in my room, but once they were still playing when I got home, in extra innings, and they pulled out an incredible win after Angels third baseman Doug DeCinces botched what would have been a game-ending catch of an easy pop fly. They'd been doing well all year, but that game really got me going. *My god*, I thought, *could 1986 really be the year?* I allowed myself to envision my deepest wish coming true. Yaz wouldn't be there, but Jim Ed still would be. Dewey still would be. And there'd be pandemonium in the streets, and confetti raining down, and me and my brother in the middle of it laughing and screaming.

And I think of Dwight Evans slowly striding to the plate with the game reaching a crucial stage, me on my grandfather's orthopedic bed, my grandfather safe and sound in his La-Z-Boy. The next summer he'd be in a nursing home. The summer after that he'd be gone. I think of Dewey working the count to 3–1. I hear the chant of 33,000 people on the television. My grandfather joins in. The crowd noise blooms into a great wordless roar that covers the hum of the oxygen machine. My grandfather bobs a loose fist in time to the chant, the tip of his trumpet mouthpiece sticking out through two purple-splotched fingers. He turns to me, grinning, his eyebrows raised.

"Dewey . . . Dewey," he chants, and he won't look away until I join him.

Topps 1977 #521: Bob Grich

Comic books and baseball cards, the primary pillars of the fantasy world in which I spent most of my childhood, come together in this 1977 Bobby Grich card, which has always reminded me of Marvel comics artist Jack "King" Kirby's lantern-jawed, dimple-chinned heroes, who often paused amid dire intergalactic battle to fill the entire comic frame with their chiseled heads and deliver clear-eyed pronouncements of urgent courageous purpose, just as Grich seems to be doing here. Most baseball cards imply that the next moment beyond the moment of the photo will be a few batting cage swings or a saunter to the outfield to shag some flies. But here it seems more likely that Grich—as soon as he is done uttering something along the lines of "He has gone mad with power and MUST BE STOPPED!"—will in the next rectangular frame chronicling his adventures leap high into the sky on superpowered legs to collide with a dark muscular other-worldly destroyer with dead eyes and ornate Aztec-inspired headgear.

As far as I know, Grich never tangled with Galactus or Modok or the Red Skull; he did once scream at Earl Weaver for pinch hitting for him too often when he was a rookie, but no blows were thrown by either man. Mostly, Grich quietly went about his job, over the course of his career creating a body of work bettered by only a few second basemen in major league history. (Bill James, a longtime advocate of the underrated Grich's estimable worth, ranked Grich as the twelfth best second baseman of all time.)

This card heralded the beginning of Grich's stay with the Angels. (Note the blotchy, doctored uniform piping, Topps scrambling to adjust for his free agency defection from the Orioles.) Interestingly,

I have no memories of Grich besides this card until a moment at the very end of his Angels sojourn. The reason the latter moment, which came during the Angels' 1986 American League championship series tilt with the Red Sox, stands out in my memory is that once again Bobby Grich seemed like a character who'd be at home in the pages of a superhero comic. I don't recall exactly when the moment occurred, but it was either after the Angels' third win, which put them up three games to one, or after the Angels took a commanding lead in the next game. The California sun was shining down, the home fans were screaming joyously, and Grich leapt into the air to give a seismic high five to a teammate, who in my memory was, fittingly, the Angel with a superhero's bulging musculature, Brian Downing. Both Angels seemed larger than life, especially Grich, as if with a couple uncanny Hulk-like leaps he could bound all the way across the continent to New York to finally participate in a World Series.

He shrank back down to human size soon enough, I guess. He became like the rest of us once again, who only ever fly in our dreams. I don't remember noticing him as the Red Sox clawed back to beat the Angels and win their first pennant since 1975.

Not that I was looking for him. I was too busy flying.

Topps 1978 #473: Bill Buckner

BILL BUCKNER

The little color television in the corner of the dorm room seemed to be emitting the kind of gamma rays that center superhero origin tales. The three young men with me in the room—Steve from Peterborough, NH; Tom from Marblehead, MA; and John from Norwich, VT—were all glowing, as if they would soon be able to shoot fire from their fingertips or stop bullets with their chests or topple a building with one punch. And I seemed to be levitating several inches off the ground. In a few seconds we'd all be invincible.

We had a two-run lead in the bottom of the tenth inning of Game Six of the 1986 World Series. The first two Mets batters had made outs. No one was on base. We needed to record just one more out for the deepest wish of our childhoods to come true. I started wondering how I was going to get to Boston for the parade, and if my brother would be able to meet me there.

"Where can we get champagne this time of night?" I said, and Gary Carter stroked a sharp single to left.

It's easy to try to make sense of it all now. To soberly and magnanimously absolve everyone involved from blame. To claim I'd never assigned blame in the first place. To claim I never wished grave ill on John McNamara or built a lexicon of mockery around the sad failure face of Calvin Schiraldi or evaded the question of who was responsible for the ball skipping to the backstop and allowing the tying run to score, Bob Stanley or Rich Gedman, by simply throwing them both onto the noxious dump fire smoldering for years and years in my mind. To claim that because I had almost completely stopped believing the game could still be won by the time Mookie Wilson's ground ball bounded toward Bill Buckner, and because I was not one of the idiots who harassed him and his family until he fled Boston for Idaho, or one of the idiots who years later held up a sign saying they forgave him, as if he had something to be forgiven for (*Forgive us, Bill Buckner*, the signs should have read), that I was somehow not complicit in the crushing weight of history that came down on Bill Buckner's shoulders, obliterating the achievements of a career that included 2,715 hits and 1,208 RBI and a .289 lifetime batting average and an All-Star berth and a batting title and a division crown and a pennant and a moment just a few moments away from invincibility. To claim the thought of Bill Buckner never prompted a sharp ache to spread through my chest. To claim I wasn't overwhelmed by a bitterness that severed a connection to the closest thing I had to a religion in such a way that the connection, though it would survive, would never be fully repaired.

Steve from Peterborough, NH, swore and cried. Tom from Marblehead, MA, smashed empty beer bottles against the wall. John from Norwich, VT, climbed into his bed and curled into a fetal position, pulling his covers over his head. I just stood there looking down at a phlegm-colored institutional rug, a painful, skeletal grin on my face that I couldn't get rid of, a corollary to the painful beating in my head: *What the fuck? What the fuck? What the fuck?*

Topps 1975 #385: Dock Ellis

I thought childhood was over. I thought I'd lost the touch of the gods. It was a cold late morning in January 1987. A friend handed me and a couple other friends each a tiny perforated cardboard square imprinted with a yin-yang symbol. We placed the cardboard onto our tongues.

We were near a playground. As we started to feel something in our limbs, a giddy electric shivering, we got on some swings. Childhood returned, and not just the memory of childhood but the full feel of it, the narrow, deep glee of simply *swinging*.

You can just get by from day to day or you can swing. Dock Ellis swung. He spoke up loud and clear when something bothered him. He wore hair curlers on the field during pregame warm-ups. According to the book Dock Ellis collaborated on with poet Donald Hall, *Dock Ellis in the Country of Baseball*, he once announced before a game against the Reds (whom Ellis felt had established a psychological edge over Ellis's Pirates), "We gonna get *down*. We gonna *do* the *do*. I'm going to *hit* these motherfuckers," and then in the first inning he backed up his words by drilling the first three Reds batters before throwing six straight balls to Tony Perez and Johnny Bench, who had temporarily given up baseball for dodgeball. (At that point Ellis's manager finally removed him from the game.) Off the field, he visited prisons and befriended and helped the inmates, laying the groundwork for a post-baseball career as a devoted and talented social worker. Even when he was near the very top of the game, he spilled over the sides of it. Early in his career, on an off day, Dock Ellis met up with a friend who had some tiny perforated squares of cardboard.

I wanted to follow the footsteps of another character determined to spill over the sides of life, Sal Paradise. And just like the narrator of *On the Road*, I had an old boarding-school roommate who, by living in California, offered a suitably faraway point B. I rode a Greyhound bus all the way, having no adventures to speak of, the vast land that was the star of my favorite book scrolling past the dirty bus window like stock footage in a dimly lit documentary.

Once I got to California, I soon ran so low on money that I had to exist for a while on tortillas and cream cheese that I stole from a small grocery store. I got so desperate I applied for and, because they took anyone, got a job once again fundraising door to door for an environmental protection organization. I was worse than ever at it, and one day in Lompoc I hit a new low, unable to get a single penny from anyone. Near the end of my shift I knocked on a door and a thin guy with aviator glasses answered. I began reciting the official spiel in my customary hesitant monotone.

"Hey, let me ask you something," the guy said, cutting me off.

"Okay," I said.

"How would you like to experience something a thousand times better than any acid trip?"

I looked down at my clipboard, at my watch. I looked back up at the guy. I went inside and chanted Nam Myoho Renge Kyo with the guy and his Asian wife for a while, the three of us kneeling in their living room.

"Wow, huh?" the guy said afterward. I assured him that he'd changed my life, even though I still felt the same. Before leaving his porch I tried to finish my spiel and get a contribution. He was leaning in his doorway. He waved a hand around like he was shooing a bug.

"We've moved beyond all that," he said. "Don't you see?"

A few days later I got a job at a gas station. I worked there for a month and a half and quit in time to spend my last couple weeks in California smoking pot, meditating on a cliff overlooking the Pacific, and reading books that in various ways affirmed that the whole wide world was an illusion.

While the rest of his teammates and the team they would be playing slept, Dock Ellis, eyes wide open, marveled through the night and into the next day at the whole wide world far below.

"I might have slept maybe an hour," Dock Ellis recalled in *Dock Ellis in the Country of Baseball*. "I got up maybe about nine or ten in the morning. Took another half tab."

As he regained the full altitude of his orbit, he realized that, in just a few hours, back down on earth, he was scheduled to pitch. No one had ever attempted to pitch a major league game while experiencing the hallucinogenic effects of LSD, but Dock Ellis ran toward life no matter what. He arrived at the ballpark with only enough time to watch the ball leap from his fingers a few times before the Star-Spangled Banner was played.

My brother met me in California at the end of the summer. He was about to drop out of college for a while and work, but before donning the UPS browns he wanted to get a taste of the big wide world. To spill over the sides. He and his friend Dave had taken a meandering route west, and the plan was that the three of us would drive all the way back east together. By the time they picked me up they had built up a bond from all the miles, their in-jokes and references to road experiences making me feel like an outsider. I was hoping that on the drive east I'd become a full partner in the trip. Also, I hadn't yet learned how to drive and was hoping (and dreading) that I'd get a chance to practice as we shot across the continent. I imagined that somehow on the long drive I'd free myself of all my limitations; somehow I'd no longer be myself but someone better.

Before heading east, we detoured north for a two-day outdoor concert featuring Santana and the Grateful Dead. The line getting into the parking lot was never-ending, long enough for us to purchase three hits of acid from some guy, long enough for us to talk over how best to use our new acquisition, long enough for us to dismiss the rational choice of waiting until the next day so that we could take the hits just before the concert in favor of an alternative and more immediate time of liftoff, because at the present moment we were bored out of our skulls, inching along at a mile an hour if we were moving at all. So, still paralyzed in traffic, we just said *What the fuck*. Onto our tongues went the little squares of cardboard.

A long night devoid of stories ensued. Dave had a particularly bad trip and kept saying that he was cold, *so cold*. Even after we finally escaped the clutches of the traffic jam, we spent a lot of the night in or very near the car. For an eternity I sat on the ground against the car, leaning against a tire, and stared at my pant leg, praying for it to reflect the light of dawn.

Dock Ellis was wild that day. During the night he'd been listening to Jimi Hendrix, and maybe the snarling, snapped-power-line frenzy of Hendrix's guitar was still ripping through him. Through the first five innings, he walked five batters and hit a sixth. But no one had scored, despite all the baserunners dancing around behind him like jackals. No one had made any solid contact, either. Through five: no hits. Through six: no hits.

As the sun began to rise, my brother and I left Dave in the car, still shivering under all his clothes, and went to an open area and threw a Frisbee. Before you are born you are one with the universe, after you die you're one again, but when you're alive you're like a piece of the whole that's come loose and is falling. That's how I felt for most of that acid trip. A chunk of flesh plunging through the dark. But when I played catch with my brother I no longer felt that way. There was just an old indestructible connection, the disc a bright shared pulse in the dawn.

In the seventh, as Dock Ellis's whole body thrummed like something connected to the apocalyptic heartbeat of the universe, a Padres pinch hitter stung one through the box, but second baseman Bill Mazeroski dove and made the catch, preserving the oval on the scoreboard below the letter H. In the eighth, as his pitches continued to snarl and sneer, Dock Ellis surrendered his eighth walk of the game but then got the next batter to ground out to the shortstop, ending the inning. In the ninth, all the colors of the rainbow huddled behind the muted tones of the gray, misty day like giggling guests at a surprise party, about to leap out and start screaming. Dock Ellis stood at the center of it all and realized that all he had to do, all he ever had to do, was play a simple game of catch.

The car died before we even got out of California, on a long uphill part of the highway just outside Truckee, causing us to abandon our cross-country drive and fly home. When I got back to college I found that the ranks of my party buddies, which had been shrinking at the transient school since the end of my first semester, had dwindled to nothing. A few weeks in, telling myself I was aiding my writing by

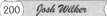

further exploring the inner reaches of my mind, I flew solo through a sheet of acid one hit at a time.

During one trip I played pickup basketball and found it impossible to miss. I sank every shot I took, even ridiculous sprawling heaves meant to test the limits of my hot streak, which ultimately seemed not to be a hot streak at all but a temporary glimpse of who I really was, unencumbered by all the layers of failure and doubt and guilt.

Most often I spent the trips staring at the wall or into some damp woods behind the house where I was renting a room. I was hoping for a vision, or for a return of that feeling of childhood I'd had during my first trip. That feeling never did return, however, and the closest thing I had to a vision was when I was wandering around campus and some faroff mountains briefly turned into a pair of dirty Converse All-Stars.

Finally, I reached the end of the sheet, taking what would be my last hit of acid on Halloween 1987, at a Phish show at Goddard College. It was a bad trip—narrow, jittery, alienating, laced with the smell of my own burning synapses—and I spent most of it crashing around alone through limb-scraping brush in the dark woods behind the art building, where everyone was having a fantastic time dancing and laughing together, all the revelers wrapped in colorful costumes, the guitarist and bass player hopping up and down in jester hats, the drummer in a matronly dress. All I had on was my Josh Wilker suit—ripped jeans, T-shirt, army jacket, dirty Converse All-Stars, skin—and if I could have I probably would have taken it all off and set it on fire.

Maybe I'm haunted by boundless possibilities. Maybe I always have been. My earliest years, the late 1960s and early 1970s, came in a time and place bubbling with the idea that anything was possible. The ecstatic visions of Jack Kerouac seemed less an elegiac psalm to an evaporating world than a prelude to a world yet to come. You could be whomever you wanted to be and each day was going to be a new transformation, the promising light of the present moment giving way to even brighter, warmer, wider light. In the early 1970s, you could, as Dock Ellis did late on the night before a day game against the Padres, take a hit of acid and be unbeatable, untouchable, unhittable. You could be the best possible version of yourself, all your lesser costumes burned clean away.

Topps 1979 #359: Dan Spillner

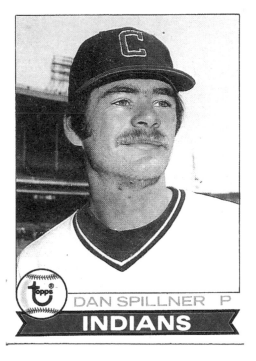

When I finished college, in 1990, there weren't any major or minor league teams knocking down my door, so to speak. My BFA in creative writing was as useful, professionally speaking, as a degree in pointing at clouds and saying what they resembled. I had no skills, no connections, not even much ambition beyond a hazy collection of vague hallucinations about a future involving writing, some shattering moment of spiritual enlightenment, rooms full of people cheering for me, and fucking.

I gave away my records and most of my books and threw away anything else I couldn't carry on my back. Luckily, my baseball cards had been transferred a few years earlier to the storage facility. I like to think if I had them with me I would have held on to them as I prepared to blindly flee from the beginning of Life, but I was in something of a panic of self-abnegation. Maybe I would have chucked them in a Dumpster. But maybe then I would have seen Dan Spillner smiling back at me through the Dumpster stench. Maybe, moved by some combination of his vaguely familiar name and bland mustache and friendly smile and neck acne, I would have climbed in after Dan Spillner and his cohorts and begun this rescue mission years earlier than I finally did.

Instead, I took a trip to Europe, where I spent my little wad of savings as sparingly as possible. After a couple months I was broke, the two notebooks I'd filled still lacking any sort of lasting story. Besides a few stray conversations, my only human contact had been one drunken youth hostel breast grope in Scotland, near the end. I can't even prove the trip happened, as there's no visual record of it. I hadn't brought a camera. I'd visited many places where cameras were always flashing, and after several weeks of solitary travel I began to wonder if my true self resided, if anywhere at all, solely in partial glimpses of myself in other people's photographs. I was the blurry elbow of the stranger passing through.

By the time Dan Spillner smiled for the camera in his 1979 card, he had managed to stick around long enough for the evidence of his minor league struggles to have disappeared. This was common. At a certain point, if you were able to hang on for a while in the majors, your minor league records, no longer needed to fill space, disappeared from the back of your card. Gone was any evidence of anonymity and strife, of any kind of a past that may have seemed to be leading nowhere. And who knew what the future held? As yet, for Dan Spillner, there had been no defining moment, no gleaming triumphant connection, no indestructible story. But there were still some years to come, and maybe they would engrave the name Dan Spillner in the books.

The day after I returned from Europe, I got a temporary holiday-help job as a UPS driver assistant. I started chipping in on the rent with my brother for my mom's railroad apartment on Second Avenue and Ninth Street in Manhattan, which he'd been living in alone since Mom had gone to France to work on her PhD. When the holidays ended I switched to loading trucks at the UPS warehouse on Tenth Avenue and Forty-second Street. My shift started in the middle of the night. My job was to grab packages coming down a long, groaning conveyer belt and sort them into one of four trucks parked behind me. Four others also worked the conveyer belt, each with four trucks to load. Five loaders facing us worked a second conveyer belt. A cheap boombox played "Everybody Dance Now" over and over. The loader to my right shadowboxed during the occasional lulls in packages coming down the line. I was the only white guy besides the harried supervisor, who rushed around in a short-sleeve button-down shirt and tie. The only thing we ever had that remotely resembled a conversation was when he noticed the Red Sox cap I'd worn to work.

"Rico Petrocelli," he barked, hurrying past. Then, over his shoulder, his voice mostly blotted by the conveyor belts, he seemed to say the name Carl Yastrzemski.

As it turned out, the most notable moment in Dan Spillner's long career as a reliever on perennial also-rans came in 1983. I'd watched it in the TV room of my boarding-school dorm. He'd been the blurry elbow of the stranger passing through, the journeyman with the bland mustache, the last man to ever face Carl Yastrzemski.

It was tiring, monotonous work. The boxes turned my hands black and all my clothes gray. During the nightly ten-minute break, I sat in one of the trucks and read Dante, hell then purgatory then paradise as the months went by. At quitting time I walked home down the west side and cut across Twenty-ninth Street past towering early morning prostitutes, spent condoms strewn all over the sidewalk like kelp left behind by the receding tide. Near home I yanked a newspaper out of the trash and read it back at the apartment while eating generic three-for-a-dollar mac and cheese and drinking cans of beer, the blinds shut against the morning light.

One day near the end of my walk home I stopped at a light and looked across Third Avenue and saw my brother standing there, staring back at me. He was on his way to his office job. A heavy duffel bag weighed him down. I had my newspaper from the garbage. We both started laughing. One minute you're a kid and the next you're chained all night long to a conveyor belt. And your brother, your hero, is lugging a duffel bag full of undone work back to an office where his biggest thrill in many months has been finding and correcting a misspelling of the proper noun *Yastrzemski*.

Topps 1978 #36: Eddie Murray

EDDIE MURRAY

My brother worked steadily. He took after our father in that way. Every morning up and off to the grind, day after day, week after week. I shied away from joining him. I didn't think I was competent enough to work a job that required skills beyond anonymous, temporary lifting and carrying. Also, after all my Kerouac worship and my childhood surrounded by adults (besides my father) doggedly trying to exist outside steady jobs, I feared that steadiness would lead me to a life without value. I'd be like a card in a new pack that you barely notice as you flip through searching for some kind of promise.

Eddie Murray's 1978 card had promise, evidenced by the gleaming ALL-STAR ROOKIE trophy in the bottom right corner. This trophy showed up on a few cards each year and then, in the coming seasons, depending on how the recipient of the trophy had fared, it would either stand as a rich silver harbinger of the good things that had come to pass or as a glum tin comment on the trophy winner's failure to deliver on their potential. When you're in your early twenties, life carries the burdensome imprint of that trophy. Will it come to mock you? Will you squander the promise of beginning?

I quit the truck loader job and fled back to Vermont for a few weeks, staying at Tom's condo, where I spent an inordinate amount of time putting golf balls across the wall-to-wall carpeting at table legs. In the evenings Tom came home from his steady job as a dealer rep for a company that sold tankless water heaters and barbecued on his deck as the two of us drank and looked at the man-made waterfall twenty feet away. He was glad to have me there.

"How's Jenny?" he sometimes asked, meaning my mom.

When I wasn't staging table-leg golf tournaments, I found time to write a young adult sports novel that, I later would come to understand, drew far too heavily on my childhood love of *The White Shadow*. As soon as I finished the thing, I returned to my brother, who had moved to an apartment in Brooklyn, making way for my mom, who had come back from France. On my first day there, I took a long walk from the apartment to the Brooklyn Heights promenade and stared across the East River at the Manhattan skyline, imagining that I would soon enough bring the city to its knees with my undying work about teenaged boys shooting baskets. I never did sell the book, but as I waited for it to sell I got what I figured would be a temporary job at a liquor store where my brother had worked while attending NYU.

Eddie Murray won the Rookie of the Year award in 1977, but it should have gone to Mitchell Page, who nearly led the league in stolen bases while also easily besting Murray in the two most telling of the basic offensive production categories, on-base percentage (.407 to Murray's .336) and slugging percentage (.521 to Murray's .470). Which of the two young sluggers would rapidly decline with each succeeding year, banished from regular playing time by 1981, and which player would eventually join Hank Aaron and Willie Mays as only the third man to ever amass more than 3,000 hits and 500 home runs? When the 1978 cards came out, you couldn't know the answer to that question. By the early 1990s, of course, as I took my first steps as an adult, Mitchell Page was long gone while steady Eddie Murray was still driving in his 90 to 100 runs a year, a perpetual standout always just shy of superstardom, seemingly immune to the ups and downs that threatened and confused and defined the lives of everyone this side of the Hall of Fame.

My mom worked a temporary job in the print department at the Metropolitan Museum of Art. Going back to graduate school had been even harder than she'd imagined, but she had stuck with it, steady as a Hall of Famer, despite the mountains of reading and endless memorizing of facts and writing of papers and contending with ambitious, moneyed fellow students, most of them young enough to have been her children.

Her biggest ally along the way had been the same guy she'd separated from two decades before. She and Dad had never shown any antipathy for one another that I had seen and, beyond staying friends, had in fact, for reasons I never quite understood, never even bothered to get a divorce. When Mom moved to New York for graduate school they began to see more of one another, and Dad was so encouraging about her studies that when she finally completed her dissertation on Honoré Daumier she dedicated it to him.

She was still working to complete that dissertation while she was employed at the Met, but after many years she was in the home stretch with her studies and working, albeit temporarily, at one of the greatest museums in the world. She was a worrier, though, and worried that she'd still somehow be unable to finish her dissertation and that she'd be unable to find work after her temporary job ended. She worried about Dad. She worried about Ian. She worried about me.

"How's Tom?" she sometimes asked.

Everything seemed to have within it at least a hint of aftermath, and sometimes much more than a hint. My liquor store job was no exception. The store had once been successful, but since two large warehouse-style liquor stores had opened nearby business had waned. Sometimes people stuck their head in the door just to tell us that we were selling something for considerably more than one or the other of the warehouses. Sometimes, just for something to do, we took empty individual-sized boxes of Absolut and used them to cover up large gaps in our shelves. This practice of covering up the empty shelves increased as the years went by until eventually most of the store was empty boxes.

"Wow, you guys really have a lot of Absolut," a customer would sometimes observe.

When I wasn't filling empty spaces, I was filling empty time. Sometimes I'd read the baseball encyclopedia we kept in the back. Sometimes I'd glare out the window, sorting passing women into imaginary piles, fuckable and unfuckable. Sometimes I watched baseball games on the television behind the counter, both New York teams perpetually playing out the string, Charlie O'Brien grounding out to second, Steve Balboni staring into space, Eddie Murray padding his prodigious career RBI numbers with a sacrifice fly to plate Bill Pecota late in a 7–3 loss.

I worked most shifts with a married adjunct philosophy professor named Dave. On Fridays, Dave took a twenty from the register and we bought Italian food from a restaurant around the corner and ate it in the back with a bottle of wine. Dave did most of the talking, and he also took care of the refilling of our chipped coffee cups. Once the bottle passed its halfway point, the conversation turned from sports to memory lane—to Dave's memories, that is, or to be even more specific, to the difference between Dave's girl-glutted past and my gnawingly lonely present. Dave spun great expansive tales of romantic adventure and seduction that always seemed to begin with him leaving the liquor store with a bottle of wine in his satchel and always seemed to end with him smoking a joint with some beautiful, sensuous she-beatnik on a rooftop below the gentle caress of the 3 a.m. night. I loved the stories, loved how he told them, loved feeling a little drunk at work on the free wine, loved the way the whole ritual seemed to beckon for a wider world than the one I was experiencing in most of my waking hours. Later, before we locked up the gates for the night, I dutifully tried to follow Dave's lead, jamming a bottle of wine into my backpack next to the Dostoevsky and the Mead Wireless notebook filled with my feverish screeds. But my Friday nights, instead of ending on a rooftop with a girl, always ended while waiting with my brother in a stink cloud of bum urine for the F train to Brooklyn after last call.

Ian and I went to games sometimes. Most of the time, baseball in the early 1990s seemed to me like the Merle Haggard song: "It's Not Love (But It's Not Bad)." We spread ourselves across several seats in a half-empty stadium in the Bronx or in Queens and watched with detached bemusement as a fly ball conked Deion Sanders in the head or Vince Coleman pulled a hamstring or Scott Kamieniecki served up a few gopher balls or John Franco walked in the go-ahead run.

Sometimes we still went to a game with more at stake than simply wanting to pleasantly kill an afternoon. My brother wore a Red Sox cap and I wore, more often than not, the painter's cap with YAZ on the front that Ian had bought outside Fenway a few years earlier. One Memorial Day, thusly clad, we ventured to Yankee Stadium and watched from high above the left-field foul line as Red

Sox pitcher Danny Darwin gradually surrendered most of a big early cushion, the stadium crowd getting louder and louder, nearing its transformation into the Beast. Finally Jeff Reardon was summoned from the bullpen in the bottom of the ninth, and Mel Hall ripped Reardon's meaty offering high and deep. The shrinking white pill disappeared into the right-field stands like a catalytic tablet into a witch's cauldron. The Beast erupted. Its closest tendril, a cackling blonde woman, pummeled the two of us, Ian on the shoulder and me on my Yaz-capped head, amid the thunderous noise as Mel Hall strutted from base to base.

After Hall finally touched home plate, it took so long for my brother and me to get to the subway that I'm not entirely sure I'm not still there, insane, dreaming all subsequent events. We took a wrong turn upon exiting the stadium and had to circle the whole giant palace of horrors through an endless circling thicket of Yankees fans, the subway nowhere in sight. Ashen-faced, our Red Sox caps stuffed in our pockets, my brother and I said nothing, just trudged. I remember seeing one young sunburned and well-lubricated Red Sox fan flailing against the Beast.

"*Fuck* Bucky Dent!" he kept shouting as he stumbled through the heckling throng. Veins stood out in his forehead and his voice cracked. "Bucky Dent *sucks!*"

You poor crazy bastard, I remember thinking, not without some admiration. It was like watching someone try to start a fistfight with an oncoming train.

My dad's apartment was only a couple blocks from the store. He had retired and sometimes stopped by on his way to or from killing a few hours at the NYU library.

"Here are some vitamins," he said one day, shoving a container the approximate size of a watercooler across the counter to me.

"Here's a carbon monoxide protector," he said another day. "It's important that you and Ian have one of these in your apartment. You must read the instructions on how to use it correctly."

"OK," I said, like he was telling me to brush my teeth.

Sometimes I saw him on the weekends, too. It was a good part of those years, getting to know my father. Once we went out for dinner and after a bottle of wine I asked him about the day we had all moved away from him to go to Vermont.

He stared down at the table for a long time, and I thought he wasn't going to say anything.

"That night," he finally said. Then he shook his head and didn't say any more.

Eddie Murray bats right, according to the listings on the back of his rookie card. Eddie Murray bats left, according to the photo on the front. Eddie Murray stares at the viewer in this photo, many years away from becoming the career RBI leader among switch-hitters. Nothing has been settled. Nothing is known. The world is uncertain, riddled with mistakes. How do you proceed when you don't want to proceed, when you want to stay a rookie forever?

Most days I had nothing in particular to do until my shift started in the evening. Some days I'd write, some days try and fail, some days who the hell knows. Watch *Charles in Charge*, sleep, pace, beat off, worry, do a few push-ups, stare out the window at a sliver of sky. One of those days I spilled out of the building to go to work and a passerby peered at me and remarked, "*Damn*, look like you getting your *ass* kicked by *life*."

At the store, I had to learn to hide this ass-kicked-by-life face behind a more implacable mask. The door was open, and anyone could come in, and sometimes the people who came in were asking or begging or probing for a weakness to exploit or just plain looking to steal.

"No," I learned to say. But it only worked if you filled your whole body with the word.

Behind the counter, we had a baseball bat hanging by the knob from two nails, Jeff Burroughs's autograph engraved in the barrel. I took it off the nails and hefted it sometimes, whenever I felt the armor of the word "No" wearing thin. I no longer imagined, as I had when I was a kid hefting a bat, that I was smacking triples and doubles and home runs, but instead that I was cracking kneecaps and shattering ribs. The daydream's backbeat: *no, no, no.*

It's one thing to be able to look back at the rookie card of a legend and appreciate the card's faint aura of uncertainty. It's another thing to be taking your first steps in adulthood without any sort of notion at all about where you're going to end up. You begin to imagine your own possibilities as something you could hold in your hands, like a rookie card, so as to imagine tearing that card to pieces, as if by doing so you could rid yourself of the oppressive weight of possibly amounting to nothing instead of something.

And even if there's nothing to grab on to, nothing specific to tear into shreds, that won't stop you from trying. In October 1992, for example, my brother and friends and I reacted to the Toronto Blue Jays winning the World Series by gouging Canada from the map of the world that hung on the wall in the back of our favorite bar, the International. It's not that we hated Canada but that the Blue Jays winning the World Series had been unthinkable when we'd been kids, and if the unthinkable was now happening, it must mean that our childhoods were truly gone without a trace. But more than that it was just something to destroy, and something is better than nothing.

By the following year, our disenchantment with the world had grown, and once again we transferred that disenchantment to baseball. Baseball no longer held us like it once had, back when nobody knew if Mitchell Page or Eddie Murray would turn out to be the better player. We knew we were changing and that baseball was basically the same, but we couldn't gouge at ourselves like we'd gouged at the map in the International, so we decided to Blame Baseball. And in 1993, my brother and I and two friends went to a game we dubbed—not without some awareness that we were full of shit (all four of us have attended many baseball games since then), but also not without some real vitriol—the Last Baseball Game Ever. We were all suffering through varying degrees of loneliness and either unemployed or lashed to repetitive menial jobs of one stripe or another. So why not at least pantomime the killing off of the last of the haunting, painful hopes of childhood? Why not declare that centerpiece of our younger years, baseball, forever null and void?

We chose for the Last Baseball Game Ever the second-to-last Mets home game of that team's disastrous 1993 season. The game turned out to be the longest and most uneventful game I've ever seen. Not even a single run was scored for sixteen innings, and while sixteen innings of scoreless ball might seem a likely home for one after another of pressure-packed clutch pitching performances, game-saving fielding gems, and fascinating managerial moves, it was in fact a game in which nothing whatsoever seemed to happen. Batters grounded softly to second and popped out to left field a lot, maybe. I'm not sure. But it went on and on.

After the eighth inning, they closed the concession stands. Sobriety set in, coupled with gnawing hunger. The zeros kept growing across the digital scoreboard. I began to hope they would stretch on forever. This hope combined with our ever-increasing mobility throughout the stadium to make me feel as if a state of damp, cold, mediocre grace had descended upon us. At some point late within the regulation nine innings, we'd ventured down from our seats in the upper deck to tentatively test out the mostly empty sections in the loge boxes. Nobody said anything, the ushers apparently too deadened by the abject misery of the Mets' season to even try for bribes anymore. And as the game edged into extra time we moved even closer, until by the twelfth or thirteenth inning we were mere rows from the home dugout on the third-base side.

We were surrounded for the first time all night by other fans, and there was mixed into the hundred-loss malaise a feeling of giddy excitement—none of us belonged here, and yet, *here we were!* The people who usually sat in these seats were far, far away that night, at some event that mattered, and we finally had our chance to See What It Was Like.

I realized at some point that the closest player to me as we sat in those seats was the Mets third baseman, well-traveled veteran Chico Walker, who in what seemed like another lifetime had been the young player dispatched to replace Carl Yastrzemski in left field on Yaz's last day. Our proximity to the field and the relative quiet of the stadium introduced the rare opportunity to say something to a player on the field that he would hear. As I was trying to think of something Yaz-related to shout to Chico Walker—as if he could always be used as a cosmic conduit to Yaz—I noticed the identity of the one person in uniform even closer to me than Chico Walker. The Cardinals' third-base coach shared the last name and physical description of a former player whom I like to believe, against the mounting evidence to the contrary, was long ago sliced into tiny bits in a wood-chipper accident. There he was, just standing there straight and tall, as if nothing had ever happened. I found myself half-standing out of my seat, the ache that had long ago settled in my chest flaring sharply up my throat and out into the air.

"Bucky Dent, you ruined my life!" I yelled.

The zeros kept spreading as if by mitosis across the scoreboard. We shifted over to an even sparser gathering of fans on the first-base side. It was at this point that the game really seemed headed toward infinity, and I stopped shivering in the damp fog as a calm came over me, as if I were about to drift into fatal hypothermal slumber.

Unlike my brother and me, the two friends who had come along with us were full-blooded Mets fans, and so they couldn't as easily embrace my vision of an everlasting game without a winner. Because of that, they eventually struck up a rendition of "Meet the Mets."

At first, just their two voices were singing the song, but then a third shaky voice that seemed to be coming from the thin, damp fog itself joined in. For a brief moment, there seemed to be no one connected to that other voice, but then this slight, gray-pallored guy in a dirty Atlanta Braves cap appeared on the fringes of our ragged congregation.

He spent the remaining moments of the game in our company, a guy about our age with lank dirty hair down almost to his shoulders and an aura about him of either being someone who lived in his parents' basement or, perhaps more likely, who had recently been evicted from his parents' basement, leaving with a broken-zippered duffel bag containing a change of clothing and the tattered edition of the baseball encyclopedia from his childhood.

In the weeks and months and years to follow, he appeared periodically on the fringes of our gatherings as if from nowhere. He always remembered us from the Last Baseball Game Ever and acted briefly like he was a familiar part of our group before wandering off. He materialized without exception on nights when the element of directionlessness in our lives seemed even more pervasive than usual. The last time I saw him was years ago, but I'm still not sure I won't see him again. He briefly wandered into a bar on Second Avenue near Houston Street dressed in a replica of Michael Jordan's short-lived number 45 Bulls jersey and matching Bulls shorts, vaguely acknowledged us, and then wandered back out into a night that was way too cold to be dressed in a remaindered basketball uniform.

On the night of the Last Baseball Game Ever, he faded back into the ether from whence he came moments after the game finally ended in the bottom of the seventeenth inning, as if he could exist only while things were undecided, nothing but zeros on the board. Eddie Murray, the only player present who had appeared on one of my childhood baseball cards, started the rally with a leadoff single. After a sacrifice bunt and a Chico Walker popup, Murray loped around third and toward home on a Jeff Kent shot into the gap. But before he became the winning run, the only run, the Last Run of All Time, Eddie Murray tiptoed to a stop a step away from scoring. The on-deck hitter, Joe Orsulak, had to shove him across the plate.

Topps 1977 #260: J. R. Richard

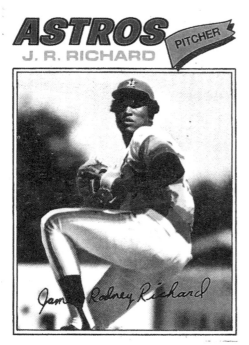

I spent a lot of my twenties in the International. More often than not, my brother was there. We had a lot of good times there, and we had a lot of times where it seemed like we were waiting for something to happen. *That door will swing open and my life will begin.* I wanted it, dreaded it, feared it. The days went by, the weeks, the years. I worried that my brother and I were destined to live together forever, like Miss Emily and Miss Mamie, the desiccated spinster sisters from *The Waltons*. Since I'd left college, we'd already shared three apartments: the narrow railroad in Manhattan, a dump in Brooklyn that constantly trembled from the vibrations of the nearby Brooklyn-Queens Expressway, and a railroad in Brooklyn where my brother slept in the living room and I crammed myself into a loft bed in a converted closet a few feet away, as close to my brother's bed as I'd been as a kid. When we finally got home from last call at the International, dawn breaking, I'd fall unconscious below dim glow-in-the-dark stars left over from when previous tenants used the loft bed for a young child.

J. R. Richard spent his early to mid-twenties trying to find the strike zone, and then suddenly it was like whatever he had been looking for found him, seized him, changed him. He began taking long, loping strides toward Cooperstown.

He was 6′8″, threw blazingly hard, wore the dazzling colors of the distant, exciting, up and coming Astros, had a cool, mysterious name, and once he became a star he always seemed to be featured by Topps in one of their rare action shots, the photos making him seem even bigger and more electrifying than the increasingly impressive numbers on the back of his card suggested.

Back in the heyday of J. R. Richard I sometimes passed entire afternoons wondering who could beat up whom in the Marvel superhero universe, and though I understood that the worlds of baseball and comics did not overlap, J. R. Richard (last name virtually identical to Reed Richards, leader of the Fantastic Four) was an exception, and I thought of him as if he could be placed somewhere in the penultimate tier of the Marvel rankings, able to trade skyscraper-rocking blows with the likes of Spider-Man, Iron Man, or Luke Cage: Power Man. And even the three top Marvel strongmen—the Thing, Thor, and the Incredible Hulk—though perhaps too powerful for J. R. Richard to hold off in a fistfight without the help of some lesser masked functionary such as Hawkeye or the Falcon, could not, if the situation were ever to arise, touch one of the lightning-bolt fastballs that sprang from J. R. Richard's giant superpowered hand.

My brother was even more mesmerized with J. R. Richard than I was and modeled his pitching motion on the one shown in this 1977 card: high bent-kneed leg kick, hands held tight to the chest, scowling eyes locked on the catcher's target. He perfected the motion while hurling a tennis ball at the strike zone he'd duct-taped to our wooden garage door. The sound the ball made when hitting the door got louder as the years passed, my brother amid the seismic epicenter of his puberty seeming to get bigger by the day: 6'1", 6'2", 6'3". By the time he had reached his full height of 6'4" and no longer played organized baseball and was openly longing to leave home for good, the scowling, bent-kneed windup and gunshot report of the garage door had become the primary elements in a ritual of imagined escape, each pitch a prayer for an impossible transformation from cornered teenager into the pure violent beauty of J. R. Richard throwing heat.

Sometimes my brother didn't show up at the International.

"Where's Ian?" I was asked.

I never really knew. I tried throughout my twenties to make time stand still, the two of us side by side at home and at baseball games and on barstools. I tried not to feel anything if I could help it, but I felt the ache in my chest whenever he failed to show up. I rarely found out where he'd been or what he'd been doing on those nights,

but one night, as he later told it, he was wandering around the city, getting angrier and angrier. Rich pricks everywhere. Hipsters, yuppies, predatory phonies. The whole city one big exclusionary enterprise, roped off by velvet to keep the likes of him out. He went into a Korean grocer and bought a persimmon, about the size and weight of a baseball. He continued his walk, hefting the fruit, continuing to stoke his rage, and when he came to a velvet-roped club not far from our dank, smoke-glutted lung, the International, he shouldered through the front door, yelled, "This is *hell!*" and hurled the persimmon with all his might and all his J. R. Richard inspired technique.

We got into a drunken fracas at the International once. I don't remember how it started, if I ever knew, just that the narrow bar was unusually crowded that night and Ian took umbrage at what he perceived to be the arrogant attitude of some random skinny cool guy and his friends, which unlike our own lonely gathering of mutterers included some girls. What I discovered is that while I generally go to great lengths to avoid confrontations, I won't hesitate to jump into the middle of things to defend my brother. It turned out to be nothing more than a shoving match centering around Ian attempting to strangle his smirking adversary, but I think it still deserves to be noted because it was the only time in my life that I can remember jumping into action without first thinking about it. Soon the shoving cooled to a shouting match, which ended for me when a pretty woman in the other group referred with scorn to the theme-restaurant sweatshirt I was wearing.
"Calm down, Hooters," she said.

The great majority of the time, however, nothing really happened. My brother and I and our friends generally loitered until last call at 4 a.m., the favorite part of the night occurring near that time, after we'd all released the burden of hoping that something would happen to change our lives. Some song on the jukebox would hit like Novocaine and it no longer mattered that life was sliding past like scenery in a cheap cartoon. In fact, it felt pretty fucking good. My brother once put words to the feeling: "Numberless nights at the International Bar began their stretch run thusly: It's 3:52 a.m., I've got a headful of static from drinking cheap swill, and Peggy Lee starts teetering through 'Is That All There Is?' on the ol' Wurlitzer. And through all those painful years, I was comforted each time; I'd feel a crooked, fallen smile take shape: 'Yessir, that's all what she wrote.' Various harpies would leave me be and I'd relax into appreciation of what was. McKenna gesticulating wildly, maybe. Or 'That Guy.' Or just Rose behind the bar, humane and beautiful and flatly real. Who needs the transcendent greener grass when opening to What Is is so rewarding? (Of course, I'd forget that five seconds later, or at least by the next morning, and shoulder the misery again.)"

My brother decided he was going to learn how to play the cello. He liked the melancholy sound of the instrument, so he rented one from a music store and signed up for lessons with a recent Juilliard grad, a young, stern Asian woman who was openly incredulous about his intentions. He wanted to use the cello to wrest some beauty from his life, but he rarely got around to taking the thing out of its case. Soon another entry was added into the endlessly rich lexicon of euphemisms for masturbation (e.g., Question: "Where's your brother?" Answer: "He's 'practicing the cello.'"). Nonetheless, he lugged his albatross to and from work whenever he had a lesson, shoehorning himself and the obese case into the jammed F train at rush hour all the way from our neighborhood in Brooklyn to his job editing travel books on the Upper West Side. This went on for a couple months. One Sunday just before he finally admitted defeat, he roused himself from an "Is That All There Is?" hangover to practice his assigned homework, another lesson and its accompanying scolding from the Asian woman looming. The apartment looked, as usual, as if it had been ransacked. It may have been around the time when we had a rotting jack-o'-lantern with carved-out drunken Xs for eyes collapsing into itself next to a bottle of Jim Beam on our "dining room" table. Bleary-eyed, unshaven, wearing only his boxer shorts and a wife beater dotted with Ragu stains, my brother performed his first and last opus, a halting, truncated, off-key rendition of "Mary Had a Little Lamb."

My brother started seeing a woman, and almost immediately it became serious. Had I any sense of what was going on inside me, I would have understood that this development frightened me. I didn't want to be left out or left behind. A few weeks into the relationship, his girlfriend, Kelsey, made a sweet and innocuous suggestion that he get a kitten.

This has gone too far, I thought, as if he'd told me she'd convinced him to sell all his possessions and join the Hare Krishnas.

"Don't you think maybe she's having too big an influence on you already?" I said. "I mean, don't you think things are moving too fast?"

I got angry when I learned that he immediately passed on to Kelsey my reservations. He was on another team now. I swallowed my hurt and anger and insecurity and let it all fester, all the while continuing to cling to my brother. I leaned on him emotionally and financially (in all the years we shared an apartment he always paid more of the rent) while groping for a way to stand on my own before I got left behind.

In those years, I often fantasized about lucking into the creation of the perfect opening sentence of a novel. I'd be like J. R. Richard when the awesome power that had always been lurking inside him finally bloomed. I imagined the blazing mythic fastball of a sentence would have the power to crack a hole in the dam that was holding everything back. An entire book-length fictional world would then gush from the widening hole. By the time the 1990s were half over I had filled up a cello-high stack of notebooks with jagged scribbling, thousands of pages blackened and blued with self-lacerating complaints that the magical dam-breaking First Sentence had yet to come and deliver me from my life. On particularly frustrating days I Hulked it up a little, flying into nearsighted ectomorphic rages that metamorphosed me from a timid high-strung liquor store clerk into a rampaging beast with the gamma-ray-infused strength to rip Mead Wireless college-ruled notebooks into tiny terrified shreds.

Besides waiting in vain for genius to strike, I also daydreamed, as did my brother and at least one of my friends, of escaping from the city. My brother's vision included only the first step of his getaway: Driving without the slightest warning to anyone through the Holland Tunnel, never to return. A friend's more detailed vision involved reversing the path taken by Joe Buck in *Midnight Cowboy*: Instead of leaving a small, scorpion-infested Texas border town to come to New York City, my friend, a lifelong New Yorker, dreamed of leaving New York City for a small, scorpion-infested Texas border town, where he'd wash dishes in a diner, shack up with a divorced, embittered, chain-smoking waitress, and catch up on his reading. My own version of flight involved taking a map of the U.S., plunking my finger down on it randomly, and then taking a bus to that spot to get a job somewhere "sweeping up," as the wistfully forlorn Bill Bixby managed to do at the beginning of every episode of *The Incredible Hulk*.

I rarely left the city. There was no such thing as vacation time at the liquor store, but I occasionally took a few unpaid days off. In earlier years I'd hoped for adventures like those in *On the Road*, but things weren't working out that way. A few years into my long stint selling liquor, and not long after my brother turned in his rented cello, I told my boss, Morty, that I needed a week to go out west. I met up with my fellow Kerouac-loving former roommate from boarding school, Bill, in Santa Barbara, and the two of us drove to Utah with a pair of mountain bikes on the roof of Bill's car.

We spent a couple days camping and hiking in Zion National Park and then set out across the state, heading for the mountain-biking mecca of Moab. I had never actually mountain biked before, but I figured it couldn't be that hard. After driving for hours across a desert, and with several more car-bound hours still ahead of us, we stopped at a rest area that turned out to be nothing more than a tin outhouse perched at the edge of a long, rocky ridge. There was not so much as a telephone there. After I took a leak, I came out of the outhouse and saw that Bill was unhitching his bike from the rack.

"Let's take a break from all the driving," Bill said.

"Sounds good to me," I said. I didn't yet know how to drive a car at that time and so Bill had been doing the whole job himself while I performed such vital tasks as unscrewing the cap on the water bottle and manning the volume on the tape player. For the past couple hours we'd fallen into a silence that in retrospect seems a little haunted to me, the unending barren wilderness outside the windows taking away our words. I still had a song stuck in my head from the tape that had been playing when we'd pulled in, Willie Nelson and Merle Haggard singing Townes Van Zandt's "Pancho and Lefty."

Bill set out first on his bike and I followed behind as soon as I got his sister's bike off the roof. Neither of us bothered to put on our helmets. The ridge was about fifteen feet wide, maybe narrower in parts. It appeared to be relatively flat. It wasn't.

By the time I began hurtling down the bumpy, deceptively steep incline, Bill had wrenched his own bike to a halt and was running toward me and shouting at me to try to do the same. I didn't see him, and anyway it was too late. The handlebars had turned into a jackhammer. I was going too fast to think. Ten seconds into my mountain-biking career I flew off a cliff.

You pray for something to come and change you. It will. In 1980, in the midst of his best season yet, J. R. Richard began noticing stiffness in his back, shoulder, and arm. He mentioned it to team trainers, and in June he began begging out of games early. Nobody could find anything wrong, but nobody was really looking very hard.

J. R. Richard's second-to-last start in the major leagues was in the 1980 All-Star Game. He deserved to start: He was by then the best pitcher in baseball. He threw two scoreless innings, striking out Carlton Fisk, Reggie Jackson, and Steve Stone. His last start was six days later: July 14, 1980. He sailed through the first three innings, giving up no runs and just one hit while striking out four, and in the bottom of the third, in his final major league at bat, he drilled a double off Phil Niekro. But with one out in the top of the fourth inning he walked off the mound and into the clubhouse, complaining of dizziness.

A few days later, Richard gave it another try, but after playing catch with a teammate, he rested for a few minutes, then returned to the field to throw some more and collapsed with a near-fatal stroke. Emergency surgery saved his life. He tried a comeback. It didn't go well. *Not yet*, he must have been thinking, even as minor leaguers were pounding his offerings all over the yard. *It can't be over yet.*

I hadn't found love yet. I hadn't written anything good yet. I hadn't done anything to make Mom and Tom and Dad proud of me yet. I hadn't stood with my brother at a Red Sox victory parade yet.

With the rocky world about to vanish from beneath me, there was no room in my mind for a thought outside the tiny core of blank panic, a wordless distillation of all my unreached wishes.

Not yet.

My friend Bill estimates that I dropped twenty-five or thirty feet before hitting the steep embankment, then bounced and tumbled another hundred feet or so. When I stopped somersaulting I was in a forward-swaying seated position, a thin ribbon of blood pulsing in what seemed to be slow motion from my head out onto the scree, like how guys bled from mortal bullet wounds in Sam Peckinpah movies.

No clouds in the sky. Some dry desert brush here and there. Bill seemed to arrive at my side almost instantly, more scared than anyone I've ever seen.

"Holy *shit*, Josh! Holy fucking *shit!*"

A couple had pulled into the rest area just before I'd flown over the cliff, and the woman drove off to find a telephone so she could call an ambulance while the man made his way down. I made small-talk with the man who'd come to my aid as he and Bill each took one of my arms and half-lifted, half-dragged me toward the highway. He was an air traffic controller. He and his wife were on their way to Colorado, where he was starting a new job.

"Colorado's beautiful," I said.

Bill and the air traffic controller set me on the ground by a shallow roadside ditch. As we waited for the ambulance I started to go into shock. Unfortunately, I didn't know that I was going into shock. All I knew was that I was beginning to feel very cold on a warm sunny day, and my vision was going white and grainy, like a television tuned to a station losing its signal. I thought I might be dying.

After his failed comeback, J. R. Richard's sizable baseball earnings gradually dwindled closer and closer to zero, eroded by two divorce settlements and some bad business decisions, including an oil-well scam that cost him hundreds of thousands of dollars. Looking for a job, he approached the team whose cap he would have worn on a plaque in Cooperstown. They said they'd get back to him. The days went by. The weeks. The years.

The paramedics strapped me to a gurney, carried me into the ambulance, and hooked me up to IVs. According to Bill, who tailed us the whole way, we went one hundred miles an hour for the forty miles to the closest hospital. Once there, I felt okay with Bill by my side as a kind nurse filled me with painkillers, removed rocks embedded in my knees, knuckles, and head, and then sewed up the larger gashes. But that quiet fear I'd felt when descending into shock returned when an orderly wheeled me away from Bill for head x-rays.

I lay on the stretcher alone in a shadowy metallic room. My thoughts wandered. Maybe there was internal bleeding. Maybe a massive secret blood clot had formed and was just waiting for the right moment to fatally clog some vital artery. It happened all the time. One minute you're tossing the ball around with a teammate and the next minute everything fades.

Finally two x-ray technicians came in. I wanted them to talk to me, to talk me through it, but they were busy bitching.

"He thinks his crap don't stink," one of them said.

"I pulled enough overtime the last month," the other said, seeming to talk past him. "I got what's known as a life."

"And that big smile on his face all day?" the first one said. "Lord."

They never acknowledged me, even when they were inches away, repositioning the stretcher. It was a chilling little preview. The world will move along just fine after you're gone. As they x-rayed me, a shred of "Pancho and Lefty" was still echoing around in what I considered at that moment to be my possibly hemorrhaging brain, the haunting part near the end of the song where a ghostly chorus joins in to help tell the doom-limned tale.

All the federales say, they could have had him any day.

Any day. That day. Broken neck, shattered skull, subject of a phone call to the next of kin. As it turned out, every inch of my body hurt and I was stitched up like Frankenstein and I could barely move, but I hadn't broken a single bone, and the x-rays found nothing. I was free to limp out of the hospital, leaning on Bill. Everything glowed. We got a motel room. I called my mother in her apartment, my father in his apartment, Tom in his condo, my brother at the number we shared. I wanted to tell them I loved them. I wanted to gather them and tell them they were everything to me. I tried to write postcards to say it all but it hurt too much to hold a pen.

We headed back toward California, but after several hours of driving we ran out of daylight on the outskirts of Las Vegas. We got a room at a Motel 6 near the strip and decided despite my condition that it would be ludicrous to pass through that city and not gamble a little. I loaded up on codeine and we made our way to Circus Circus.

Inside the casino, I lowered my bandaged body down in front of a slot machine. Bill found a spot farther down the row. Trapeze artists and tightrope walkers occupied the spaces high above all the flashing and chiming and the low-lit humans solemnly trying to be lucky. Once in a while you see how singular life is, how virtually impossible, how blessed and inane. "And yet we were always being found innocent for ridiculous reasons," writes Denis Johnson in *Jesus' Son*. It was a spring night in 1995 in Vegas. I looked as if I'd fallen into a Dumpster-sized blender. I fed the machine and pulled the lever. J. R. Richard was in Houston, broke and homeless. After a few pulls, bells started ringing and coins began spilling onto my lap.

1975 Topps #363: Carmen Fanzone

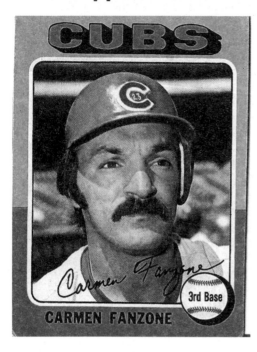

My mother got a temporary job at a college art museum back in Vermont, within a fairly short drive of Tom's condo. They had a lot of shared history, a lot of good memories. They decided to give it another try.

A year or so into this second try, in the summer of 1995, my mother's temporary job at the college art museum ended, and she spent most of the summer away from Tom, back down in New York, sleeping on the "guest mat" in my dad's apartment and finishing her PhD thesis. She had paid the rent on her vacated apartment in the Vermont college town throughout the summer, however, so I invited myself to stay there for several weeks, thinking of it as a "writer's retreat" and, more generally, as something to snap me awake from an adult life that to that point, my twenty-seventh year, hadn't amounted to much. I had no specific idea about what I would do with the time, but I hoped—blindly, desperately—that when I got back to Vermont, back to the green mountains that had mothered all the many bright colors of my childhood, a novel of great genius would begin flooding out of me.

A creeping panic began when I got my first glimpse of the tight, sullen face staring back at me from the bathroom mirror. It was a small, hot apartment with a low ceiling and no view and a clock that went tick tick tick. I didn't have any means of escaping myself. I didn't know anyone in the town. I didn't own a car, or even know how to drive one.

Every day, I walked to the nearby college library, where I read old issues of *Sports Illustrated* in between attempts to write in my notebook that invariably ended with me either knifing deep gashes in the pages with my pen or scrawling dire threats against myself. Back at the apartment, I watched reruns of *Home Improvement*, perhaps the worst sitcom ever made, to help cross the chasm of the late afternoon. With evening in sight, I started drinking and ate gigantic mounds of generic macaroni and cheese with sliced-up generic hot dogs.

At night I lay awake, staring at the ceiling, dreading the next day's blank page. Sometimes I was able to sink into a torpor vaguely resembling sleep by jerking off to memories of the sex I'd had with an ex-girlfriend just before leaving the city. As the summer wore on, I began to build that cursory encounter into something monumental, almost religious, one bright shard shining in a polluted sea of gray. In sheer desperation, I began to convince myself I was falling in love.

My mom came up to visit two or three times. On one of these visits I went with her and Tom to a lake for one of their canoeing outings. They canoed a lot, much more than they ever had in their first go-round. There was a lack of conversation during the car ride to the lake. By that point my mom may have gotten the news that she had another temporary job waiting for her in the fall, at a college museum in Ohio. I can't remember. I also can't remember if I'd yet started to have conversations with Tom in which he confided to me that he was struggling with the idea of continuing a relationship with Mom if she moved that far away. Either way, the silence during the drive seemed heavy to me, as if things were about to fall apart.

But once we got to the lake, and put the canoe in the water, and got in, and shoved away from shore—the very moment we shoved off—the burden dissolved. For the first time all summer, I felt okay. I sat in the middle of the boat without a paddle, Mom was up front, and Tom was in the back. They had once built a whole life together, had created a home, had raised two boys. Little wonder they were like two parts of a whole in a canoe. As we crossed the lake I felt blessed, for the first time in a long time, as if we were afloat in one of those rare safe pockets in life, the diminishing gray future and the unreachable primary brightness of the past gone, dissolved into a pale blue stillness. Nobody spoke, as if the moment was so fragile it would break under the weight of any sounds beyond those faint clacks and burbles marking our movement across the reflection of the sky.

Near the end of the summer, my mom came up to start gathering things for the move to Ohio. It seemed a particularly uncertain moment for both of us, for everyone. The "novel" that I'd hoped would change my life was nothing more than a notebook that looked as if it had been mauled by a pit bull with ink on his fangs. My mother was edging into more of an unknown than she had in many years, perhaps ever, going off alone to a part of the country far away from where she had spent her whole life. Nothing had been resolved between her and Tom as far as what would happen between them when she moved away, but from what happened next I can be sure that my mother was counting on the relationship, that quiet, bittersweet canoe ride, to continue.

What happened next was Tom broke up with my mom. As I understand it, they had tried once before, during the mid-1980s, to keep things going while living in two separate places, and it hadn't worked. Tom didn't want to try that again.

For a long time, one of the longest nights of my life, I lay in the dark on a cot outside my mother's bedroom in the apartment that had already established itself as the location of my most abject failure. I couldn't help overhearing my mother's side of the phone calls. All night long and into the sickly first light of a new day, that rotary dial sound: Zick. Zicka. Zickaaaa. Zick. Sometimes the phone calls ended with a slam. Sometimes they ended as if the phone fell from a dead hand. The worst was when the phone was put down with tenderness, as if tenderness could coax something gone to return. As for the sounds that were made by the human voice in between the beginnings and the endings of those phone calls: I'm not going to say a goddamn thing.

The next day, we went to the storage facility a few miles away from our old house. My weeping mother held the steering wheel in one hand and a damp wad of tissues in the other. The storage facility, a converted barn, gray and lopsided, eventually came into view.

The dark interior of our storage cell was clogged with the last of the residue of our Back to the Land dream. Broken homemade furniture, rusty garden tools, garbage bags full of faded tie-dyed scarves and silk-screened T-shirts, dust-covered cross-country skis, disintegrating books about gurus and canning and sociology and New Games, warped records by the Beatles and the Firesign Theater, the rolled-up canvases of all my mother's giant bright paintings, Tom's old blacksmith tools. Box after box of the things that carried us only so far.

The box that contained my baseball cards was among that detritus. I opened one flap and the brightness of the cards inside stung me. I carried the box out of the room, the flap still open, the faces of baseball

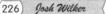

players staring up at me. Outside, we had been making two piles: a small pile to go to Ohio and a much larger one for the dump. I understood that my box of cards belonged in neither pile. But I wasn't ready to look at the cards, either. Those bright colors. Those faces. Those names. I closed the flap with one hand so that my box of cards was just a box again, but then I held it to my chest for a while, delaying my return to the dark room where my mother was sneezing and crying.

I carried the box with me to Ohio, where I helped my mom get settled. Eventually she stopped breaking into tears every few minutes and I got on a bus headed back east. I waved to my mom from the Greyhound window, the box of cards on my lap, where it stayed through the whole ride. I still hadn't been able to look through them, but I opened the flap a couple times and felt a terrible pull that seemed too much for me to handle.

When I got off the bus in New York, I went to the liquor store and begged the owner, Morty, for my job back. It turned out there was an opening for me as big as a canyon. I would start pulling long shifts six days a week and living in the apartment owned by Morty above the store.

With that position secured, I stomped off to my ex-girlfriend, the one I'd had sex with just before leaving for Vermont, and begged for her to take me back, too. As with the job, I'd been the one to break things off. Neither the job nor the relationship had seemed to be right, then, but after my miserable summer I was convinced that what I needed was the life of a Regular Joe. I needed to behead my ridiculous aspirations. I needed a job. I needed a girl. The options I had recently abandoned seemed to be my only options, so I pursued them with a tenacity that I have seldom displayed before or since. My ex-girlfriend was particularly skeptical of my turnaround, but I kept pleading, promising her that I was a Whole New Guy, until she finally relented.

While I was taking a week or so to set up my new life as a person without any problems, I was staying at the apartment I'd shared with my brother for several years. The day before I left to move to the apartment above the liquor store, I finally got the courage to pull open both flaps of the box I'd found in the storage facility.

My brother was in the room with me when I started rooting around in the box. Since I had collected cards because of him, my cards were really *our* cards. This was our coauthored youth, right here, one card at a time. But somehow the cards that had been the center of my earliest waking years remained estranged, even as I held them up one by one in my hands.

I didn't understand it then, but I still had more fucking up to do before the gods would finally speak to me again. My return to the liquor store wouldn't work out, nor would the revived relationship with the ex-girlfriend, nor would any of the jobs or relationships to follow for year after year after year. When my job at the liquor store ended, I moved back in with my brother, the untended weeds of our lives continuing to tangle even as the same estrangement infecting my baseball cards seeped into our brotherhood.

Maybe I knew that things wouldn't work out at the liquor store, that since I wasn't bleeding internally the invisible Siamese connection to my brother hadn't truly been severed, that I'd eventually return to a corner of his apartment, a corner of his life. But it seemed at the time that I was finally striking out on my own, finally leaving the past behind. I wanted to find some glowing, definitive, triumphant piece of it as I sat with my brother and pulled baseball cards from the box I'd found in the storage facility. But nothing was happening. Many of the faces seemed unfamiliar. It was all just cardboard.

A certain stunted suspense began to preside. It was a more concentrated version of the definitive mood of our disappointing adult lives to that point. Night after night, week after week, year after year, and now, in miniature, card after card, the question arose.

Would nothing ever happen to us?

Eventually I pulled Carmen Fanzone from the pile. I felt something in my chest, like the flicking of a latch. When I showed the card to my brother, we both erupted, laughing until tears started leaking from our eyes. It was the kind of laughter that kept multiplying, finding new detonations in and around the very idea of Carmen Fanzone. The melancholy deadpan. The gag-store mustache. The comedy-sketch name. But it was more than all that, more even than the Rowland Office laughter of brotherly laughing fits. The laughter was that type that hits you just a few times in your life, seismic laughter, sprung from the fault lines of the questions you can't answer.

What happened to our childhood? Who are these impostors? How could the onetime center of our lives offer up such an absurd unknown?

My brother was the first to be able to speak.

He said, "There was never no goddamn Carmen Fanzone!"

Topps 1981 #221: Bob Davis

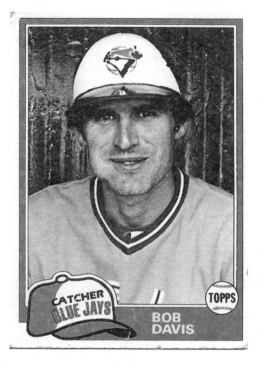

Some time after I moved back from the apartment over the liquor store into yet another apartment with my brother, he and I and another friend, Pete, drove upstate for a court date. On an earlier trip, Pete had gotten arrested for being the point man in our absurd drunken scheme to steal a poster from a movie theater lobby. The poster featured an ape wearing glasses and playing chess. Pete was apprehended by blond, tan, gum-chewing teenagers in national movie theater chain golf shirts. They held him until the cops arrived.

On our return trip for the court date we passed Yankee Stadium. This was during the era when the Yankees won the World Series every year. We all felt like there was no place in that city for conquered misfits like us, two Red Sox fans and a Mets fan.

Fuck you, Yankee Stadium, we said, our middle fingers high.

On the drive home after the court hearing, at which Pete was lectured by an incredulous ninety-year-old judge and charged with criminal mischief, we were tired and silently drifting into our own orbits, bracing for the indignities of the days and weeks to come. No one said anything for a long time. I remember that the song on the radio was that insipid virus of a ditty, "Walking on the Sun," a clear sign that we had ceased giving a shit. Let whatever comes, come. My brother was at the wheel, driving the used car he'd bought with advance money for a travel book he would never complete. We crossed over the Macombs Dam Bridge, Yankee Stadium behind us.

I remember you scumbags, Yankee Stadium must have said, squinting down at us.

If memory serves, there's a somewhat unusually placed traffic light at the end of the Macombs Dam Bridge. Or maybe it isn't normally there and Yankee Stadium put it there just for that moment. Anyway, it changed from yellow to red. My brother's mind was elsewhere. A car barreled straight at us, eyes wide in the faces of its passengers. Brakes squealed, then came the surprisingly soft sound of crunching metal.

Amazingly, no one in either car was hurt in the head-on collision. But after my brother nursed his convulsing vehicle to the shoulder, where a battalion of muscular young Bronx residents from the other car commenced screaming at him, I watched my brother age before my eyes. His posture sagged. His face went gray. He was barely getting by as it was. He had let his insurance payments lapse. He was getting screamed at. His car, which he needed to complete the travel book he had been contracted to write, was clearly now no more than a few heartbeats away from flatlining. Pete and I looked on, Pete freshly saddled with the criminal mischief charge, me with the sad feeling that came from watching my older brother, whom I'd always idolized, standing there in the middle of it all like a pitcher with nothing left and no help on the way, a mop-up man who has to stay in the box and take a beating as the boos rain down.

I applied for a job as an adjunct professor at the college I'd attended as an undergrad. I didn't have any teaching experience, but the recommendation of two of my old writing teachers helped me get the job anyway. Or maybe they just needed a body. I was given two classes, Basic Writing and College Writing. The pay was meager, but that had never held me back before.

Terror crested four times a week in the firing-squad minutes directly preceding every meeting of my two classes. Each flare-up of terror gave way to a kind of public seizure that gripped me for ninety minutes before casting me back to my solitude sweaty and stunned, my voice raw, as if I had spent the entire hazy interval sobbing. The students gone, I sat at the head of the empty class until my legs stopped trembling. I usually felt ashamed about one or another of the things that had tumbled from my mouth during the ill-planned lesson.

Most of the other adjuncts at my college also seemed to be just passing through. There were a couple of longtimers, but they had fit their adjunct duties into a sturdy arsenal of chisel-jawed remunerative pursuits, one guy teaching a couple of classes when he wasn't leading tours through the Amazon rainforest and selling photographs to

National Geographic, another guy maintaining his on-campus reputation as a ruthless grammarian between professional jazz trumpeting engagements. Most of the others seemed to view the low-paying, no-insurance, no-security job as a stepping-stone to something better. I may have entertained that thought, too, early on, but in the same blurry, hypothetical way that I daydreamed about someday winning a National Book Award or owning a house or ceremonially passing my baseball cards down to a son. It soon became apparent that the job was merely another in my long line of crumbling ledges to cling to by my fingertips.

That year I finally got my driver's license, and in the summer I drove to Ohio, where my mom was still living and where my father had moved, too. At first he had gotten an apartment of his own a few blocks away from her, but by the time I got there he had moved into the guest room in her little house.

"All those years he looked out for me," my mom told me one night. "Now I'm going to look out for him."

In August I returned to Vermont, and just before classes and my ledge-clinging resumed I moved into a cabin in the woods. The cabin had no electricity, no running water, a small woodstove for heat, and a big plastic lime-coated barrel for my excrement. I needed somewhere, anywhere, to live, and so My Year in the Woods began as much out of desperation as out of a desire to follow in the heroic footsteps of Thoreau. But the idea did appeal to me. Maybe in solitude I'd be able to penetrate the essence of All Things. Maybe when that fucking tree falls in the forest and no one's around to hear it, I'd be there to hear it.

My friend Charles sent me off to my year of solitary purity with a gag gift of a battery-powered television about the size of two decks of cards. I went through a lot of batteries that year. Another vice I cultivated at the cabin grew out of another gift from Charles, a small orange plastic propeller toy. You use both your hands to spin the stem of the propeller and it flies through the air for fifteen or twenty feet. It's the type of thing you might try a couple times before moving on with your life, but during my year in the woods I created a golflike game that involved trying to hit a series of trees around the cabin with the flying propeller in the fewest "strokes" possible. Then, reverting to a practice that had devoured huge tracts of empty time in my childhood, I populated the game with an ever-growing catalog of intricately conceived imaginary personalities revered by millions of imaginary fans for their prowess in the hallowed, physically taxing, mentally punishing, spiritually grueling sport of Twirly Propeller.

Instead of completing the novel I'd been hoping to finish (about a directionless liquor store clerk), or taking assiduous egoless note of the natural phenomena all around me, or resolving to pretzel my stiff, inflexible body into a straight-spined lotus position and chant sutras until the top of my head split open to guzzle nirvana, I enacted Twirly Propeller tournament after Twirly Propeller tournament, each a harrowing marathon with several elimination rounds that gradually built to the breathless white-knuckle tension of the Championship Match. It's all gone now, but throughout my year in the woods I kept in my head the entire history of Twirly Propeller, all the single-match, yearly, and lifetime records, all the famous rises and falls, all the improbable limping heroic Comebacks from Complete Oblivion.

But sometimes I just sat and listened to the woods. And I loved coming back to the cabin on a clear night when the moonlight was shining down on the birch trees. And I loved being able to drive a little ways and see Tom at the house he and his new wife, Susanne, had bought, a beautiful place halfway up a mountain, the dream of a stable life in the country finally come true. And I loved one day that spring, sitting on the porch of the cabin, sun melting the last of the snow, a fat biography of Elvis Presley on my lap, but me so glad to be alive I couldn't read. And every once in a while I was able to put a few words together in my notebook that tugged at something inside me, something below the ache that had long ago settled in my chest.

The deepest tugging sensation grew slowly, as if sprouting from a planted seed, out of a practice I started halfway through the year to stave off insanity. I began selecting a baseball card from my collection at random and laying it on the table by the door, where I would then look at it for a few days in the morning light and the dusk light and the light of a guttering kerosene lamp and the light of loneliness and the light of being a brother and the light of being a son and the light of being a failure and the light of a guy who was running out of money and the light of a guy who kept forging on through the snow and the mud and even the painfully tender first sounds of spring.

Thoreau did not spend his year in the woods staring at baseball cards, but I wasn't Thoreau. I was someone who had leaned on my cards throughout childhood and who had since childhood felt an ache in my chest as if something was missing. After a few days, I tried to put down a few words in my notebook about the card that I'd randomly pulled from my collection and placed on the table. Words didn't surge forth as in my long-held dream of a Kerouackian volcano of creation. But I could tell that something was there, a faint but perceptible tugging.

Bob Davis's 1981 card was one of the most haunting of my random selections. Maybe it's because Bob Davis's expression seems like that of a man who's trying to remain cheerful in spite of the tiny constant ringing noise that's made his sanity into a thin, fraying, tightly stretched rubber band. Or maybe it's because of the clammy gray catacomblike background, such a stark contrast to the overwhelmingly predominant baseball card backdrop of blue sky as to suggest something about Bob Davis's extremely peripheral, ogrelike isolation on the far fringes of major league baseball. Or maybe it's because of the discovery I made that Bob Davis, clinging for dear life to the thin pleasure of a tobacco wad, shares my birthday. As a kid, I hadn't noticed that any god shared my birthday. Probably Bob Davis had been too anonymous to draw me into a close inspection of his card, especially in 1981, when baseball cards were ceasing to be the center of my life and my life was proceeding without a center. Maybe he'd been in the last pack I ever bought as a kid, a gray particle on a screen showing a TV station that had fallen almost completely into static. Probably I hadn't looked past his anxious grin on the front or his .198 lifetime average on the back before tossing him into my box of cards with the others, only to find years later that even this ignored obscurity on the expansionary fringes of my neglected heaven had some significant connection to me, that even the least of a great forgotten beyond was capable of answering a prayer.

Topps 1980 #: 482: Rickey Henderson

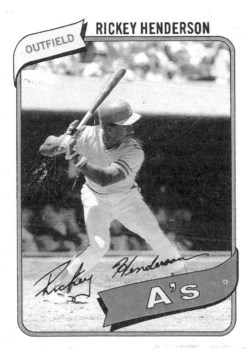

When my year in the cabin ended, I was broke. The adjunct thing had left me worse off financially than when I'd started. I didn't know what to do or where to go. I called my brother, who calmed me down. He had been in plenty of bad spots himself. He was like a hitting coach talking to a player in a deep slump, encouraging him to keep looking for his pitch.

If I could have moved back in with him I probably would have, not knowing what else to do, but he had moved into an apartment with Kelsey. His leaving our old apartment, which he had shared with our friend Pete while I'd been in Vermont, did open up a spot for me. Once again, I returned to where I'd been before, more or less. I had my notebooks, my box of baseball cards, and a credit card tab that made me feel like I was on the brink of mathematical elimination.

The photo on Rickey Henderson's 1980 rookie card was taken during 1979. He made his debut that year in a midseason doubleheader that the A's lost, part of Henderson's career-opening seven-game losing streak. Henderson finally played in a major league win, then the A's promptly lost Henderson's next three games, won one, lost five more, won one, lost five more, won one, and lost five more. The A's record in Henderson's first 29 games was 4–25. This was not that far off par for a rancid team that went 54–108 on the year. If anyone was going to start mailing in his efforts, it would have been a player finishing out that dismal campaign. And yet here is Henderson, the rookie, locked in, ready to battle.

Pete helped me get a job at the bookstore where he was working. I remember standing at the store's raised information counter and staring across the store at one of the cashiers. She had dyed one lock of her hair bright pink. I felt another faint tugging at something below the ache that had long ago settled in my chest. It was like finding the card of an unknown rookie in a pack, maybe near the end of a pack, maybe near the end of the last of four packs you bought at the end of the last full summer of the gods, the end of an era of awe, and something about the card pushed back against that feeling of everything ending and made you wonder.

I don't know if there's such a thing as love at first sight, and I can't remember the moment I discovered Rickey Henderson's 1980 card in a pack, but I'm sure the card made me wonder. The rookie's odd crouch differed not only from the posed wax-figure stances that had populated most of my cards to that point but differed also from the feeling that mathematical elimination was unavoidable, that life itself was a losing season. Here was an electric moment, full of possibility, a young man who'd so far known nothing but losing in the majors but who nevertheless was about to treat the next pitch, the next moment, as if it could not be more important.

One of my tasks as a clerk was to periodically go behind the counter and retrieve the milk crate filled with customer returns and reshelve them. I met the cashier with the lock of pink hair during this task. If it had been up to me I would have said nothing and skulked by her to get the crate of books, then maybe thought about the moment later, revising the part where I let the pitch sail by. Luckily, she had a more direct approach to life. She shoved her hand at me.

"Hi, I'm Abby," she said.

By then, all my gods were gone except one, heaven eroded but for Rickey Henderson, who persisted into the new millennium, on a new team every season or every half-season. You began to assume that you could always pick up a page with box scores and find his name somewhere. You began to assume that since he'd been around so long, he'd be around forever.

How long can anything last? My brother and I still saw each other occasionally, and if I was slumping he'd always make me feel better, but the halts and pauses in our conversations kept growing.

"Rickey Henderson is still kicking," I told him one day. We'd been sitting on a park bench, drinking Budweiser tall boys out of paper bags. We hadn't said anything for a while. I'd started gazing at the box scores in the newspaper that had been poking out of the bulging satchel he always lugged everywhere.

"Rickey Henderson," Ian said. "You don't say."

"Seattle, of all places," I said. Ian raised his bag of beer.

"To Rickey Henderson," he said. I tapped my bag of beer against his and we drank.

Abby and I spent a day together just walking around. It was nothing special. It was one of the best days of my life. We went into an aquarium store and looked at the fish and petted a black cat that was sleeping on one of the tanks. We went to a couple shoe stores looking for and not finding a pair of the kind of suede sneakers I like to wear because they remind me of the 1970s. She bought some cheap sunglasses at an outdoor bazaar. We got something to eat at an Italian place, then sat and drank coffee in a narrow, empty space in the back of a small café. We walked to the subway, and she kissed me good-bye as her train to Queens was rolling into the station.

Topps 1976 #135: Bake McBride

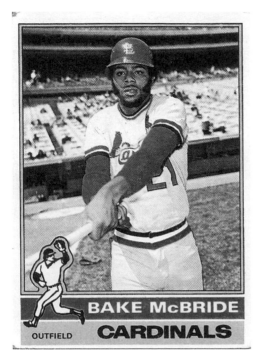

Bake McBride is one of those names that I'll never be able to say without feeling a flicker of happiness. There are others. Oscar Gamble, Jim Bibby. Dick Pole, Pete LaCock. Mario Mendoza, Mario Guerrero, Bob Apodaca, Biff Pocoroba. César Cedeño and Sixto Lezcano and Omar Moreno and Mark Lemongello. The Penguin, the Hammer, Toy Cannon, Quiz. You say the name and a door opens wide. You remember that world. You remember that time. You say Bake McBride and he's there, faster than any human could ever be, fast as you need him to be.

I had always been afraid I'd say my brother's name and find I'd been left behind. I had always been pulling on him, clinging to him, allowing absences in my own life to be filled by presences in his, day after day threading my life so intricately into his that eventually it got to the point that when either of us moved so much as a muscle the other felt it as a ripping of internal threads.

I can tell you what Bake McBride hit as a rookie and in what round he was drafted and how much he weighs and with what arm he throws. I can even tell you that my brother, like me, always loved Bake McBride, the player, the name, the way the two things match: the line drive contact of a .300 hitter in the hard consonants, smooth, effortless gliding in the long-vowel finish. *Bake McBride.* But I can't tell you if my brother might have had fears similar to my own about being left behind. All I have ever really known for sure is the kind of thing you could put on the back of a baseball card. Numbers. Places. Years. Season after season, we lived together. Through childhood, through most of our twenties. Even when I went away for brief periods, I always circled back. It never occurred to me that it wasn't only my weakness and uncertainty that might have maintained this circle, and that I wasn't the only one who worried that someday that circle might get broken.

On the rare occasions in my life when I'd had a girlfriend, my brother had gotten a slightly stricken look on his face, as if he were watching someone bicycle through a red light into the path of a speeding truck. I can't fault him for that, considering not only how my relationships usually ended but also the hesitant, uncertain, awkward way I entered into them in the first place. After all, the look on his face might have been a reflection of my own.

Still, as my life began to intertwine with Abby's, I resented Ian's careful tight-faced hints that I slow down and think about what I was doing. I wanted to tell him about how good it felt to simply walk around an aquarium store with Abby, but I couldn't find the words, partly because we'd never talked about things like that, and partly because I resented that I needed to defend my decisions. At that time, my brother, who for years had been struggling far more than I'd been willing to notice, was working hard at discovering why his life was the way it was, and a shaky evangelical zeal for this work colored our interactions. One evening, as we were sitting on a park bench, he sensed my resistance to his hints to slow down and began nudging the conversation in a more general direction, toward the whole big box of cards of our lives, from birth on up.

"We *have* to figure this shit out," he finally said. But the word *we*, the very thing I had clung to from my first conscious moments long into adulthood, felt suffocating.

"I don't have to figure out anything," I said.

Eventually the hinting and denying of hints led to my brother asking that I meet him at a place called Mullins. We sat at the bar. A baseball game was on.

"So look," he finally said. "I'm going through some things right now. Some really rough water. And I just can't be around you and her right now."

We finished our beers and walked together to the subway. When I got home I would be unable to sleep. I would stare at the ceiling all night thinking that what my brother said, however it was intended, amounted in my mind to an ultimatum: *me or her.*

But as we waited for the train, I only wanted there to still be something between us, something to say. I remembered the fantasy basketball league that we were both in. The draft was coming up soon.

"So who'd you rank first?" I asked.

"Hm? Oh, Tracy McGrady," Ian said. "Big year."

"I got him one, too," I said. "He can give you something in every category."

We weren't making eye contact.

"Yup, Tracy McGrady," he mumbled. He leaned over to see if a train was coming.

"Tracy McGrady," I said. My stomach started to hurt in the ensuing silence. *Is this it?*

"Troy O'Leary," I said, like casting a line into the water. My brother checked his watch.

"Ed O'Bannon," I said, trying again. The tunnel started rumbling, the train on its way. The light got brighter. My brother said something, but it was lost in the clattering arrival.

"What?" I yelled. He waited for the brakes to stop screeching.

"Willie McCovey?"

I nodded.

"Willie McCovey," I said. We were both looking at the doors. They opened and we got on. The train started moving. There was just enough space for us to sit down but we remained standing. I only had two stops until I transferred.

"Donovan McNabb," I said.

"Shaquille O'Neal," he said. We pulled into a station and the doors came open. Nobody got on or off. The doors closed. The train started moving again.

"Lynn McGlothen," I said. My brother held on to a pole with one hand and tapped his chin with the other, looking down at the grimy floor. He had a big satchel full of undone work around his shoulder. I had a feeling we were missing something obvious. The train arrived at my stop. The doors opened. I got off and turned back toward my brother. Our eyes met. The doors closed and the train pulled away, the best one forgotten, the best one left unsaid. So say it now, two voices in tune, two voices as one. Say it and he's here: Bake McBride.

1980 Topps #720: Carl Yastrzemski

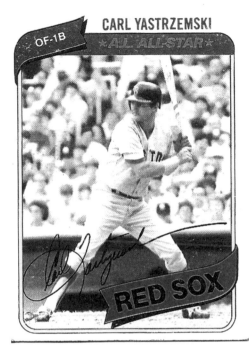

I moved out of New York with Abby, to somewhere else altogether, attracted to the idea that it was unfamiliar, a place beyond the reach, so I tried to believe, of any personal echoes.

And yet in this new place, Chicago, I started almost immediately to dig deeper into my childhood baseball card collection, as if I'd finally decided I had to figure this shit out. I taped the card I loved most to the wall by my writing desk. Yaz at bat.

Dig in. Stay balanced. Wait.

The statistics on the back of the card provided further instruction. The tiny type, the many seasons, the stunning number of hits, the even more stunning number, hidden but revealed by simple subtraction, of outs. *You've got to fail. No way around it. You fail and fail. You keep trying.*

The deeper I dug, the more I noticed strange, inexplicable absences and other strange, inexplicable presences. Team checklists that I'd filled in thirty years earlier no longer seemed capable of accuracy. I didn't have some cards that the checklists said I should and had other cards that according to blank checklist boxes should not have been in my shoebox at all. Just whose cards were these, exactly?

Unpacking another box, which had been taped shut since before I'd gone away to be an adjunct professor, I discovered Ian's Yaz cap.

At my brother's request, I got on a plane to fly to a family therapy session. I sat in a small white room with a therapist, my mother, my brother, and Kelsey. Dad had opted not to come, citing his age and his hatred of air travel. I don't think Tom had been asked to come, maybe out of deference to my mom, who had burst into tears the last time she'd seen him, some years earlier, at a reading of one of my pile of unpublished short stories.

The therapist used a whiteboard and a black marker to map out a family tree that included the unusual configuration of our family during the early 1970s, while we were living in the experimental three-parent house in New Jersey. There my brother and I were, on the same branch, below the unusually augmented parental branch, three names above us instead of two. All of us except the therapist sat as if we were bracing for a blow to the head.

"What was life like for these two?" the therapist asked. She pointed at the lowest branch.

"Painful," Ian said.

She asked other questions. She had to raise her voice at times above the sound of a lawn mower outside. The grass must have been wet because the mower kept clogging and almost stalling, but then whoever was pushing it eased off, and it sputtered and spat back to life. It made me think of our house in East Randolph. I mowed the front yard and part of the side yard, and Ian did the back and part of the side. It also made me think of Tom. When I'd lived in the cabin, I'd gone over to his house once in a while and helped him mow his lawn, and after that whenever I went back to visit in the summer I'd always try to fit in a couple hours with the mower.

I don't know who we all are to one another exactly, but at least I can mow a fucking lawn.

Eventually the sound of mowing receded to a faraway moaning and hacking and then finally went silent, and the therapist asked me how I would characterize my childhood. A word came out of my mouth, followed by others. I had a thought partway through: *What the fuck am I saying?* Speech suddenly resembled my recurring dream of having to parallel park a semi: huge, unwieldy, impossible. My voice finally sputtered to a stop, and I sat there with no firm idea of what I'd said beyond the first word. Even the first word confounded me. It didn't seem like something I'd say. But I'd felt the need to explain that those years, my childhood, our childhood, weren't only the roots of destructive need. Those years weren't only pain. Those years were the opposite of pain. Pain was that ache in my chest. Pain was the slow severing of one voice into two.

"Happy," I'd said.

Afterward, we played miniature golf. Around the turn to the back nine, as we were waiting for a big family with a lot of laughing kids to finish the tenth hole, Ian and Kelsey stepped over to the snack counter to get ice cream and my mom walked behind a miniature church and started weeping.

"What's wrong?" I said. She waved her putter vaguely.

"All the other normal families here and then . . . us," she said.

We parted saying it had been good and helpful, but I still don't know what to make of it. The thing I carried away in one piece was a moment when I watched my brother and Kelsey walking together, each with an ice-cream cone in one hand and a putter in the other. I knew my brother had been going through a tough time, and something about the way they leaned their heads toward one another as they walked and talked looked like the opposite of that. Here was something still beginning.

My brother and I had vowed during the family therapy session to keep talking, and for a while we stuck to the plan to speak at least once a week on the phone. But the conversations had hitches in them. We were trying to figure out what came after the end of two boys with one voice.

I didn't mention the Yaz cap, even though I kept feeling like, in the new era of hashing everything out in therapy, I should. But a thorough inventory of hurt and blame and every last entanglement wasn't what we needed, even if it had been possible, which it wasn't.

What we needed was a win.

I wore the Yaz cap to a Red Sox bar in Chicago to watch Game 4 of the 2004 World Series with Abby, the Red Sox one win away. When Keith Foulke lobbed a throw to Doug Mientkiewicz for the final out, Abby looked up at me and started crying and we hugged in the middle of a beer-raining mosh pit. I wanted to run through the streets. I wanted to call my brother. But what I needed to do more than all of that was relieve the tremendous pressure that had built up through the course of the game in my bladder. As I wriggled through the packed bar to go take my first piss as a champion, arms reached out from the crowd to pat the top of my Yaz-capped head.

"Yaz!"

"Way to go, Yaz!"

"We finally fucking did it, Yaz!"

It was a great moment, but since it was my brother's cap, it should have been my brother's moment. I tried to assuage my guilt with the hope that I'd soon be handing the cap back to him. There had always been the idea, at least in my mind, that we'd meet in Boston if there was ever a parade.

Even as I got my plane ticket I didn't know if it was going to work out. I didn't know if it meant as much to Ian as it meant to me. But when I got off the plane the day of the parade, there he was: my goddamn brother.

As we were walking into the parking garage I reached into my backpack.

"Here, man," I said. I handed him the Yaz cap.

"Yaz!" he said, beaming. He took off his regular Red Sox cap and put the yellowed painter's cap on. He had a bulging bag hanging from his shoulder, as always, and he stuffed the Red Sox cap in there.

I looked up at the Yaz cap that I'd taken from him and clung to for all those years.

"Look, I just want to say I'm sor—" I mumbled.

"I present to you," my brother said as we rounded a corner, "Yaz-mobile!"

His outstretched hand indicated a gray sedan with a big home-made flag hanging from the antenna and red and blue banners all over the sides and back. The flag announced that the driver of the car was a member of "the Church of Yaz." The banner on the back said, in Red Sox lettering, "We Won!" Big banners on both sides of the car also used Red Sox lettering to declare the vehicle's name. Later, as we were driving around, smiling, a driver passing us on the right lay on his horn and leaned his shining face out the window. He was about our age.

"Yazmobile!" he shouted.

I still have the largest Yazmobile banner from my brother's car, folded up and stored in a plastic container with other keepsakes. I try to hold on to things like that, especially now that I have had so many things like that disappear that it makes me wonder if I would even still have Carl Yastrzemski's autograph had he ever written back.

My brother's first child, a daughter, was born in October 2005, on the very last day of the Red Sox' championship reign. His second child shares a first name with the general manager who had overseen the victory. As for me, I sent an invitation to my wedding to every member of the Red Sox, who were scheduled to play an afternoon road game against the White Sox just a few miles south of the evening ceremony. Like Yaz, they never replied. But Tom was there, standing with me alongside my two closest friends, and my mother and father were there, sitting side by side in seats up front, and my brother stood closer to me than anyone, holding the rings, as Abby walked toward me down the aisle.

On the day of the parade, my brother and I joined a mob a few blocks up from Faneuil Hall and cheered our throats hoarse as the champs rolled by. After all the duckboats passed, we walked around dazed for a while. It had happened. Every coin ever chucked in a fountain. Every candle on every birthday cake. Every scattered dandelion seed. Every wishbone. It had happened.

A pack of shirtless teenaged boys staggered past with a crudely rendered cardboard sign that read "Show us your boobs!" I bought a championship T-shirt from some guy with a garbage bag full of them. We passed a big guy in a Pedro Martinez jersey and an Afro wig saying into his cell phone, "So you get the bail money yet?"

Eventually my brother and I found ourselves packed in with a crowd on a bridge stretching over the Charles River. The parade was still going on. It had moved to the water. We sacrificed our frayed voices some more as the duckboats floated by beneath us. They continued to move up the shore, a continual roar following them from the throng at the water's edge and echoing across the river and up into the cold gray sky. Winter was on its way, but for the first time in our lives my brother and I were going into it side by side as champions, and the roar rippling up the shore sounded exactly like the first crowd prayer I'd ever heard, as a seven-year-old at Fenway, that one long unbroken syllable, as if the whole world were yelling as loud as humanly possible for Yaz.

FOR YOU

Parent

LOUIS WILKER

FOR YOU

Parent

TOM BYRNE

FOR YOU

Parent

JENNY WILKER

FOR YOU

Brother

IAN WILKER

FOR YOU

Wife

ABBY THEURING

Deepest thanks to Mac Squires, J. Andrew Squires, Lillian Wilker, Charles Wilker, Joe Wilker, Helen Pepperman, Sam Pepperman, Dave Wilker, Paulina Wilker, Bob Squires, Ellen Drysdale, Anne Squires, Conrad Squires, Bonnie Bishop, Dana Wentworth, Barbara Ernst, Bill Ziegler, Matt Pavoni, Tony Whedon, Neil Shepard, Frank Iovino, Pete Millerman, Charles Bender, Morton Gaber, Terrance Dolan, Sean Dolan, Mark Rifkin, Ellen Scordato, Akim Reinhardt, Ofer Rind, Jim Cotter, Rose Ortiz, Kelsey Goss, Leslie Daniels, Susanne Byrne, Rick Zand, Chris Noel, David Ebenbach, Carol Anshaw, Fay Dillof, Phyllis Barber, François Camoin, Ellen Lesser, Dory Adams, Patty Theuring, Skip Theuring, Samantha Theuring, Evan Wilker, Theo Wilker, Darren Viola, Jon Daly, Ken Arneson, Bob Timmermann, Scott Long, Alex Belth, Jon Weisman, Craig Calcaterra, Rob Neyer, Kate McKean, Laura Downhour, David Gomberg, Robert Kempe, Junko Miyakoshi, and Peter Thomas Fornatale.

Thanks to everyone who has ever joined the conversation at cardboardgods.blogspot.com, cardboardgods.baseballtoaster.com, and cardboardgods.net.

Thanks to baseball-reference.com.

Special thanks to Travis Peterson at punkrockpaint.com for his card-doctoring wizardry.

JOHNNY WOCKENFUSS

Goodnight, Johnny Wockenfuss, wherever you are.